Brotherhoods and Secret Societies
in Early and Mid-Qing China

DAVID OWNBY

Brotherhoods and Secret Societies in Early and Mid-Qing China

THE FORMATION OF A TRADITION

STANFORD UNIVERSITY PRESS

STANFORD, CALIFORNIA

1996

Stanford University Press
Stanford, California
© 1996 by the Board of Trustees of the
Leland Stanford Junior University
Printed in the United States of America

CIP data appear at the end of the book

Stanford University Press publications are distributed
exclusively by Stanford University Press within the
United States, Canada, Mexico, and Central America;
they are distributed exclusively by Cambridge
University Press throughout the rest of the world.

Preface

It is startling to realize that research for this book began more than a decade ago. At the outset, the doctoral dissertation that makes up the core of the present volume was to be an examination of the interplay of class and kinship in late imperial Southeast China, illumined by in-depth study of the lineage feuds for which the region is famous. I found the impersonal, commercialized aspects of the feuds particularly intriguing. Kinship groups frequently hired outside mercenaries to fight their battles, and compensated the families of poor lineage members who volunteered to serve as "substitutes" (*dingxiong*) when feud violence prompted official investigation by confessing to crimes they had not committed. I hoped to expand on what we already knew about such practices by examining feud-related confessions and depositions housed in the Routine Memorials of the Board of Punishment Archives (*xingke tiben*), a rich source of data newly available to foreign scrutiny. Qing law required that magistrates investigate homicides, and feuds produced homicides and thus, presumably, archival documents. My seemingly simple task would be to sift through the vast number of routine memorials in order to find those relating to feuds from my chosen region. The logic was compelling enough to convince the Committee on Scholarly Communication with the People's Republic of China (as it was then called) to send me to the Number One Historical Archives in Beijing, for the 1986–87 academic year.

It took about six weeks of anxious searching through the Board of Punishment archives to realize that Qing bureaucratic methods were not what I had supposed: the information on feuds simply was not there, or at least not in sufficient concentration for my research to yield the anticipated results. Law or no law, Qing magistrates preferred not to intervene in feuds and feud-related homicides unless absolutely necessary. There was of course a certain logic at work here, since feuds were messy affairs, intimately linked to local power structures, and unlikely to be resolved rapidly and neatly. Unless a feud was unusually and visibly violent, it made sense for career-minded officials to ignore such local violence as much as possible.

Under these circumstances, I had no choice but to revise the topic of my dissertation research. Happily, the documents that I did unearth on feuds suggested possible leads. These documents frequently mentioned brotherhood groups and secret societies in the same context as lineage feuds, and new questions led to new research. I had assumed, again somewhat naïvely, that feuds and "secret societies" would belong to different parts of the world of late imperial China. Lineage feuds would belong to the realm of kinship and territoriality, already well explored by Maurice Freedman, among others, whereas secret societies belonged to what we call in the current Chinese context the "floating population," people forced by demographic or socioeconomic change to abandon their homes and seek their fortunes elsewhere, often in ways that the state defined as criminal. The fact that Qing officials writing about the problems of governing the Southeast Coast did *not* make such a distinction suggested that a closer examination of these brotherhood groups and their relationship to local society might be justified, even if this required sorting through the vast literature (in several languages) on secret societies and rebellion.

This book is the product of that examination. Although I could not have imagined at the outset the shape the book would eventually assume, it remains to some degree a study of class and kinship in late imperial Southeast China, even if neither of these important concepts receives careful and direct consideration. Indeed, throughout this volume I stress the *closeness* of brotherhood associations and secret societies to lineages, villages, and religious groups rather than the *distance* of these groups from the central institutions of rural life. There is no doubt that most members of brotherhood associations had been marginalized in important ways, and that they can be viewed as an underclass. At the same time, their own experience of "class" as well as the organizational and cultural tools they used to protect themselves drew heavily on the world whose margins they occupied. The fictive kinship ties created through brotherhood associations constitute the most obvious of these tools. I found, in short, that opposing class and kinship proved clumsy and anachronistic in the context of late imperial Southeast China.

Instead of class and kinship, this study examines the emergence and

evolution of a tradition of popular organization. I begin with the proliferation of brotherhood associations in the early Qing period, and argue
that although both brotherhoods and blood oaths have long been part of
Chinese social practices, bands of men joining together through a blood
oath and calling themselves a "brotherhood association" (*hui*) appear in
unprecedented numbers in the seventeenth and eighteenth centuries,
particularly in Southeast China. I end in the early nineteenth century, at
the time when the Qing suppression of the Lin Shuangwen rebellion in
the late 1780's forced members of the most famous brotherhood association, the Heaven and Earth Society (*Tiandihui*), to flee their homes in
the Southeast Coast, taking refuge in other parts of South China, Southeast Asia, and, eventually, in Chinatowns throughout the world. This
episode surely did much to set the stage for the violent nineteenth-century confrontations between the Qing state and secret societies, mani-
fested through frequent rebellions.

Between the beginning of the tradition and its flight from Southeast
China in the late eighteenth and early nineteenth centuries, I examine
various aspects of what I call the "early" history of Chinese brotherhood
associations. These aspects include the relationship of the brotherhood
association to local society, to popular culture, to violence and to the
state. At the risk of oversimplification, I find that many early brotherhood associations were known and recognized parts of local society, tolerated, if grudgingly, by local elites and even local officials. Their initiation rituals, so often described as "exotic," actually drew on popular
religious traditions, and would have been understood by the vast majority of commoner Chinese of the late imperial era. Indeed, the claim of
brotherhood associations and secret societies to access to supernatural
power must account for much, their attractiveness, since joining such
associations carried a considerable risk of punishment and there were
other, less dangerous, ways of pursuing mutual aid—which is what most
brotherhood members claimed to have sought in joining. In some instances, these religious "beliefs" might explain the hostility of brotherhood associations and secret societies toward the state. More frequently
the combination of state hostility to popular association, and the involvement of many brotherhood groups in predatory violence, prompted
confrontations that led to rebellions. The hostility of the state toward
brotherhood associations, as well as the fact that virtually all the source
materials used in the course of this study were produced by government
investigations into brotherhood activities, has meant that a study of
popular organization is at the same time a study of state-society relations in late imperial China. A final comparison of the roles played by
Chinese brotherhood associations in China and in the Chinese commu-

nities of precolonial and colonial Southeast Asia suggests some of the characteristics of the late imperial order in China.

The list of those who contributed to this project is long. In subject matter and methodology the study reflects preoccupations similar to those of Philip Kuhn, my mentor and dissertation adviser. My debts to him will be obvious to all those who know his work.

The Committee on Scholarly Participation with the People's Republic of China, the Fulbright Foundation, the Foreign Languages Area Scholarship Fund, the Whiting Foundation, the Center for Chinese Studies in Taipei, and the University Research Council of Southern Methodist University all provided funding.

Chinese libraries and institutions that facilitated research include: the Qing History Research Institute in Beijing; the Number One Historical Archives in Beijing; and the libraries of People's University, Beijing University, Beijing City, and the Institute of Sciences, all in Beijing. In Fujian, I was fortunate to be able to make use of the libraries of Fujian Normal University, Fujian Provincial Library (both in Fuzhou), as well as the library of Xiamen University. In Taipei, the libraries of Academia Sinica and the Taiwan Provincial Library all proved useful. In North America, I have exploited the holdings of the Harvard-Yenching and Widener libraries at Harvard University, as well as the libraries of Southern Methodist University, Princeton University, McGill University, and the Université de Montréal. The kind and competent souls at the Interlibrary Loan Office of Southern Methodist University's Fondren Library deserve special mention for their unfailing efforts on my behalf.

In China I benefited enormously from the assistance of Chen Chunsheng, Chen Kongli, Chen Zhiping, Dai Yi, Ju Deyuan, Kong Xiangji, Li Hua, Lin Tiejun, Liu Ruzhong, Liu Wei, Liu Yongcheng, Luo Ming, Wang Lianmao, Wang Sizhi, Wei Qingyuan, Yang Guozhen, Zheng Zhenman, and the members of the History Department and the staff of the Rare Books Library at Fujian Normal University, in Fuzhou. In Taiwan, Lin Man-houng was a gracious and informed host. Chen Ch'iu-k'un and Ch'en Yung-fa were also extremely helpful at Academia Sinica, and Chuang Chi-fa was yet again a *junzi* at the National Palace Museum.

People who read all or part of the manuscript at various stages include: Robert Antony, Peter Bol, Timothy Brook, Tom Buoye, Sharon Carstens, Timothy Cheek, Kenneth Dean, Josh Fogel, Barend ter Haar, Mary Heidhues, Philip Kuhn, Harry Lamley, Dian Murray, Susan Naquin, Dan Orlovsky, Evelyn Rawski, John Shepherd, Woody Watson, Jim Wilkerson, and Jane Kaufman Winn. Their assistance is warmly acknowledged. Muriel Bell, Bobbie James, John Feneron, and Shirley Taylor of Stanford

University Press deserve thanks for their professionalism and affability in preparing the manuscript for publication.

It is customary on occasions such as this to thank one's family for their forbearance. However, neither my wife nor my two sons knew me *before* I began this project, so it is perhaps more appropriate for me to express my hope that they will not be overwhelmed by a liberated husband and father.

D. O.

Contents

Maps and Tables

A Note on Conventions

All place names, personal names, and Chinese terms are rendered in pinyin. Dates are given according to the Chinese calendar in the following manner: QL 35.5.3 (1770). The reign periods of the Qing emperors are abbreviated as follows:

Shunzhi (SZ)	1644–61	Daoguang (DG)	1821–50
Kangxi (KX)	1662–1722	Xianfeng (XF)	1851–61
Yongzheng (YZ)	1723–35	Tongzhi (TZ)	1862–74
Qianlong (QL)	1736–95	Guangxu (GX)	1875–1908
Jiaqing (JQ)	1796–1820	Xuantong (XT)	1909–11

Map 1. Taiwan and adjoining areas of Southeast China

*Brotherhoods and Secret Societies
in Early and Mid-Qing China*

Chinese Brotherhoods and Secret Societies Through the Opium War

In the early 1990's, while teaching in Dallas, Texas, I was invited by a community college at some distance from the metropolitan area to give a general lecture on "China." This lecture was part of a semester-long series of events designed to bring the culture of the larger world to a somewhat inaccessible part of the American Midwest; if memory serves, "China" was to be followed the next week by a performance of the *Nutcracker Suite*. After my slide slow, calligraphy demonstration, and Chinese lesson (all well received), and a brief lecture on "Confucian Influences on the Chinese Revolution" (less well received), I opened the floor to questions. One of the first had to do with "Chinese ninja," by which the student meant, of course, Chinese secret societies.

As this anecdote suggests, many people otherwise ignorant of China and Chinese history are aware of and intrigued by Chinese secret societies. And despite its inaccuracy, the manner in which the student referred to secret societies—as "Chinese ninja"—reveals much about the nature of this continuing fascination. Chinese secret societies, together with Fu Manchu and Bruce Lee, Chinatown Asian gangs, and world-wide Triad-run narcotics networks, connect China and the Chinese to images of sinister violence. Such images, as Harold Isaacs has shown, make up an important part of the larger package of American stereotypes of the Chinese.[1]

I wish that I could promise that this study will rip the cover off Chinese secret societies, exposing the terrible mysteries at their core. In a way, I suppose it does, but the "secret" of "secret societies" here revealed is unlikely to satisfy those seeking exoticism and mystery. Instead, the present volume uses Qing archival information to restore Chinese secret societies to the social, historical, and cultural contexts that gave rise to them. Although from a contemporary perspective these contexts are distant, and hence exotic, secret societies themselves lose much of their mystery when understood in the framework of late imperial Chinese society and culture. In a nutshell, I argue that secret societies were informal, popular institutions, created by marginalized men seeking mutual protection and mutual aid in a dangerous and competitive society. The goal of this book is to chronicle the emergence and proliferation of these organizations, to examine their relationship to local society and popular culture, and to probe their relationship to the Qing state.

Let me begin with definitions and precisions. The "secret society" is more properly understood as one variety of the "brotherhood association," a category I have created to encompass a range of popular fraternal organizations that flourished in the early and mid-Qing period. In China proper, I identify three types of such organizations, although in the Chinese diaspora, brotherhood associations also took the forms of the *kongsi* of Southeast Asia and the *tong* of North American Chinatowns, important additions to the lexicon of brotherhood practices. Within China, the least complex brotherhood association was the simple brotherhood, established by a small number of people for the immediate purposes of mutual aid. One good illustration of this simple brotherhood was the burial society (generally known as Father and Mother Society— *fumuhui*) in which relatives or neighbors contributed small amounts of money to a common fund so that they could bury their parents. Other simple brotherhoods facilitated protection of crops, or self- and mutual-defense for members. Still others could be predatory rather than (or as well as) protective. There is no reason to assume that all brotherhoods, however small and simple, began in innocence.

Alongside the simple brotherhood was the named brotherhood, groups that banded together and selected a specific two-character name for their group, followed by the character *hui*, meaning "society." Some of these differed little from simple brotherhoods; others, like the Tiandihui, were secret societies employing rituals and symbols with apocalyptic and occasionally political connotations. The decision to name one's brotherhood clearly meant something, if only a slightly more formal elaboration on age-old brotherhood practices.

Secret societies, which emerged in the mid-eighteenth century, were one variety of named brotherhood; every secret society we know of used the three-character formula associated with the named brotherhood. Secret societies were groups that employed "esoteric" symbols and rituals to attract followers, and they are distinguished from simple and named brotherhoods by their special language and symbolism. However, not all bands that used this formula can be called secret societies in any meaningful sense, and even groups like the Heaven and Earth Society, which appear to conform to the definition of secret society in some instances, take on other meanings in other contexts.

Blood oaths provided the cultural means by which fraternal organizations bound themselves together. A blood oath frequently accompanied the formation of even simple brotherhoods, although there are instances of simple brotherhoods formed without blood oaths. Virtually all named brotherhoods and every secret society I have ever encountered also employed a blood oath. The decision whether to employ a blood oath to cement a brotherhood was important, for blood oaths often signified more than mere "fictive kinship" at both the popular and elite level. On the one hand, blood oaths carried connotations of solemn purpose in dangerous circumstances, and they were frequently associated with rebellion. On the other hand, blood oaths also carried the taint of barbarian license, or dark, dangerous, heterodoxy.

Blood oaths and simple brotherhoods have long pre-Qing histories. Rebellions, which require considerably more organization than simple brotherhoods, have throughout Chinese history employed blood oaths as well as some variety of what might be called "brotherhood ideology." An important finding of this book, however, is that named brotherhoods and secret societies appear rarely in pre-Qing China, and only begin to proliferate during the eighteenth century. This is the basis of my claim that we are dealing with a new social institution. I locate the initial impulse behind the proliferation of such associations in the violent and mobile society of late imperial China's Southeast Coast, where, according to archival records, they first appeared in significant numbers.* In this region, the wars of the dynastic transition and the demographic explosion of the eighteenth century, among other causes, served to marginalize significant numbers of men—often younger men—from the structures of lineage and village life. Some took to the road; others were simply pushed to the edges of community life. In either case, such men frequently founded brotherhood associations to seek mutual assistance and protection in a precarious world.

The seemingly innocent pursuit of mutual aid in eighteenth-century

---

* Catalogues of archival documents concerning "secret societies," a subcategory of "popular movements," available at the Number One Historical Archives in Beijing, reveal that the vast majority of such cases of which the Qing were aware occurred in the Southeast Coast. There were surely similar developments in other parts of China. It is intriguing, nonetheless, that Entenmann 1982: 229–32 cites evidence suggesting that the very similar *guluzi* bandits in eighteenth-century Sichuan may have had their roots in the Southeast Coast.

Southeast China cannot, however, explain a keen interest in Chinese ninja in late twentieth-century Texas. The pursuit of mutual aid does not seem to require secrecy, nor is it generally exotic in any sense of the word. Indeed, the rise of mutual benefit societies during a similar period in Western Europe led, among other things, to the formation of trade unions and the birth of modern actuarial science (to facilitate calculations of how much to invest in funds dedicated to members' medical benefits).[2] Although these are both important topics, I suspect that neither was of particular interest to my audience in Texas. Another important aspect of this book is thus to explore the connections between mutual aid and the more spectacular history of secret societies: their "esoteric" rituals and symbols, their frequent involvement with crime, and their role in violence against the state.

Some of these connections are neither spectacular nor esoteric. The same impulses that drove marginalized men to band together in pursuit of mutual aid could also lead them toward crime and banditry, and there is little reason to highlight the particular contributions of brotherhood associations in this context. Similarly, crime and banditry often prompted state intervention, which in turn often prompted resistance from brotherhood associations and secret societies. Again, this structural explanation of the involvement of secret societies in anti-state violence requires little attention to the special organizational or cultural characteristics of the societies themselves.

Such a structural explanation is incomplete, however, and we cannot understand the connections between mutual aid and brotherhood associations without considering ideological and cultural factors. For example, an important ideological factor was the Qing decision to prohibit and indeed severely punish a wide variety of organizational practices associated with brotherhoods and secret societies. Here, indeed, is one reason why eighteenth-century Chinese in search of mutual aid might band together in *secret* organizations: such organizations were illegal and carried significant risks. At the same time, however, Qing laws were nuanced, despite their overall harshness; one could pursue mutual aid *without* employing the rituals and symbols that aroused the anger of the state. The fact that many chose to employ just such rituals and symbols even though they were well aware of the risks involved suggests that we take these rituals and symbols seriously. Secret society members drew these rituals and symbols from the realms of popular religion in order, as they believed, to add a layer of supernatural protection to the more secular protection sought in joining a brotherhood association. From the perspective of the Qing state, the propagation of such charismatic religious beliefs meant that secret societies were "heterodox" as well as simply illegal. At a certain level, the exorcistic and shamanistic aspects of secret society ritual practices *can* be understood as a cosmological challenge to the power of the "son of heaven" and the state apparatus he commanded.

The Lin Shuangwen uprising of 1787–88 on Taiwan, which provided the historical context in which secret societies took on their specific meaning for the Qing state, stands as the central event examined in this book. Though it was founded in the early 1760's, the Heaven and Earth Society (Tiandihui), the most famous of Chinese secret societies, did not achieve notoriety—indeed, was not even known to the emperor and most Qing officials—until Lin's rebellion. Lin was himself a Tiandihui member, and elements of his uprising clearly drew on Tiandihui symbolism, even if we cannot attribute the cause of the rebellion to the Tiandihui. Lin's uprising lasted more than a year, and its suppression counted as one of the Qianlong emperor's "ten great campaigns."[3]

The Qing state unsurprisingly placed the blame for the uprising on the Heaven and Earth Society, and it devoted enormous energy not only to suppression of the rebellion but also to the search for the society's origins. This search involved frenzied efforts in southern Fujian and northern Guangdong to locate the society founders, and in some areas took the form of house-to-house investigations. The many arrests and summary executions occasioned by these investigations prompted resistance on the part of desperate members of brotherhood associations, some of which had apparently been devoted solely to mutual aid before finding themselves caught in the Qing dragnet. The last decade of the eighteenth century thus witnessed a protracted confrontation between the state and brotherhood associations in the Southeast Coast: arrests, rebellions, and executions punctuated the end of the reign of the Qianlong emperor and the beginning of that of Jiaqing. This decade of confrontation, along with the scandalous corruption of Heshen and the death of the Qianlong emperor, may well have signaled the end of the long period of High Qing peace and prosperity and the beginning of the troubled nineteenth century.

A more concrete result of this decade of confrontation was the flight of secret society masters and members from the original Tiandihui base areas in the Southeast Coast. Initially, most sought refuge in inland areas of South China, spreading the influence of the Tiandihui through Jiangxi, Guangxi, Hunan, Guizhou, Yunnan, and elsewhere. Others followed the increasing migration to Southeast Asia, where the Tiandihui joined other brotherhood associations that flourished throughout the nineteenth century as important sociopolitical mechanisms for the growing numbers of Chinese who migrated to the kingdoms and colonies of the region.[4] The same forces brought Chinese secret societies to the Chinatowns of Europe and the Americas, where they began to take on their modern image as "Chinese ninja."

It would be an exaggeration to describe the Lin Shuangwen rebellion and its aftermath as a transformative moment in the history of Chinese secret societies. After all, secret societies employing heterodox rituals and symbols had existed before Lin's rebellion, and innocent brotherhood associations devoted to mutual aid continued to exist after Lin's rebellion. Yet there is no doubt that these episodes redoubled the Qing hostility toward the Tiandihui and other such societies, and that Qing suppression not only spread the influence of the society throughout many parts of China but surely also forced the society in the direction of consistent resistance to Qing authority.

This study examines the emergence and proliferation of brotherhood associations as informal institutions created by young men marginalized by the violence, mobility, and socioeconomic changes of the region and period, and it studies the relationship of these associations to the orthodox structures of the social order, to popular culture, and to official ideology. The early history of the brotherhood associations was diverse: brotherhoods could be large or small, innocent or predatory, quiescent or rebellious. It was also a fragmented history and should not be reduced to a single narrative. It might be possible, were one seeking such a narrative, to view the proliferation of the brotherhood associations as part of the changes associated with China's "early modern" order, when young men, marginalized by demographic and socioeconomic change, sought protection and security in new social forms. But brotherhood associations never fulfilled this potential: the Chinese state continued to condemn and harass brotherhoods, and the kinds of economic development that might have reabsorbed marginalized groups did not occur until well into the twentieth century. Brotherhood associations thus remained an important organizational resource for desperate, frightened men, but could not offer the promise of lasting security. Most associations and secret societies appear from archival records to have been small and ephemeral, easily initiated, and just as easily disbanded.

I conclude my research before the first Opium War, and examine only some of the initial waves of the flight of Tiandihui members out of their original base areas. This means, unfortunately, that further research will be required to link the implications of the present work to our understanding of the great wave of mid-nineteenth-century rebellions and indeed to the decline of the late imperial order. My choice to focus on the early history of brotherhood associations and secret societies grew in part out of the fact that, with the exception of extremely detailed research into the date and venue of the founding of the Tiandihui, this early period has been relatively neglected, particularly in English-language historiography. Methodological considerations also played a role; I have tried, where possible, to place brotherhood associations in their local settings, and therefore an expansion of the research focus would require inclusion of more such settings, thus unduly encumbering an already dense work. The remainder of this introductory chapter discusses the various settings—historiographical, geographical and historical, and documentary—that have guided the research and writing of this book.

The Historiographical Setting

A brief summary of the historiography of brotherhood associations and secret societies will bring into sharper focus the interpretive perspectives already suggested. Such a summary is particularly necessary in a field as crowded as that of Chinese secret societies, where the historiographical setting is as important as the historical and documentary environments. Happily, Dian Murray's *Origins of the Tiandihui* provides a masterly synthesis of the huge literature on secret societies, thus liberating other historians to pursue more narrowly focused research.[5] For the purposes of this introduction, I thus reduce this vast tradition to four major schools: Republican-period Chinese-language scholarship, most frequently identified with the works of Xiao Yishan and Luo Ergang; Western-language scholarship of the 1960's and 1970's, generally associated with the work of French scholar Jean Chesneaux; research produced at various points during the nineteenth and twentieth centuries by Western scholar-officials in the employ of colonial governments (or treaty port authorities, in the case of China) often attempting to govern substantial Chinese populations; and, most recently, scholarship carried out by Chinese (and some foreign) researchers in both the People's Republic of China and Taiwan, based on archival materials located in both Beijing and Taipei.

My research builds on the recent work of the archival scholars. The patient labors of these talented researchers have largely discredited the interpretation of the Republican-period Chinese scholars as well as that of many Western scholars associated with the Chesneaux school, by tracing the roots of secret society activities to the local pursuit of mutual aid rather than to national or class politics. At the same time, archival scholars have yet to provide a convincing explanation of popular motivation for joining such societies, given the considerable risks involved and the possibilities of seeking mutual aid in ways that did not excite the animosity of the state. Some of the work of the colonial sinologists is relevant in this context, but for reasons of language and history, the two schools have rarely been joined together. The present work thus offers a synthesis of the approaches of the archival school and the colonial sinologists, and attempts to ground the experiences of brotherhood associations and secret societies in popular culture.

Republican-period Chinese scholars depicted secret societies as anti-Manchu, nationalist rebels, the earliest and most enduring scholarly characterization. Although the frequent use of restorationist slogans such as "overthrow the Qing and restore the Ming" by rebellious secret societies during the eighteenth and nineteenth centuries already suggests this depiction, and nineteenth-century versions of the Tiandihui origin myth trace the establishment of the society to Qing perfidy, the scholarly characterization actually developed in the early twentieth century out of the political needs of Sun Yat-sen.

Exiled from China in 1895 for revolutionary activities, Sun traveled the world, visiting communities of ethnic Chinese, asking their help in toppling the Manchu regime and establishing a modern republic.[6] Frequently, he found that courting—and even joining—local secret societies was essential to mobilizing the resources of the communities. To encourage such mobilization, Sun praised the supposedly nationalist, anti-Manchu origins of secret societies, hoping to rally the latent patriotism of North American and Southeast Asian societies, historically closer to mutual benefit societies than cabals of rebels-in-waiting. In his contacts with mainland secret societies, Sun again found it useful to stress their anti-Manchu rituals and heritage, hoping to redirect the activities of the frequently xenophobic societies away from foreigners and toward the Qing.

A scholarly edifice grew up to support Sun's efforts. Around the time of the 1911 revolution, "scholar-revolutionaries" such as Tao Chengzhang and Hirayama Shu put together popular, journalistic histories of secret societies that reflected Sun's political intentions.[7] After the revolution, a great many scholars, such as Xiao Yishan and Luo Ergang, began to comb the historical record for genuine evidence to substantiate Sun's claims and to validate the populist, nationalist posture of the regime in the face of instability and disintegration.[8] These scholarly efforts succeeded where the Republic itself failed: most Chinese continue to believe that the Heaven and Earth Society was founded in the early Qing, out of ethnic revulsion at the prospect of barbarian rule, and that secret society–led rebellions throughout the Qing period expressed this same sentiment.

A second, complementary, characterization of secret societies as "primitive revolutionaries" developed during the 1960's and 1970's, largely through the work of scholars associated with Jean Chesneaux. Determined to bring "history from the bottom up" to the study of the Chinese past, Chesneaux argued that secret societies opposed not only the Manchu regime but oppressive elitist regimes throughout Chinese history: "Chinese secret societies were an essential component of the 'anti-society,' an opposition force whose dissent was better organized, more coherent, and better sustained than that of the bandits, the vagabonds, and the dissident literati."[9]

Consistent with this belief, Chesneaux broadened the focus of research on secret societies. Whereas Republican-period Chinese scholars had concentrated narrowly on the early Qing history of the Heaven and Earth Society, Chesneaux treated White Lotus sectarians, Heaven and Earth Society members, and adherents of a wide array of popular organizations as part of the same general phenomenon—popular opposition to oppression, either at the hands of the state or by the wealthy and powerful gentry. Chesneaux's interpretation may not have achieved the wide-ranging influence of Republican scholarship, but his *Popular Movements and Secret Societies in China* remains a standard work in the field.

A third school consists of what might be called the colonial sinologists—a rather loose category that includes a wide range of authors, from twentieth-century police officials in colonial East and Southeast Asia, to missionaries and educators in nineteenth-century China.[10] Although this group was widely scattered in time and space, we can still identify two common threads that bind together much of their scholarship. First, most of this scholarship was directed toward the achievement of greater colonial control over the activities of Chinese secret societies, and in this sense was not wholly different from the efforts of Qing officials. Schlegel's famous translations of secret society documents helped Dutch colonial authorities develop policies to deal with local Chinese associations. The authors of several important studies of Chinese secret societies in Malaya compiled significant portions of their data while serving in the colonial police force and government.[11] Regardless of their thoroughness, intelligence, and objectivity, the quality of this research could not but be influenced by the political setting in which it was carried out.

Second, the scholarship of colonial sinologists often took the form of translations and annotations of society documents.[12] Such translations and annotations stand as some of the first genuine efforts to interpret society-generated materials on their own terms: Republican-period Chinese historians, for example, read them as coded references to anti-Manchu resistance. As a result, much of the work produced by this school retains its value today primarily, but not exclusively, as reference material.[13]

The fourth school of interpretation developed in the 1970's and 1980's through the work of Chinese historians in both Taiwan and the People's Republic of China.[14] These historians, whom I call collectively the archival school, have made important revisions to our received understanding of secret societies. These historians have convincingly illustrated that the Heaven and Earth Society was not established until the 1760's, rather than being, as often contended, an early Qing invention. These historians also argue that Han nationalism is not the dominant theme of early secret society activity, even though some anti-Manchu elements do appear in early written materials of the Heaven and Earth Society. Instead, the archival school depicts secret societies as fraternal associations grounded in the search for mutual aid. This argument restores secret societies to a more plausible context as part of local social history, by removing the burden of protonationalism thrust upon them by Republican-period scholarship, as well as that of class consciousness celebrated by Chesneaux.

All these characterizations have their value. Anti-Manchu slogans *did* constitute an important part of many secret society–led rebellions, even if secret societies did not originate as protonationalist organizations. Secret societies *did* lead attacks on local elites and the Qing government, even if they found their motivation in traditional Chinese sources rather than in class-conscious ideologies. And most society members *were* attracted by the promise of mutual aid, even if this leaves unexplained the importance of brotherhood and secret society rituals and the connection between brotherhood associations, violence, and rebellion.

At the same time, all these characterizations leave important questions unanswered. I have no desire to fault these scholars for their choice of emphasis, but I might note nonetheless that none of these schools provides a satisfactory explanation of popular motivation for joining a secret society—unless one is willing to accept debatable assumptions concerning late imperial popular culture. Republican-period scholarship assumes that many peasants were antiforeign, that they expressed this sentiment in ways that suggested modern nationalism, and that they were ready to organize to pursue their goals. Chesneaux likewise assumes that peasants were dissatisfied with their lot and that this dissatisfaction led them in the direction of conscious dissent and political organization. Xenophobia and chronic dissatisfaction are not implausible assumptions, but there is much research to suggest that, even in rebellion, nationalism and class consciousness competed in popular mentalities with other less "modern" elements.[15] In addition, the efforts of the

Chinese communists to build a revolution on the backs of traditional forms of discontent illustrate the ideological and organizational distance between "traditional" and "modern" notions of "protest."[16] Even the archival historians, who have been more respectful of the historical context in which secret societies developed and flourished, have nonetheless failed to explain why peasants chose this particular manner of pursuing mutual aid, given that there were other ways to achieve the same ends without incurring the same risks.[17]

In short, unless one is willing to accept the image of the Chinese peasant as nationalist rebel, class-conscious revolutionary, or risk-hungry daredevil, the appeal of the secret society to many of those who joined remains somewhat mysterious. What must still be explained is the connection between Qing brotherhoods and past forms of popular organization, as well as the cultural meanings attached to the various aspects of the brotherhood tradition—blood oaths, initiation ceremonies, and "esoteric" rites and symbols. These meanings, deeply rooted in popular culture, will help to explain the ongoing appeal of membership, in spite of the danger involved.

The Geographical and Historical Settings

Popular culture is of course rooted in geography and history, even if the precise nature of the connections between history, geography, and culture remains ambiguous. As one of China's nine "macroregions," as defined by G. William Skinner, Southeast China (or the Southeast Coast; I use the two interchangeably) includes parts of southern Zhejiang and northeastern Guangdong, as well as all of Fujian. The region is divided by north-south mountain ranges into the lowland coast and the upland mountains. The coastal areas were historically marked by orientation to the sea, as well as by greater population densities and more intensive agriculture, but the macroregion as a whole is not particularly well suited to rice agriculture: most of the land in Fujian is mountainous, and even the flatter, coastal areas have rocky, sandy, thin soil that needs considerable fertilizer to produce adequate yields. In the eighteenth century, the surplus grain produced in the northwestern inland prefectures of Jianning, Yanping, and Shaowu supplied the coastal deficit prefecture of Fuzhou.[18]

As an island, Taiwan obviously constitutes its own macroregion, but ties of history, economy, population migration, and culture justify its inclusion in this study. The high mountain ranges of the interior are the island's defining topographical feature, dividing it into east and west and determining the flow of the rivers that carve up the western plains. All of Taiwan lies south of the double-cropping line, and by the mid- to late eighteenth century, the fertile alluvial plains between the sandy western coast and the mountainous interior supplied rice-deficient areas of southern Fujian with important supplies of grain.[19]

The natural environment of the macroregion shaped the development of a diversified economy. Fishing and salt production have long been part of the coastal economy. Timber in the mountainous upland regions encouraged the development of a papermaking and book-publishing industry, and also contributed to the development of coastal shipbuilding. The development of long-distance sea trade is the most important characteristic of the region's economic history. Merchants from the Southeast Coast traded in luxury goods with distant markets in Japan and South and Southeast Asia, and engaged in domestic trade in staple goods and some luxury items with port cities to the north. The coastal cities of the Southeast Coast served as important transshipment points for much of this trade. In addition, seafaring generated its own light industries in the development of shipbuilding, porterage, stowage, brokering, and other services, and the availability of distant markets allowed peasants within the marketing systems of the port cities to make use of comparative advantage. Nonetheless, long-distance trade was a chancy business; in addition to the expected risks of piracy and bad weather, merchants along the Southeast Coast operated at the sufferance of the court in Beijing, which at various times and for various reasons over the course of the centuries attempted to proscribe foreign trade. Depression was the frequent result.

Aspects of the history of the late imperial Southeast Coast are well known. The Ming-Qing dynastic transition, which lasted a full forty years in the region, has attracted a good deal of attention, and we can speak with some confidence about the brief reign of Prince Tang of the Ming in Fuzhou in the 1640's as well as the career of Zheng Chenggong and family.[20] The effects of the coastal evacuation, ordered by the Manchus in the 1660's in an attempt to defeat Zheng Chenggong, are known, at least in broad outline.[21] The revival of the commercial fortunes of the region in the early eighteenth century has been well chronicled, as have the Han colonization of Taiwan and the resulting commercial relations between the mainland and the island.[22] Furthermore, sophisticated studies treat a wide range of topics, from commercial contracts and their role in the rural economy, to lineages and local power structures, the development of multiple rights in land ownership, and the importance of local religious traditions.[23]

Still, the present state of research does not provide a detailed explanation of the links among regional economic cycles, population growth, and the emergence and proliferation of brotherhood associations. Indeed, I am not sure that the data exist that would make such an explanation possible, and in any case, the present study, based on documents written by Confucian officials who assumed that crime and violence had above all moral causes, can hardly hope to sort out the complexities of the various factors involved. Instead, this narrative emphasizes *movement* and *violence* as central features of the world of eighteenth-century Southeast China as experienced by members of brotherhood associations, suggesting that the relationships between mobility and violence, both as causes and as effects of social change, form the backdrop for the emergence and spread of the brotherhood association.

Mobility characterized the society of the Southeast Coast long before the late imperial period. Han migrants from north and central China settled Fujian in the Tang, bringing the region into the Chinese cultural and political world. The early blossoming of the Southeast Coast in the Song relied as much on the daring of seafaring merchants as on the brilliance of local scholars. Such daring even prompted some Chinese of the Southeast Coast to take up residence in the commercial entrepôts of the South Seas; from the very beginning, the Chinese diaspora in Southeast Asia (and elsewhere) has been largely made up of migrants from Fujian and Guangdong.

Nonetheless, one gets the sense that the mobility of the society of the late imperial Southeast Coast was exceptional. The volume of this mobility was surely unprecedented. The busy late-Ming movement of people and goods between Fujian and Southeast Asia, however important to the economy of the region, remained the province of a small number of coastal traders.[24] The size of this group increases if we include the merchants engaged in seaborne domestic commerce, but it is doubtful that maritime trade "mobilized" large numbers of peasants and craftsmen in a physical sense, even as local economies responded to the opportunities provided by trade.[25]

Mobility in the late imperial period, on the other hand, involved large numbers of people from many regions and social classes of the Southeast Coast. The eighteenth-century incorporation and population of Taiwan is one of the most telling indications of this movement. The population of the island grew from a mere 100,000 in 1660 to almost 840,000 in 1770, and perhaps 1.2 million by 1824.[26] Since Qing immigration policy prohibited family migration, and sex ratios on the island remained highly imbalanced until the end of the eighteenth century, the majority of the population growth before the nineteenth century resulted from migration from southern Fujian and northern Guangdong.

The hundreds of thousands of migrants to Taiwan are the most outstanding example of mobility (as well as the most easily measured), but there are many more. Large numbers of migrants from the Southeast Coast continued to settle in Southeast Asia (and more engaged in cyclical migration) during the eighteenth century, setting the stage for the great waves of this movement in the nineteenth; Han Yulin, governor-general of Fujian-Zhejiang, reported in 1733 that one to two hundred thousand people from the Zhang-Quan region had already settled in the Philippines.[27] Fujianese and Guangdongese settled the Jiangxi highlands during the seventeenth and eighteenth centuries.[28] Many Fujianese moved to Sichuan in the early Qing to fill the void created by late Ming rebellions.[29] Fujianese merchants established *huiguan* in all major commercial centers.[30]

Movement *within* the region was surely even more pronounced than these long-distance population flows. In the late seventeenth century, migrants from Zhangzhou and Quanzhou prefectures in Southern Fujian flocked north to Zhejiang to grow hemp and indigo. As early as the late seventeenth century, Quanzhou natives did virtually all the metalwork, carpentry, dress-making, and haircutting in the inland Fujian county of Longyan.[31] Skilled craftsmen migrated to large cities to cater to the desires of the urban wealthy for homes worthy of their status.[32] So-called drifters, chiefly from coastal areas of the region, harvested the annual tea crop in mountainous northwest Fujian, and then carried the crop to market.[33] Shop assistants and peddlers in the major commercial towns spoke in the varied accents of the linguistically diverse region, and contributed to the wave of urbanization that by the 1840's made the Southeast Coast China's third most urbanized macroregion.[34] Because much of this migration, both internal and external, was seasonal rather than permanent, society became more rather than less mobile.

The causes of this mobility are complex. An optimist might see in this movement a happy "emancipation of labor" from previous conditions of "feudal" bondage, a "free labor market" in service to the healthy expansion of the "early modern" economy and its "sprouts of capitalism." A more immediate cause, at least for the late seventeenth and early eighteenth centuries, might be located in the wars and violence of the dynastic transition. Battles with foreign and domestic "pirates" in the sixteenth century already signaled the difficulties of controlling the distant, ocean-oriented region, and the Ming government began to lose its hold on the Southeast Coast by the 1620's.[35] The region subsequently fell into the hands of trader-militarists such as the Zheng family, whose battles with the Manchu forces have been well chronicled elsewhere.[36] The extended dynastic transition lasted until the 1680's, when the Qing finally subdued the remnant Zheng forces and established control over Taiwan.

In the sixty-year interim, the Southeast Coast experienced repeated bandit attacks on virtually all the county seats, occupation by the Southern
Ming court during 1645–46, invasion by Qing forces in 1647, occupation
by these armies during a thirty-year standoff with the armies of Zheng
Chenggong, the evacuation and ruination of the coastal areas from 1661
through the mid-1680's, and a 1674 rebellion led by Geng Jingzhong, descendant of the Han bannerman Geng Zhongming, who had been
awarded feudatory control over Fujian in 1648.

The effects of this protracted transition are easy to catalogue but difficult to measure. Military occupation always brought high taxes, arbitrary exactions, and disruptions of commerce. The coastal evacuation
alone destroyed the local infrastructure—irrigation works, polders, markets, houses, ships, fortresses—so that even after the relaxation of the
evacuation decree and the reopening of foreign trade, the situation returned to normal only gradually. Between the late sixteenth and the late
seventeenth centuries, the population of Fujian as a whole may well
have decreased from 9.5 to 7.7 million people.[37] Even the inland prefecture of Jianyang recorded staggering losses: figures from gazetteers indicate that the 1694 population was only 36.79 percent of what it had been
during the Ming Wanli period (1573–1620).[38]

Violent attacks on the region by outside forces prompted violent responses from within. Some of those thrown off the land or out of their
market stalls by armies of occupation formed predatory bandit gangs.[39]
Elites responded by organizing private militia (which often amounted to
hiring their own bandits). Indeed, the dynastic transition witnessed yet
another wave of militarization in a violent frontier society where many
local lineages felt compelled to construct veritable forts for their protection.[40] Violence, or the threat of violence, marked the resettlement of the
coastal areas following the rescension of the evacuation decree, as those
who had been displaced from fields, polders, and water fought newcom-
ers seeking to profit from the disruption for control of valuable resources.[41] One measure of the decimation of the coastal areas is that local officials had to recruit nonnatives to restore the fields even after the
local population was allowed to return.[42]

Violence still continued to characterize the region after the trials of
the dynastic transition had passed. We have archival records of the activities of some 140 brotherhood associations in the pre–Opium War
Southeast Coast, and most of these records owe their existence to violent
activities in which the brotherhoods engaged.[43] In Taiwan alone, we also
find 32 cases of feuding in the period before the Opium War,[44] and local
officials on the mainland Southeast Coast complained constantly of
similar practices by which large, well-armed lineages used violence to

oppress smaller, weaker groups. Frontier Taiwan was further said to suffer "a small rebellion every three years and a large uprising every five," only a slight exaggeration.[45] The mainland Southeast Coast witnessed its share of rebellions too, if not as many as Taiwan.

Whether the eighteenth-century Southeast Coast was more violent than other regions of China is difficult to say. There is always a danger of exaggerating the violent nature of a premodern society, particularly when working with sources generated by crime and violence. Aggregate comparative data suggest that Fujian and Guangdong were indeed the most violent provinces in the late Ming, but that by the nineteenth century this distinction had passed to Nanzhili and Shaanxi.[46] Research under way on comparative levels of violence in eighteenth-century China (measured by estimated rates of execution for capital crimes) seems to accord with the findings for the nineteenth century, suggesting that Fujian and Guangdong provinces were somewhat more violent than the national average but not the most violent.[47] The same research indicates, nonetheless, that the northeastern counties of Guangdong, which belong to the Southeast Coast rather than to the Lingnan macroregion, were much more violent (again in terms of estimated executions) than the other Guangdong counties.[48]

Whatever the aggregate picture, it is beyond question that Chinese officialdom considered the region to be violent. The Yongzheng emperor, for example, noted in a sacred edict of 1734, "The local people of [Zhangzhou] and [Quanzhou] are accustomed to violence and love to fight."[49] Similar remarks appear in many local gazetteers. Chen Shengshao, who served in various counties of the Southeast coast in the 1820's and 1830's, paints a chilling portrait of a society numb to the moral dimensions of violence:

> [The people of Zhaoan county, Zhangzhou prefecture] purchase a poor man's son or a beggar. They give him food and clothing, and . . . treat him as their own son. . . . But should they come to hold a grudge against a rich man, or simply to covet what they cannot have, they kill their "son" and deposit the corpse in the "son's" home village. At first they pretend that he is out late and hasn't come back, but they later "learn" of his death. They cry and curse, saying "So-and-so killed my son." The rich man [named by the blackmailer] gets wind of this, and fearing that a pettifogger will emerge to plague him . . . decides to bribe his way out the dilemma.[50]

Yao Ying, an 1808 *jinshi* who served in both mainland Southeast China and Taiwan in the early nineteenth century, suggests one response of the state to such a violent society, a response that could only exacerbate the problem: "Before coming to Zhangzhou, I had heard that when troops [in

Zhangzhou] surrounded and arrested [a criminal], they sometimes destroyed the homes and burned the lairs of those they arrested. I at first thought that such practices were excessive, but after having served there myself for some time, I realized that there was no choice about the matter."[51]

Such a violent atmosphere surely contributed to mobility (just as a mobile society contributed to violence, as I shall argue below). Even the rumor of an impending feud sufficed to inspire the flight of weaker villages. Government intervention to suppress ongoing violence often provoked the flight of those who feared arrest or implication. Losers in interlineage battles over land or water often had to go elsewhere. And there is no way to count the numbers of frightened, marginalized men and women who took to the roads to avoid a confrontation with a landlord, an employer, or a bully.*

A contributing factor to both violence and mobility was surely the rapid growth of the population throughout the eighteenth century, even if the relationship between overpopulation, conflict, and movement is difficult to pin down. As is well known, the population of China as a whole nearly doubled between the mid-seventeenth and the mid-eighteenth centuries, jumping from 150 million in 1650 to 270 million by 1776.[52] The Southeast Coast shared in this demographic explosion, once the losses of the dynastic transition were made good. The population of Fujian, which had dropped to perhaps 7.7 million in the late seventeenth century, reached 11.2 million by 1776; that of Guangdong reached 14.8 million[53] after having been recorded as 6.4 million in 1749.[54] Although population figures from early nineteenth-century Fujian and Guangdong are implausible, every indication is that the region continued to share in "the unique chapter of population growth that did not end until the outbreak of the Taiping rebellion in 1851."[55]

However, although there is little doubt that the population of eighteenth-century Southeast China reached unprecedented levels, overpopulation is a relative concept. Because Ming officials frequently undercounted population and early nineteenth-century population records for Fujian and Guangdong clearly overcounted, it is possible to calculate frightening declines in the important man/land ratio. Ng Chin-keong, for example, gives unadjusted figures for mid-sixteenth-century Minnan as 5.0 *mou* per head in Zhangzhou and 8.4 *mou* per head in Quanzhou. By 1812, the ratio for Fujian as a whole had dropped to 0.93 *mou* per head, and given greater population densities in the Minnan region, the ratio must surely have been worse there.[56] Against the Malthusian

---

* Such themes are extremely common in the depositions included in routine homicide memorials (*xingke tiben*) from this period.

gloom cast by these figures we should also recall, first, that European travelers to the region in the Ming were astonished by the size of the regional population; and that the population of the region has of course continued to grow throughout the nineteenth and twentieth centuries.[57]

Nonetheless, numerous signs of distress suggest the seriousness of increasing population pressure during the eighteenth century. Grain prices in Southeast China rose over the course of the eighteenth century, just as they did in much of the rest of China.[58] Furthermore, Fujian Governor Wang Shu (served 1740–42) noted as early as the 1740's that "Fujian is mostly mountainous, and the fields are scattered. . . . Even if the people can reclaim a *mou* or two, it is always at the corners of [already cultivated] land, or on the tops of mountains."[59] The fragmentation of landholdings to which Governor Wang alludes can suggest that poverty drove more and more smallholders to sell portions of their land. Increasing acreage planted in sweet potatoes reveals ongoing incorporation of marginal land, surely driven by lack of fertile paddy land, as well as by hunger.[60] This evidence suggests that the situation in Fujian, chronically rice-deficient since the Song,[61] worsened in the face of eighteenth-century demographic growth, in part because there was little land to reclaim.

The question of hunger probes the important issues of poverty, misery, and marginalization. Qualitative evidence—stories of beggars, banditry, desperation—is not lacking, but the same is true of any premodern society (and many modern ones, including our own). Indeed, the depositions of many brotherhood association members speak eloquently to these concerns. In addition, many officials involved in the largely illegal migration to Taiwan made relevant observations. Shen Qiyuan, writing in 1729 against the ban on immigration in force at that time, argued:

> The homeless [*wuji zhi min*] of Zhangzhou and Quanzhou should not be barred from migrating. They have no land to till, no skill to sell, and no food to eat. Those who do well on Taiwan become wealthy, and even those who do less well can feed and clothe themselves. . . . When we tell the people to remain where they are and starve to death, rather than come to Taiwan where they can make a living, we are not acting as father and mother of the people.[62]

Another passage (with eerie contemporary overtones) reveals the danger of the passage to Taiwan, suggesting the desperation that drove these people:

> There are agents [*ketou*], who are in league with pirates and other bad characters of the water world. They use small, leaky boats, stuff hundreds of people into the hold, board it up, and refuse to let the people out. They

set sail at night, and if they meet up with a storm, they wind up in the bellies of the fish. If they run aground on arriving at the Taiwanese shore, they simply abandon ship out of fear of detection. They call this "liberating living creatures" [*fangsheng*, a Buddhist act of merit which includes, among other things, purchasing live fish at the market and returning them to the water]. . . . If the passengers get stuck in deep mud, this is called "planting cassava" [*zhongju*]. If the passengers get caught in high tides, the agents call them "fish bait" [*eryu*]. These bandits are only out for money, so they have no conscience. But people on the mainland are poor enough to take the risk and fall into their trap.[64]

The many temples on Taiwan to the souls of the unburied dead [*youyinggong*] who failed to survive the passage are testimony to the perils of these desperate migrants.[64]

If the violence of the dynastic transition and the growth of the population during the eighteenth century contributed to the creation of a society of unprecedented mobility, the consequences of this movement, in turn, could not but affect the texture of local society. Again, we find the clearest examples of this in the context of the social order (and disorder) of Taiwan, where movement to and within the island added the wildness of a new frontier to a regional culture that still retained certain features of its own frontier heritage.

Compared with the increasingly crowded mainland Southeast Coast, Taiwan was, at least until the end of the eighteenth century, underpopulated and undergoverned. This situation encouraged a certain flexibility in practices of group formation and social organization, and even, in some cases, genuine social mobility. As one commentator noted in the context of the early eighteenth century: "It is not the set pattern that the sons of gentry remain gentry forever; nor that the sons of peasants remain peasants forever. If the fathers and elder brothers of today's elegant Taiwanese gentry were not peasants and workers, then they were merchants and peddlers. No more than one or two out of one hundred inherits his father's occupation."[65] Other commentators repeated these themes, not without a certain Confucian approbation: "[The Taiwanese] make no distinction between noble and base, and all dress in beautiful, colorful clothing. They are embarrassed to wear cloth boots or stockings, and instead have their footwear embroidered, discarding it at the first hint of a blemish. Even the porters and yamen lackeys wear silk trousers."[66]

Another example of the social fluidity of frontier Taiwan is the ethnic (or "subethnic") collaboration through which early eighteenth-century migrants from the Zhangzhou, Quanzhou, and Hakka regions of the Southeast Coast reclaimed the rugged Taiwanese countryside.[67] Even if this collaboration was prompted by the more immediate ethnic conflict between Han and aborigine, it is no less true that such collaboration was rare in the rural areas of the mainland Southeast Coast. We find further evidence of flexibility in the formation of surname groups on Taiwan, where, in some cases, those of the same surname were welcomed even in the absence of close genealogical ties.[68] Religious ties, organized through temple communities called *shenminghui*, competed with family organizations for the allegiance of the Taiwanese population.[69] Brotherhood associations had an obvious role to play in this society marked by shallow, overlapping spheres of social organization; as illustrated below, members of brotherhood associations and secret societies could also be members of surname groups and temple societies. Such flexibility was not necessarily confined to Taiwan (and perhaps not even to the Southeast Coast). Nonetheless, the fluidity of Taiwanese society was surely more marked than that of the mainland, well known for its powerful lineages.

Such fluidity could of course result in violence. The conditions of immigration, for example, gave rise to what James L. Watson has called in the context of the nineteenth- and twentieth-century Hong Kong New Territories a "bachelor subculture," although in the case of Taiwan this subculture appears to have dominated important aspects of social life until well into the nineteenth century.[70] As already noted, many Taiwanese throughout the eighteenth century were bachelors by necessity, because formal Qing immigration policy and the dangers of frontier life combined to discourage female migration. Such bachelors were known in Taiwan as "arhat's feet" [*luohanjiao*]:

> *Luohanjiao* is a Taiwanese slang expression for those who have no land or property, no wife or children, who are not officials, farmers, artisans, or merchants, and who do not labor. They gamble, they steal, they feud, and they rise up. So what is a *luohanjiao*? He is single and roams the land, forming bands [*dang*] wherever he goes, never owning both shirt and trousers at one time, remaining barefoot his entire life. In large cities and villages they number no less than several hundred; in small cities and villages they number at least several tens. This is why Taiwan is difficult to govern.[71]

Many Qing commentators bemoaned the lack of a restraining female presence on the men of the island, which left them free to fight, whore, gamble, and drink as they pleased.

Again, one imagines that such a social atmosphere differed only in degree from that of the mainland Southeast Coast (or of much of late imperial China in general). Writing about early nineteenth-century eastern Guangdong, Cheng Hanzhang commented: "In every village, after the late rice has been harvested and placed on the threshing floor, local riffraff [*wulai*] put together a festival to repay the spirits [*choushen*]. They collect money to . . . hold an opera, and the riffraff take a percentage of the gambling that takes place. The drinking and gambling continue for ten days to half a month. It is a terrible custom."[72] Cheng's comments concerning the popular culture of the region suggest a truculence and readiness for violence that surely served migrants to Taiwan well (and to which the Taiwanese frontier experience surely contributed):

> Local troupes present operas dealing with disloyal servants and rebellious [subjects]. They completely ignore ethics and principle and stress only strength [*haoqiang*], jumping and fighting throughout the performance. There are a hundred variations on the same theme. But the ignorant masses know no better than to roar their unanimous approval. This is teaching the people to be rebellious. . . .Local officials should also keep an eye on the book markets, where the publishers are selling lewd novels and tales of mountain rebels. These should all be burned.[73]

The instability of frontier life in Taiwan could only aggravate the general tendency toward rowdiness inherent in a "bachelor subculture." The constant threat of attacks by the aboriginal tribes, who found themselves pushed ever farther from their traditional hunting and farming grounds, counseled that all men be armed and ready at all times with the "cudgels, fowling pieces, and beheading knives" that constituted the major weapons of the epoch.[74] In addition, by the mid- to late eighteenth century, the relative ethnic cooperation (among the Han) that had marked the initial reclamation of Taiwanese farmland gave way to large-scale ethnic feuds. In these feuds, violence could ravage large areas of the island, as villages mobilized and fought simply on the basis of ethnic identity (Zhangzhou, Quanzhou, or Hakka).[75]

Such a violent atmosphere surely affected the character of interpersonal and familial relationships. During the Lin Shuangwen rebellion, enemies on occasion dismembered their captives, revealing a shocking degree of dehumanization (*TDH* 1: 351–52). Less shocking but still relevant, rebel leader Lin Shuangwen's wife noted plaintively in her deposition to Qing authorities: "My husband has a crude and violent nature, and was never peaceful with me. The year before last when [he] wanted to rise up, I urged him several times not to, but he wouldn't listen, and took a knife and said he was going to kill me" (*TDH* 4: 437). At the other end of the spectrum, collective violence in the region frequently provoked the repression of the state. Indeed, the habits of overworked officials, who often ignored rumors and even officially lodged complaints of violence until such a posture became untenable, and then intervened with fairly massive displays of force, must have made violence seem all the more justified. The brutality of the techniques employed by the military in the region—burning the houses of villagers suspected of harboring alleged criminals, for example—could only add to such an impression.

Movement and violence, violence and mobility. Whatever the underlying socioeconomic forces behind the "dislocations" that stand out so clearly in the archival documents, movement and violence must have been an important part of the popular awareness of these forces. One can easily understand the appeal of brotherhood associations in such a fluid and dangerous environment, to those struggling to survive in new and unfamiliar terrain as well as to those who found themselves prey to the threatening, wandering strangers.

The Documentary Setting

As important as the historiographical, geographical, and historical settings is the documentary setting, particularly in the case of a study claiming to interpret the life experiences of an underclass by means of documents written by an elite, and particularly when these documents treat "criminal" activities. This study is based almost entirely on Qing archival documents, many published, some not. These documents consist of the depositions of arrested society members (and those of their neighbors and family members) and written materials in the possession of association members, as well as Qing commentary on the nature of the associations and the means taken to apprehend and extinguish them. The number of such documents is large, but not overwhelming. I have already noted the 140 cases of *hui* or secret society activity in pre–Opium War China located by Zhuang Jifa, chiefly in the Qing archival holdings on Taiwan. Many of these cases are very carefully detailed.[76] Qin Baoqi's edited collection of documents from the Number One Historical Archives in Beijing on the pre–Opium War Tiandihui comes to seven volumes and hundreds of documents.[77] Hundreds, if not thousands, of other documents treating other varieties of secret societies are also available for perusal at the Number One Historical Archives in Beijing and at the National Palace Museum archives in Taipei (although many of these are in the process of being published).

The Qing state was extremely sensitive to brotherhood associations, which, of course, accounts for the impressive number of documents concerning them. For historians, at least, this sensitivity is a boon, not the least because Qing officials faced with brotherhood activities frequently produced more thorough and less formulaic documentation than when dealing with more routine crimes. In addition, secret societies themselves also produced substantial amounts of written materials: handbooks, membership certificates, banners, seals, charms. When we add the society-generated material to the Qing memorials and interrogations, we have a multitextured richness of documentation rarely found in the context of more straightforward criminal activities. Finally, brotherhood associations swore blood oaths, circulated rebellious proclamations, used apocalyptic symbols, and engaged in quasi-religious rituals, even as they engaged in mutual aid, criminal violence, and, on occasion, rebellion. The cultural complexity of these activities focuses attention on the interplay between social history and popular culture, between the "objective" socioeconomic forces connected to the late imperial order and the cultural and organizational resources available to those compelled to respond to these forces.

The inherent bias in the archival documents that make up the core of this history generally precluded sympathy on the part of Qing officials and limited the nature of the questions officials asked of those they arrested to a fairly narrow set of concerns ("Who recruited you?" "How did he know about Tiandihui rituals?" "Who else was present at the initiation ceremony?" "Did you recruit anyone else?" "Who are the people referred to in these manuals?"). In addition, the culture of the Chinese criminal justice system affected the nature of the documents in a number of ways. First, the widespread use of torture to secure the confession necessary for conviction calls into question the credibility of any deposition dealing with a serious crime. Second, the pressure brought to bear on local officials by the emperor and provincial- or capital-level officials often meant that arrest, torture, and conviction were more important than genuine pursuit of justice. For the same reason, distortion or suppression of information by local officials, whose careers could suffer from mishandling of mass actions, frequently accompanied forced or otherwise crafted "confessions."[78] Thus these documents, which already represent a biased sample of the activities of brotherhood associations, overreporting those involved in crime and violence, underreporting those engaged in innocent mutual aid, also give a biased interpretation of the sample.

Used with care, however, the documents can prove valuable. In some instances, they can be used in ways that Qing officials did not anticipate. For example, the large number of arrests made in the Lin Shuangwen uprising, together with the Qing practice of demanding from the rebels information concerning the age, place of birth, place of residence, occupation, martial status, family circumstances, and length of residence on

Taiwan, permit researchers to reconstruct a sociodemographic profile of the Tiandihui members and the rebels who followed Lin Shuangwen. This profile, moreover, undermines the interpretation of the rebellion advanced by Qing officials by illustrating that people long resident on Taiwan, rather than newly arrived "drifters," were at the core of the rebellion.

Furthermore, Qing officials often included along with their memorials numerous examples of written material produced by brotherhood associations (chiefly secret societies), in the form of manuals, charm books, banners, seals, certificates, and the like. In some instances, Qing officials clearly did not understand the meaning, or the degree of heterodoxy, of the materials; in other instances, they dispatched the material to prove to the emperor and higher officials just how perverse the commoners under their charge were. There are isolated indications that Qing officials might have tampered with or suppressed these written materials, but there is no indication that such practices were systematic, and the researcher can for the most part treat this material as authentic. Finally, even if many confessions were forced or false, not all confessions were, and not all parts of all confessions were. False confessions, where the arrested party provides incorrect or misleading information, are often detectable by comparison with other confessions from the same case. Forced confessions, by contrast, are usually related to Qing assumptions about the nature of associations and the sorts of crime in which they were involved—assumptions that most leaders were perversely evil, for example, and that one of the manifestations of this evil was greed, obvious in the fees charged for initiation (to cite one example); that the leaders of most secret societies were bound together by something resembling a conspiracy; that the purposes of most associations were limited to banditry and rebellion; and that most members of associations were ignorant and deluded. Confessionary information that belies these persistent Qing prejudices, or relates to questions outside the realm of these prejudices, can generally be accepted as fairly accurate (unless internal evidence suggests otherwise).[79]

The Organization of the Book

This book is organized around a theme with variations. The theme is that brotherhood associations should be understood as a popular institution that arose in response to the circumstances discussed above. The variations are the case studies for which the documentation is rich enough to permit detailed treatment of important issues.

Chapter 1 begins by tracing the pre-Qing genealogies of the social form identified with brotherhoods and secret societies (the *hui* or *she*) as well as the practice of swearing blood oaths. It then examines a number of archivally documented examples of seventeenth- and eighteenth-century brotherhoods, named brotherhoods, and secret societies in light of their "genealogies." Named brotherhood associations, though new to the Qing period, were built on earlier practices, some of which are quite ancient. *Hui* or *she* had long been part of community or lineage life, serving ritual or organizational needs under the direction of community or lineage elites. In the Qing period, young men at the margins of community life took control of the social form and began to use it for their own purposes, removing it from the control of local elites. But many brotherhood associations maintained ties to local society, existing alongside or in between legal, orthodox institutions; although they were rarely celebrated, they were nonetheless tolerated, sometimes even by the state.

The findings of Chapter 1 largely accord with the interpretations of recent archival historians that have emphasized the links between brotherhood associations and mutual aid. Chapters 2 and 3 test the boundaries of this characterization by examining some of the frequent instances of secret society involvement in violence and rebellion. Specifically, Chapter 2 treats the background to the Lin Shuangwen rebellion of 1787–88, the first Triad-led rebellion in Chinese history,* and finds that although the founders of the Heaven and Earth Society clearly used apocalyptic and rebellious symbols, and the Heaven and Earth Society was brought to Lin Shuangwen by a society member who had been in direct contact with the founders, very few of the apocalyptic or rebellious aspects of the "pure" Tiandihui appear in the Lin Shuangwen rebellion. Instead, Lin's Heaven and Earth Society seems to have been a criminal gang, and the rebellion grew out of ethnic tensions and the actions of the heavy-handed Chinese state on Taiwan.

Chapter 3 examines similar questions by comparing Lin's rebellion with the Zhu Yigui uprising of 1721. Zhu's uprising, also on Taiwan, was brought about by natural disasters and official malfeasance, and—most importantly—occurred before the creation of secret societies. Informal, ad hoc, brotherhoods (called *baiba* in the Zhu Yigui uprising rather than the later *hui*) did play a role, but they did not predate the conflict, as did Lin Shuangwen's Tiandihui, and only appeared after the tensions that led to rebellion began to mount. These defferences aside, Lin's and Zhu's rebellions are clearly more similar than different. If anything, Zhu's rebellion contains more apocalyptic and political messages than does Lin's. This does not mean that the Heaven and Earth Society could not

---

* Or, more precisely, the first rebellion in Chinese history that the Qing recognized as Tiandihui-led. See discussion of the Lu Mao and Li Amin uprisings below.

be rebellious or could not carry messianic messages, but it does suggest that the secret society tradition competed with other, less specific messianic and rebellious traditions in Chinese history, and that one should not make easy assumptions about the relationship between secret societies and rebellion.

Chapter 4 takes up the history of the Heaven and Earth Society in the period after the Lin Shuangwen rebellion. Unsurprisingly, the Qing reacted harshly to Lin's rebellion, and the final decade of the eighteenth century may well have been a watershed in the history of secret societies and their relationship to the state. During this decade, we find definitive evidence of groups that adopted the rituals and symbols of the Tiandihui for specifically rebellious purposes, and the Qing responded with escalating violence, passing harsh laws, terrorizing the countryside in search of Tiandihui leaders, and engaging in on-the-spot execution of society members. In some parts of the Southeast Coast, the violence of this decade may have confirmed the image of the Heaven and Earth Society as a vehicle of antigovernment protest, thus linking the mutual aid fraternities of the eighteenth century to the anti-Manchu rebels of the nineteenth.

A more complex story developed as the Heaven and Earth Society spread out of its original home base in southern Fujian, northern Guangdong, and Taiwan. In Taiwan and in southern Fujian the Tiandihui of the late eighteenth and early nineteenth centuries seems to have been largely a rebellious organization, and in Guangdong it became chiefly a vehicle for robbery. But in the western Fujian–eastern Jiangxi region the Tiandihui intermingled with local cults, lay Buddhism, and a range of magico-religious practices, and appears to have functioned as a variety of popular religion. Tiandihui members in this region continued to engage in robbery and criminal violence, and there is one case of attempted rebellion, but evidence from this period and region leaves no doubt that people were drawn to the Tiandihui not primarily by dreams of violence or rebellion but by the promise that the Tiandihui could provide supernatural protection from natural and human dangers. The perceived power of Tiandihui rituals may well have led marginalized young men to engage in crimes or violence they otherwise would not have been drawn to, but the charms, gods, and scriptures that accompany society practices make clear that the primary appeal of the Tiandihui was religious rather than simply utilitarian.

Chapter 5 shifts the focus of analysis to the state, examining Qing laws and the implementation of laws regarding brotherhood associations. The recommended punishments were harsh, presumably because Qing lawmakers associated brotherhood associations with heterodoxy and rebellion (although detailed justification of these harsh laws is strangely lacking). At the same time, Qing officials took pains to distinguish one sort of brotherhood, named brotherhood, or secret society from another, even including legal practices that resembled brotherhood associations but should not be punished. These careful distinctions not only reinforced the Qing self-image as benevolent, paternal rulers; they also signaled the Qing recognition that brotherhood associations were not all reducible to a devilish, heterodox plague on the Manchu house. Read sympathetically, the distinctions reproduce the range of brotherhood and secret society behavior outlined in this book. At the same time, examination of Qing implementation of the laws suggests that too often these definitional subtleties gave way as Qing officials faced with brotherhood associations opted for harshness and control.

Furthermore, archival evidence suggests that most confrontations between the Qing state and brotherhood associations involved neither rebellion nor heterodoxy but criminal entrepreneurship—banditry, robbery, racketeering, and so forth. A comparison of Qing laws and attitudes toward brotherhood associations with Qing laws and attitudes toward feuds (*xiedou*) shows that Qing officials employed similar language in their discussion of secret societies and feuds, suggesting that both were dominated by young toughs who used violence for their own ends. However, while Qing officials were quick to see criminal entrepreneurship in every sphere of secret society behavior, even when the societies are more properly understood as expressions of popular religion, they failed to interpret feuds in the same way, in spite of their own comments to that effect. Instead, Qing officials consistently linked feuds with lineages and villages, hence with lineage and village leadership. Feuds, in the eyes of Qing officials, were private violence, linked to known structures of rural society, and therefore more "normal" and acceptable than violence linked to brotherhood associations. Qing officials rarely intervened in feuds, choosing to allow local elites to manage their own affairs.

The Qing failure to note the similarities between secret societies and feuds points to a fundamental ideological decision, which helps in some ways to explain the fate of the marginalized, unconnected people who participated in both forms of violence: the Qing were not able to understand those outside the pale of lineage and village life. As a result, even innocent associations ran considerable risk of extreme punishment; young men engaged in feud violence could commit atrocious crimes, not with impunity, but often with less risk than those who joined brotherhood associations.

Chapter 6 seeks to place the data and arguments of the previous chapters in a larger perspective. Comparing the experiences of Chinese brotherhood associations in Southeast Asia with those in Southeast China proper, the concluding chapter emphasizes the power of the late imperial Chinese state to set limits to organizational innovations such as the brotherhood association, even though as a premodern state, the Qing was unable to stamp out the unwanted brotherhoods or even consistently to impose its own definition on local practice.

CHAPTER I

Brotherhood Associations in Southeast China Through the Lin Shuangwen Rebellion

Throughout Fujian, the evil habit of forming brotherhoods and secret societies [*jiehui shudang*] persists. In every village and lane, vagrants and outlaws, violent and prone to fighting, fearful of finding themselves isolated and helpless, secretly band together and set up associations, which they then name. Some publicly claim that they are worshiping a deity. Others secretly manufacture symbols that facilitate recruitment [*yinji wuse*]. . . . Some form brotherhoods according to age; others, fearing trouble with the law, eschew the "brotherhood" name. Their chief purpose is to engage in mutual aid in the event of trouble, but their strength and numbers allow them to oppress the weak and the few. . . . [There is little harm] in the villagers' establishing devotional associations such as incense societies [*xianghui*, generally part of pilgrimages]. . . . In addition, there are ignorant commoners who, out of mutual affection, band together in numbers of no more than a few. But if they begin to recruit others and set up named brotherhoods [*hui*] . . . then we must suspect their intentions. (*GZD QL* 22: 804)

So wrote Fujian Governor Dingchang in the tenth month of QL 29 (1764), as part of a long memorial to the Qianlong emperor on the subject of brotherhoods and secret societies. Having been at his post for three years, the governor took care to preface his remarks with the general observation that the overall level of violence in Fujian had recently dropped "with the passage of strict laws"—an impressive achievement, given that Fujianese "popular customs have long had a reputation for willfulness and perversity." Brotherhoods and secret societies, however, remained a persistent problem, requiring further legal solutions, which the governor discussed at length. Dingchang's memorial is thus important in the history of Qing laws against secret societies, and it raises a number of intriguing questions.

First, the fact that Dingchang felt compelled to compose a complex memorial on the legal penalties to be applied to various kinds of brotherhoods suggests that something about these brotherhoods was new to him, and perhaps new to the eighteenth century. Other evidence supports this view. James Tong's exhaustive work on Ming collective violence does not mention secret societies or *hui*.[1] As is well known, the Qing passed the first laws in Chinese history against blood-oath brotherhoods and secret societies. By contrast, there were at least 45 incidents of *hui*-related violence in Southeast China in the eighteenth century.[2] C. K. Yang's nationwide survey of violence in nineteenth-century China locates 611 secret society "mass action incidents," accounting for 9.2 percent of all mass actions during the nineteenth century.[3] These figures certainly suggest that brotherhood associations, or at least brotherhood associations that engaged in violence, began to proliferate in the eighteenth century. On the other hand, Dingchang links brotherhood associations to more innocent practices of popular religion, pilgrimages, and mutual aid, all of which have histories that go back well before the Qing.

Second, Dingchang juxtaposes the innocent pursuit of mutual aid with frequent and worrisome violence, without providing a convincing explanation of the connections between the two. His discussion distinguishes brotherhoods and secret societies from common bandits. Again, he connects even the violent named brotherhoods and secret societies with common practices of mutual aid and popular religion, and in another, untranslated, part of his memorial he argues that the formation of brotherhood associations was simply one means by which local groups protected themselves. Indeed, Dingchang notes that brotherhood associations were to be found in "every village and lane." All this suggests that brotherhoods were embedded in the institutions of local society. Yet Dingchang clearly views some varieties of these associations as a threat to public order, arguing later in his memorial that "opposition to the state and resisting arrest also begin with [the establishment of associations], and thus I say that this evil habit is truly the origin of all illegal activity."

How should we understand the connection between brotherly affection and mutual aid on the one hand, and violence and rebellion on the other? How can something so embedded in the life of the community be at the same time so threatening? Why does something with such a long history require new laws for its control? How should we understand brotherhoods and secret societies, their membership, and their relationship to the surrounding social order?

The brotherhood associations that appear frequently in eighteenth- and nineteenth-century sources were not, I believe, completely new phenomena. Instead, they grew out of organizational and cultural practices of traditional Chinese communities, which provided either mutual assistance or the administration of community activities. Although many Qing brotherhood associations remained within community structures, others moved out from under the control of traditional communities and community leaders. But certain features of seventeenth- and eighteenth-century brotherhood associations were new and distinctive, and they seem to account, at least in part, for the frequent mention of these groups in Qing sources. During the early Qing period, brotherhood associations became increasingly common as informal institutions catering to the needs of marginalized young men in the Southeast Coast. Neither the men nor the institutions were always completely alienated from traditional society, nor were all these associations secret. Often the brotherhood associations existed alongside or in between traditional institutions, allowing their members to achieve a variety of ends, ranging from mutual aid to criminal entrepreneurship to, on occasion, rebellion.

Eighteenth-century Chinese knew how to form brotherhood associations because most of them derived from traditional institutions and practices. The association (*hui* or *she*) as a social form was part of traditional village life, often connected either to lineage rites, practices of popular religion, or informal structures of mutual aid. Indeed, the widespread nature of some of the organizational mechanisms associated with the *hui* in twentieth-century Taiwan has prompted anthropologist Stephen Sangren to characterize the association as more basic to the organization of Chinese society than kinship.[4] The brotherhood oath that accompanied the formation of most associations would likewise have been familiar from a variety of contexts, ranging from popular drama and fiction to marriage oaths and declarations of friendship—and to acts of collective violence.

Outside elite control, however, even the innocent aspects of these familiar practices took on new meanings.[5] Since many brotherhood associations were only partially attached to traditional, orthodox social institutions, they became potentially dangerous in two ways. First, brotherhoods were unigenerational, unlike the more typically hierarchical institutions of local society with their built-in age-based authority. Some brotherhood associations facilitated late-night drinking and acts of bravado in ways that lineages and village communities, more directly linked to the Qing political order through local gentry, did not. Second, Qing authorities viewed the blood oath itself as heterodox and dangerous, particularly when employed to cement even small numbers of men

in unsanctioned associations. Most commoners surely shared this recognition that few blood oaths were completely innocent.

The frequent connection between brotherhood associations and violence also grew in part out of their structural position in Chinese society.
Since brotherhood associations were often located between traditional
institutions, drawing membership from more than one village, lineage,
or ethnic group, association members did not always receive the protection afforded more central members of solidary groups, and members
were also freer to engage in various types of violence, if violence proved
necessary or profitable. Mutual aid in such an environment might easily
move from shared crop-watching or common contributions to parental
burial funds, to less innocent forms of "self-help." Rebels and malcon-
tents might also find themselves naturally drawn to such associations
because of their tenuous relationship to local society (providing limited protection and yet adequate distance) and their bonds of blood
brotherhood.

This chapter will illustrate more fully the variety of different kinds
of brotherhood associations that flourished in late imperial Southeast
China. Dingchang's memorial is instructive in this regard: his mention
of the "ignorant commoners" who band together in small groups clearly
refers to the "simple" brotherhoods discussed above; his description of
the practice of naming associations again corresponds to the "named
brotherhoods" discussed in the Introduction; and his mention of those
brotherhood associations that "secretly manufacture symbols that facilitate recruitment" must be a reference to some sort of secret society.
Dingchang clearly sees all these as variations on a single practice, which
I have called the brotherhood association. A significant part of the scholarly debate over the nature of the secret society, as illustrated in the discussion of the historiography of Chinese secret societies in the Introduction, has stemmed from an attempt to construct narrow generalizations
for a diverse category that included a number of different types: innocent
brotherhood associations fully embedded in law-abiding communities,
associations at the margins of society that divided their time between
legal and illegal pursuit of mutual aid, and associations that harbored
con men and rebels.

In sum, this chapter seeks to establish a more textured characterization of brotherhood associations that does not reduce their separate characteristics to those of class-conscious rebels or innocent practitioners of
mutual aid. The argument is complex and much of the evidence is difficult. Ultimately, my characterization of the late imperial brotherhood
association is founded on an interpretation of Qing archival materials
treating a variety of brotherhoods and secret societies, but I begin with a

"genealogy" of the brotherhood association, tracing the histories of the practices embodied in the association: the *hui* as a social form, and the blood oath.

Genealogies of Early Qing Brotherhood Associations

Regardless of the purpose for which they were established, most Qing brotherhood associations consisted of two components: an organization that brought members together in pursuit of some form of cooperative enterprise, and a ritual, generally including a blood oath of fictive brotherhood, that cemented the organization. The genealogies of each of these components illustrate the long history of organization for mutual aid, generally carried out within the confines of village society. The longer history of the blood oath is more difficult to trace, and possesses dangerous symbolic overtones of heterodoxy and rebellion. Though neither the *hui* nor the blood oath was new to the Qing period, groups of men at the margins of society, who for purposes of mutual aid banded together through a blood oath and called themselves *hui*, proliferated for the first time during and after the Ming-Qing transition.

ORGANIZATION FOR MUTUAL AID

Local organization for mutual cooperation in Chinese society spanned a broad spectrum of activities and generally employed terms such as *hui* and *she* as names for the organizations. The kind of local organization that eventually grew into the Qing *hui* first emerged in significant numbers in the mid- to late Tang, and was usually referred to as an *yishe*.[6] The *yi* of *yishe* refers to an artificial unit of social organization imposed from above and *yishe* thus means an "association of the *yi*," but for all practical purposes few of these seem to have transcended the boundaries of the village.[7] Another source of cooperation for mutual aid included the vegetarian societies (*zhaihui*), scripture-reading groups, and sutra storytelling practices (*sujiang*) originally attached to Buddhist temples.[8] An elite version of these associations, the *fashe*, brought together monks and local notables in the homes of the latter for discussions of the sutras, but most *yishe* maintained their concern with the character and morality of *she* members by encouraging mutual aid in a number of related activities.[9]

Agricultural production was one of the most important of these activities. Early examples of agricultural mutual-aid societies include "hoe societies" (*chushe*), which were small-scale labor-sharing organizations found in both northern and southern Song and Yuan China.[10] The well-known crop-watching societies (*kanqinghui*) of the Ming-Qing period

surely draw on this tradition too. In some instances, cooperation continued after the busy season of agricultural labor, extending to the construction of dikes and polders, the collection of stubble, and various other
chores. Some peasants shared draft animals; others made scarce tools
available to their neighbors. Still others pooled their funds to purchase
animals and tools.

The Confucian classics sanctioned such cooperation, and the state encouraged it.[11] In 1395, for example, an official in the Nanjing area sent a
memorial to the first Ming emperor arguing as follows:

> Among the peasantry there are couples who have received forty, fifty, or
> one hundred *mou*. There is much work to be done in the fields in the
> spring and summer, and if the husband is unlucky enough to take ill and
> the wife has to nurse him . . . then the agricultural chores will be aban-
> doned and the fields taken over by weeds. Even if he recovers, it will be
> too late, and the state will lose its tax revenues, while the man will have
> nothing with which to feed his family. Their poverty will force them from
> the land. . . . I request that we order the peasants of each rural area to form
> associations [*she*] of twenty to forty-five families, so that in the busy sea-
> son, if someone should fall ill there will be the collective strength of the
> *she* to help with the plowing and weeding. Thus the fields will not be
> abandoned, the people will not face famine, the populace will be harmo-
> nious, and their customs improved.

Ming Taizu approved the suggestion, and wondered if it might also be
extended to mutual aid in the event of weddings and funerals.[12] An early
Qing (1660) entry in the *Da Qing huidian shili* similarly encouraged
"the establishment of village *she*, so that the people will concentrate
in groups of twenty or thirty, forty or fifty families, who will provide
agricultural assistance during the busy season in the event of death or
illness."[13]

As the first Ming emperor suggested, weddings and funerals, as important ceremonial occasions in the life cycles of virtually all Chinese families, represented another context in which mutual aid could be significant. The burial of parents was a crucial obligation in a society that
prized filial piety, and there are many examples of associations whose
chief purpose was to help either with the organization or the expense of
parental burial. One Tang imperial edict cautions against the growth of
"private" *she* devoted to weddings and funerals, arguing that such activities placed too great a burden on the peasantry (who were presumably
expected to assist in the ceremonial affairs of the elite).[14] In another instance, the Tang official Wei Ting complained in a memorial that the
practice of forming *yishe* diverted both noble and peasant from the
proper rituals of mourning.[15]

Even with such official concerns, the expense of parental burial ensured the popularity of *she* and *hui* devoted to burials, and the number
of associations of this sort seems to have grown during the Ming. An
item in the Wanli period Ningjin county (Hebei) gazetteer notes the existence of burial *she*:

> People establish *yishe* to prepare for mourning. These *she* make no dis-
> tinction between rich and poor, and select [members] only according to
> virtue. They meet twice monthly on the first and fifteenth, and everyone
> contributes a certain amount of money. They choose someone who is hon-
> est and generous to be head [of the association]. When there is a death
> within the association, the leader calls for donations and devotions.[16]

Some of these funeral organizations, such as Tang Haoru's Society for the
Burial of Relatives (*zangqinshe*), appear to have become quite complex
during the Qing, keeping elaborate records so as to encourage reverence
and penalize financial and moral lapses.[17] Distressed by the contemporary practice of delayed burial, Tang set the maximum size of each association at 32, further subdivided into four subgroups of eight. A head
(*zongshou*) led each of these subgroups, known as *zong*, and an assistant
head (*zongzuo*) encouraged financial contributions, so that money could
be accumulated to purchase a proper plot of land, leaving no excuse for
delayed burial, for which there was a fine. The association was to last for
seven years. Later in the nineteenth century, Zhang Lüxiang further
popularized Tang's basic model, doubling its size to 64 members and
eight subgroups. One suspects, however, that most mourning societies
were less formal than the Tang Haoru model, as suggested by the following nineteenth-century example from Anhui:

> For the poor to bury their dead requires substantial contributions from
> relatives and friends, so there have always been Filial Piety and Righteous-
> ness Societies [*xiaoyihui*]. These meet for a meal once a month, and make
> common contributions, which are held [in trust] by one person. On the
> death of a grandfather, grandmother, father or mother, all members help
> to carry out the mourning and burial, using the [accumulated] funds to
> help the family in need. If there is extra interest it goes to the surviving
> members of the families. This is practiced by both elite and commoners.[18]

Many sources confirm the widespread existence of societies devoted to
the care of aging and dying parents.[19]

Weddings were another important, and expensive, event in the ritual
life cycle of the Chinese family, prompting the establishment of societies to accumulate funds to carry out weddings in accordance with the
dictates of ritual and display. Over the whole of the late imperial period,
scholars have found scattered references to "Sentiments" societies (*qing-*

hui), Happiness societies (xishe), Marriage societies (hunjiahui), Red Hat societies (hongmaohui), and Red Ceremony societies (honglishe), among others. Organizations devoted to preparations for marriage do not appear to have developed as early or to have been as widespread as those concerned with burials, however, and they should perhaps be grouped together with more general societies, such as the well-known Red and White societies (hongbaihui) as well as the eighteenth-century Henan hui, which accumulated funds for newborns as well as for funerals.[20]

Many of these organizations, whatever their stated purpose, shared a common financial mechanism: the pooling of joint funds and their investment in an interest-earning property or enterprise. Scholars speculate that this practice may have been imported from India before or during the Tang.[21] The biography of Wei Dan in the New Tang History notes that while serving as prefect of Yongzhou, Wei observed that the locals were too poor to afford oxen, so he set up one or more she consisting of some twenty families, and had each family contribute a certain amount of money to a common fund every month so that, over time, they were able to buy the oxen they needed.[22] Some of the funeral societies also appear to have made capital available to those contributing money.

However, there was no particular need to hide financial exigency behind the façade of ceremonial expense. At least from the Ming period, Chinese set up hui and she for the sole purpose of providing capital for friends and relatives in need. Ming and Qing commentators generally referred to such organizations as silver associations (yinhui) or "shaking" associations (yaohui), both of which appear to have begun as a form of gambling: "According to the customs of Jiangsu, whenever someone comes upon hard times, he gets his friends together and they all contribute a sum of money. They enclose dice inside a box and shake it, and the lucky winner takes it all. . . . [This is called a] yaohui."[23] Before long, one assumes, this custom evolved into the qianhui or biaohui, the revolving credit society familiar from modern Taiwan and from many other societies.[24] By the latter Qing period, revolving credit societies were extremely common. They bore various names, some indicating the size of the membership or the size of the expected contribution, and others simply variations on the theme of revolving credit: the Seven Star Society (qixinghui), the Seven Worthies Society (qixianhui), the Eight Immortals Society (baxianhui), the Gentlemen's Society (junzihui), the Five Tigers Society (wuhuhui), the Five Leaders Society (wuzonghui), the Eighty Dollar Society (bashiyuan hui), the Two Hundred Dollar Society (erbaiyuan hui), the Accumulated Gold Society (jijinhui), the Accumulation Society (duijihui), and the Credit Society (shehui), among many others.[25]

THE *HUI* IN COMMUNITY RITUAL ORGANIZATION

In addition to these examples of the *hui* or *she* as forums for the organization of mutual aid, we also find numerous historical references to celebratory or ritual occasions, and to small groups set up to organize such occasions, both of which were frequently referred to as either *hui* or *she*. The Song dynasty text *Wulin jiushi*, for example, refers to "gatherings" (*hui*) of troupes (*she*) of artisans and performers on certain festive occasions, and notes as well that "every monastery held a Buddha-washing gathering [*yufohui*, the eighth day of the fourth month, on the birthday of the Buddha], at which the monks and nuns competed to collect bronze images [of the Buddha] in little basins."[26] By the late Ming, in North China if not elsewhere, there were urban religious associations, usually called sacred associations (*shenghui*), which brought together significant numbers of unrelated individuals to carry out annual pilgrimages and to gather money to repair local temples.[27]

In addition, at least by the early Ming, it is clear that *hui* and *she* played important roles in community and lineage religious activities, either as subunits of the communities charged with organizing particular activities, or as the names for the activities themselves (often feasts or activities culminating in feasts).[28] Anthropologist Myron Cohen found that until very recently, lineage members of the North China village of Yangmansa, where Cohen did his field work, formed a *qingminghui* every year during the Qingming festival, in order to organize the "only mobilization of the lineage as a group in a ritual context."[29] In his examination of the intersection of religious and community organization in northern Taiwan, historian Wang Shih-ch'ing discusses a number of equally relevant organizations. First, he notes the late eighteenth-century establishment of a *chifuhui*—"eat good fortune association"— by the residents of the village of Tandi in the southwestern region of the Taipei basin. The association met "once or twice a year, share[d] a feast, and worship[ed]" the local earth god. In addition, according to Wang, the association also provided "the institutional means of organizing work parties to repair irrigation ditches and roads . . . [as well as serving as] a forum for negotiating disputes over boundaries and water rights." Wang also discusses the multicommunity spirit association (*shenminghui*), "self-selected communities in which membership is not defined solely on a territorial basis but on the basis of kinship affiliation, ethnic identity, or devotion to a particular god," which played an important role as a substitute for extensive lineage organization in the early development of Taiwanese society.[30] In many such organizations, mutual aid combined with religious practices to promote community or lineage cohesion.

In summary, these long-established practices of banding together in various contexts for mutual aid represent an important part of the tradition drawn upon by the *hui* of the eighteenth and nineteenth centuries. Most examples of this kind of mutual aid seem to have relied on natural interaction among village or lineage members or among members of subcommunity social units. Indeed, with the exceptions of organization for defense and organization for the construction of irrigation works, which were often larger, more complex, and less enduring than the associations discussed here, pre-eighteenth-century *hui* seem to have functioned largely within village society, under the fairly watchful eye of the local elite, and with the toleration and even occasional encouragement of the state.[31] Thus when, for example, peasants in 1720's Taiwan set up a Father and Mother Society to help fellow association members accumulate funds to bury their parents, they were clearly acting within a long and well-established tradition—even though a zealous Qing state arrested and executed the leaders. As already suggested, many Qing *hui* were to some degree outside community control, which meant that "cooperative" impulses could lead to illegal activities, and "mutual aid fraternities" could recruit unsavory members. But in terms of the basic motivation behind *hui* formation, there seems to have been more continuity than innovation in the proliferation of eighteenth- and nineteenth-century associations.

The Ritual of Association:
The Blood Oath of Fictive Brotherhood

An oath of fictive brotherhood binding members to one another was a second defining feature of the *hui* during the Qing period. In fact, the blood ritual was one notable difference between the *hui* of mutual aid and communal celebration and the potentially more dangerous *hui* that excited Qing suspicion. The sources collected to explore the history and variety of organization for mutual aid are silent on the subject of the rituals that accompanied the formation of such groups. Of the hundreds of sources assembled by Shimizu Morimitsu, one of the few that discuss the ritual aspects of *hui* formation is the Ming Wanli Sishui county (Shandong) gazetteer, which records: "The ordinary people of the cities and villages gather together in *hui*. To the east they make obeisance to Taishan, and to the south they make obeisance to Wudang [both sacred mountains]. In the idle period at the end of the year they form *she* by the hundreds and call these organizations incense societies [*xianghui*]."[32] This passage clearly refers to the "sacred associations," which were but one of many different kinds of associations, and one of the few that extended beyond village or community boundaries. It seems fair to assume that the sources are quiet on the nature of the ritual that accompanied the formation of the agricultural, wedding, funeral, and other societies because these rituals were subsumed in the ceremonial life of the communal group. Shimizu produces no sources that identify the ritual of blood-oath brotherhood with the formation of the *hui* and *she*.

BLOOD OATHS AND THE WARRING STATES TRANSITION

Historical sources on blood-oath brotherhoods appear earlier than those treating mutual aid associations, and the intersection of these two traditions in the late imperial period is one of the defining features of the *hui* under discussion here. The most compelling account of the early history of blood oaths is found in Mark Edward Lewis's *Sanctioned Violence in Early China*, and although several centuries separate the Warring States from the brotherhood associations examined in this volume, the information in Lewis's study is still helpful in evaluating the meanings attached to blood oaths later in Chinese history.

Lewis's study reexamines the Warring States transition from an aristocratic, "feudal" regime to a proto-imperial bureaucracy "as revealed by changes in the patterns of sanctioned violence"—warfare, sacrifice, hunting, and other "ritually coded acts of violence."[33] Blood oaths were crucial to this transformation in that they provided a mechanism of elite political and social cohesion in the wake of the breakdown of the aristocratic religious order of the Shang and early Zhou dynasties:

> [The pre-transition] elite [was] defined through sacrifice and warfare, drawn together through kin ties established by the cult of the ancestors and the ritual exchanges of meat, but riven by a segmentary division of authority among men who were devoted to an honor defined by heroism and martial prowess. Interstate wars, inter-lineage conflicts, and vendettas launched to avenge slighted honor generated incessant conflicts that broke down the old hierarchies of ritual and lineage law and replaced them with an increasingly savage struggle for dominance through armed force. In the conflicts of the Spring and Autumn period, the primary means devised to create new ties among men no longer tightly bound by the old Zhou order was the blood covenant [*meng*].[34]

In the early Eastern Zhou, these blood oaths became "fundamental to the political and social order," initially facilitating diplomatic pacts under the temporary leadership of an overlord (*ba*), later permitting alliances between powerful lineages, "alien states, and . . . the various contestants for supremacy" as the Zhou disintegrated.[35]

These covenants were binding forms of oaths designed to secure compliance to a common purpose, and they were "distinguished from ordinary oaths through the killing of a sacrificial animal and the drinking of its blood."[36] Participants sealed the covenants through purification and animal sacrifice (generally a sheep). "Blood was then sprinkled on the altar to summon the spirits, and the text of the covenant was read. This text included a list of the participants, the terms of the oath, and sometimes a curse upon those who violated the covenant."[37] The superficial similarity of these elite rituals to those used by eighteenth- and nineteenth-century *hui* is obvious.[38]

Lewis goes on to argue that these blood oaths, a private response to the disintegration of the old, "feudal" public, gave way in turn to a reimagined public sphere. In this new public sphere, the written text (now called a "bond" [*yue*]) replaced the blood sacrifice, the moral intentions of the participants assumed the roles of the sanction of the spirits and ancestors, and the hierarchical relationship between ruler and servitor, husband and wife, noble and dependent replaced the relative equality of the parties to the blood oath.[39] In other words, the transition resulted in the text-based moral hierarchy of Confucian imperial China.

BLOOD OATHS AND POPULAR CULTURE

It is unclear to what extent *popular* rituals adopted the blood sacrifice in this early period; most of the sources focus on elite behavior. Nor is it clear what happened to the practice of blood sacrifice after the Han-period transformation Lewis describes. We know that bonds and oaths of various sorts functioned in a variety of popular contexts from Han times down to the modern age. Barend ter Haar identifies four such practices by Han Chinese, all of which employ the language of bonds and covenants—*jie, ding, yue, meng, shi, jieyi*—while dispensing with the actual blood sacrifice.[40] These practices include: popular bonds promising cooperation between families and couples, generally in the context of marriage; legal bonds in which sworn oaths attest to veracity and personal integrity; community bonds, where oaths serve to cement communal ties, which likely gave rise to official attempts in the Neo-Confucian revival from Song times forward to impose "community covenants" (*xiangyue*) from above; and bonds of fictive kinship between unrelated persons. This evidence is borne out by literary references. The *Shuihuzhuan* and the *Sanguo yanyi* indicate that the process of brotherhood formation (*jiebai*) is moderately ancient and very popular: late Song story cycles and Yuan drama celebrated the Peach Garden Oath and the assembly at the Zhongyitang even before the novels reached more mature form in the Ming.[41] The first substantive chapter of *Jinpingmei* includes an account of the formation of a brotherhood.[42]

Ter Haar also finds persuasive evidence that minority ethnic groups,

including the Mongols and the Manchus in the pre-Qing period, employed blood-oath rituals strikingly similar to those of the transitional
period between the Warring States and the early imperial era throughout
Chinese history, and he also notes that blood oaths figured prominently,
again throughout Chinese history, in various violent, criminal, messianic, and rebellious contexts.[43] The most famous example during the
Ming-Qing period in Southeast China is probably that of Deng Maoqi,
the fabled "leveling king" (*chanping wang*) who led a major uprising of
disgruntled miners and tenant farmers in western Fujian in the late
1440's, and sealed his pact with his followers by killing a white horse,
drinking its blood, and sacrificing to heaven.[44] But pirates,[45] groups of
indentured servants (*nu*),[46] and bandits,[47] among others, also made use of
the blood oath. In at least one instance, a Qing official advised local can-
tons (*xiang*) in Guangdong to form alliances against bandits and to seal
these alliances with blood oaths.[48] Clearly, the blood oath, substituting
for ties of genuine kinship, could sanctify undertakings of great danger.

The history of the blood oath is more complicated than that of the
hui or *she*. First, it is clear that the history we have at present is incomplete, with important questions unanswered, particularly in the realm of
popular culture. Second, the act of oath-taking appeared in two different
contexts. The blood oath, drawing on the solemn idea of human sacrifice, seems to have been invoked in situations of great political moment—wars and rebellions. The simple oath (without blood) seems to
have sanctified bonds of a somewhat lesser order—marriage, friendship,
community compacts. However, for reasons that are unclear, many Qing
hui that were devoted to what appears to be the fairly innocent pursuit
of mutual aid chose to employ a blood sacrifice rather than a simple
oath, and in doing so, they imbued their organizations and activities
with a powerfully dangerous symbolism that the Qing state could not
ignore. One way to understand this choice is to recognize just how dangerous life at the margins of society could be, and to note that "mutual
aid" among poor young men could often translate into criminal or predatory behavior; the blood oath bound these young men to each other in
the face of potential risk, and perhaps also made them seem more fear-
some to outside groups.

The *hui* as a *named association*, a body of men bound together by
fictive kinship and some variety of blood oath, and naming themselves
through the use of the ideograph "*hui*," does not appear prominently in
these genealogies.[49] The brotherhood associations of the early Qing drew
on various traditions to construct their own version of nonelite associational life. Unfortunately, evidence does not permit us to trace in detail
the "evolution" of one type of *hui* into another, and it is unlikely that

we would find an uncomplicated evolution even if our record were more complete. Indeed, my argument is not that there was a wholesale transformation of one type of institution into another; innocent *hui* embedded in lineages and communities continue to exist in Chinese society down to the present day. Instead, those at the margins of community life borrowed the language of association and the symbolism of the blood oath to engage in a variety of practices related to their marginal position in society.

Brotherhood Associations in Eighteenth-Century Southeast China through the Lin Shuangwen Uprising

The following section, departing from the "global" approach used to reconstruct the genealogies of Qing brotherhood associations, takes up Qing archival evidence to examine the local context in which many of these associations flourished. The evidence on which I base this interpretation is difficult. Although Table 1 illustrates that brotherhood associations and secret societies did indeed proliferate during this period, particularly in Southeast China, not all the cases listed in this table are well documented. Many are mentioned only by name; some are discussed in only one document. Furthermore, the better-documented cases are those that engaged in crime or rebellion, thus attracting the attention of the state, and much of the archival evidence touching on this subject is embedded in narratives of violence, arrest, and persecution. Presentation of complete case studies therefore not only risks tedious repetition but also implicitly accepts the Qing interpretation of the nature of brotherhood associations. I present briefly the cases for which adequate documentation exists, and then go on to organize the evidence from a variety of cases under headings of my own devising. In this fashion I can attempt to look past the criminal and violent aspects of the cases and answer questions about the relationship between the brotherhood associations and the local societies of which they were a part.

THE CASES

1. Fujian Governor-General Yao Qisheng, who served in this post during an important part of the transition to civilian rule (1678–83), recorded several instances of predatory brotherhood activities throughout mainland Fujian province in his writings from the period.[50]

2. Qing officials uncovered two Father and Mother societies (*fumuhui*) in 1728 in Zhuluo county, Taiwan. Authorities had been looking for a criminal gang, and had discovered the Fumuhui by chance. It is not

TABLE I

Brotherhood Associations and Secret Societies in Eighteenth-Century China

Year	Association/ Society	Location
1728	Tiebianhui	Fujian
1728	Fumuhui	Zhuluo, Taiwan, Fujian
1729	Taoyuanhui	Fujian
1729	Zilonghui	Taiwan, Fujian
1730	Yiqianhui	Xiamen, Fujian
1731	Fumuhui	Haiyang, Guangdong
1735	Tiechihui	Huoqiu, Jiangnan
1736	Guanshenghui	Shaowu, Fujian
1742	Zilonghui	Zhangpu, Fujian
1742	Xiaodaohui	Zhangpu, Fujian
1747	Bianqianhui	Fuan, Fujian
1747	Guandihui	Yihuang, Jiangxi
1748	Fumuhui	Changtai, Fujian
1748	Beidihui	Zhangpu, Fujian
1750	Tiechihui	Shaowu, Fujian
1752	Tiechihui	Shaowu, Fujian
1761	Tiandihui	Huizhou, Guangdong
1762	Tiandihui	Zhangpu, Fujian
1767	Tiandihui	Zhangpu, Fujian
1768	Tiandihui	Zhangpu, Fujian
1772	Xiaodaohui	Zhanghua, Taiwan, Fujian
1773	Xiaodaohui	Zhanghua, Taiwan, Fujian
1774	Xiaodaohui	Zhanghua, Taiwan, Fujian
1775	Xiaodaohui	Zhanghua, Taiwan, Fujian
1779	Xiaodaohui	Zhanghua, Taiwan, Fujian
1780	Xiaodaohui	Zhanghua, Taiwan, Fujian
1781	Xiaodaohui	Zhanghua, Taiwan, Fujian
1782	Xiaodaohui	Zhanghua, Taiwan, Fujian
1783	Tiandihui	Pinghe, Taiwan, Fujian
1784	Tiandihui	Zhanghua, Taiwan, Fujian
1786	Tiandihui	Zhanghua, Taiwan, Fujian
1786	Tiandihui[a]	Zhuluo, Taiwan, Fujian
1786	Leigonghui	Zhuluo, Taiwan, Fujian
1786	Tiandihui	Raoping, Guangdong
1787	Yaqianhui	Cangwu, Guangxi
1789	Youhui	Jiayi, Taiwan, Fujian
1790	Tiandihui	Jiayi, Taiwan, Fujian
1791	Tiandihui	Zhanghua, Taiwan, Fujian
1792	Tiandihui	Zhanghua, Taiwan, Fujian
1792	Tiandihui[b]	Tongan, Fujian
1794	Xiaodaohui	Fengshan, Taiwan, Fujian
1794	Tiandihui	Longxi, Fujian
1795	Tiandihui	Nanhai, Guangdong
1795	Tiandihui	Fengshan, Taiwan, Fujian
1795	Tiandihui	Zhangzhou, Fujian
1797	Xiaodaohui	Danshui, Taiwan, Fujian
1799	Tiandihui	Fuding, Fujian
1799	Tiandihui	Pucheng, Fujian

SOURCE: Reproduced from Zhuang 1990a: 112–16.
[a]"Increase Younger Brothers Society."
[b]Invented characters employed to represent "heaven" and "earth."

clear if the societies were simple burial societies or had borrowed the name of the Fumuhui to cover more nefarious purposes. One of the groups had collected money, possibly for a common fund; the other, however, had secreted weapons and banners.[51]

3. Authorities arrested and executed leaders of the Iron Rulers Society (*tiechihui*) in Shaowu, western Fujian, in 1753. The society had been formed some years earlier, merging two smaller *hui*, and for several years it appears to have served protective functions. But in the early 1750's, for unknown reasons, it began to evolve toward a rebellious stance, seeking to sell letters of deputation in parts of the Shaowu area. Officials uncovered the society and carried out arrests before any violence could occur.[52]

4. Lu Mao formed a brotherhood in 1767 for the purposes of leading an attack on the Zhangpu county seat. Later identified as an early Tiandihui member (an identification I find dubious; see Chapter 4 below), he bolstered his credibility by claiming a relationship with Zhao Liangming, a supposed descendant of the Song dynasty. Members of his brotherhood recruited more than 300 adherents, largely through surname ties. In the third month of 1768, Lu attempted to lead his band against Zhangpu city in Zhangzhou prefecture, southern Fujian, but only 80 of his men followed. The Qing eventually arrested 365 of those connected with the abortive uprising, none of whom mentioned the role of the Heaven and Earth Society.[53]

5. Li Amin planned a similar uprising in the border area between Zhangpu and Zhaoan counties in 1770. He claimed friendship with a Ming descendant and promised great wealth to those who joined. As in the Lu Mao case, later confessions identified Li as a Tiandihui leader in confessions obtained after the Lin Shuangwen uprising, but no contemporary evidence corroborates this.[54]

6. A number of Small Knives societies (*xiaodaohui*) flourished in Zhanghua, Taiwan, during the 1770's and 1780's. These were first set up by petty merchants to provide mutual aid and protection in the face of continued abuses by local troops, but some branches of the Society eventually engaged in a variety of activities, including mercenary participation in local feuding.[55]

7. In 1786, on the eve of the Lin Shuangwen uprising, Qing authorities in Zhuluo, Taiwan, uncovered two named brotherhoods—the Increase Younger Brothers Society (*tiandihui*) and the Thunder God Society (*leigonghui*)—which had been set up by two brothers competing over the impending division of family property. The societies had been established on a mercenary basis, each brother paying the members of his society. Qing attempts to suppress the societies led to violence between Tiandihui members and the state (*TDH* 1: 170–75).

8. Lin Shuangwen led a Heaven and Earth Society in Daliyi, Zhanghua, Taiwan. He had been recruited to join the society in 1784* and had apparently used it for purposes of mutual aid and criminal entrepreneurship. When members of the Increase Younger Brothers Society fled and sought refuge with Lin Shuangwen, Qing authorities shifted their attention to Lin and his Heaven and Earth Society. Efforts to arrest Lin and his men prompted the Lin Shuangwen uprising, the first large-scale Tiandihui rebellion in Chinese history.

THE ENDURING BROTHERHOOD ASSOCIATION

Several of these cases show that the brotherhood association could be of fairly long standing. The Iron Rulers Society (*tiechihui*) of Shaowu, western Fujian, broken up by the Qing in 1753 after society members engaged in suspicious activities, had been in existence only since 1750, but investigations revealed that one of the two originally separate brotherhood associations that had joined to form the society, the God of War Society (*guanshenghui*), dated from the late 1730's; the other, an unnamed mutual-assistance brotherhood, dated from 1746. The two associations joined when a local bully attacked a member of the unnamed brotherhood. A member of the Guanshenghui who came to the aid of this latter suffered injuries as well. Even after the merger, the newly formed Iron Rulers Society remained peaceful for two more years, only beginning the recruitment and other activities that led to the eventual arrest of its members in 1752. Evidence links these societies in various intimate ways both to local society and to popular religion. Marriage ties, for example, brought some members together, and the societies met to solidify their bonds on days of popular religious festivals.

Another example of the relative permanence of the brotherhood association is the case of the Small Knives Society in late eighteenth-century Zhanghua and Zhuluo counties, Taiwan. Like the Iron Rulers Society, the Small Knives Society appears to have been a fixture of the local social scene for some ten years. In this part of frontier Taiwan, petty merchants established several Small Knives societies to protect themselves from abuse at the hands of government troops. Taiwan's troops were rotated from the mainland rather than recruited locally, and by all accounts were poorly disciplined. Green Standard forces, largely ignored by corrupt officers, were allowed to abandon their posts on a semipermanent basis and to engage in trade. If military obligations interfered with their commercial activities, officers permitted them to buy substitutes (a practice known as *baochai*) to stand in for them. Many soldiers ran brothels and gambling operations, and engaged in a variety of predatory practices.[56]

* The date is disputed in the sources. See p. 68 below.

According to records found by Fujian Admiral Huang Shijian in the Zhanghua country magistrate's office in 1782, when a large ethnic feud (*xiedou*) involving the Small Knives Society prompted Huang's investigations, the first instance of Small Knives Society activity dated back to 1772. At this time, Lin Da, a betel nut peddler who had been beaten and insulted by local troops, decided to band together with seventeen acquaintances, all of whom agreed to carry small knives—hence the name of the association—in the hope that their numbers and weapons would serve as protection in the event of future problems with the soldiers. Within a few months of the decision to form the band, the county magistrate discovered the Xiaodaohui, and had its members cangued and released.

In spite of this (mild) punishment, the idea of the Small Knives Society caught on. In 1773, Lin Asai formed a small *hui* of five people, again stipulating that all members carry a small knife to fend off unruly soldiers. The original group of eighteen set up the previous year eventually disbanded through attrition, but some members set up smaller associations, rarely exceeding five members. Other local peddlers began to imitate this style of organization. Indeed, local records reveal a proliferation of Small Knives societies from the mid-1770's. In 1780, local merchants took soldiers to court, and then set up a Xiaodaohui to protect themselves from the soldiers' revenge. Although there is some evidence of membership continuity, it is not as clear as in the case of the Iron Rulers Society. In the case of the Small Knives Society, the most obvious continuities are of name and purpose.

The history of the Fumuhui—Father and Mother societies—further victims of the Qing dragnet, also confirms that at least some brotherhood associations were relatively long-term fixtures of local societies. Qing officials uncovered two Fumuhui in Zhuluo county, Taiwan, in 1728, while searching for members of a reported gang. The first, in Bozailin village, consisted of 23 people, who noted in their confessions that they had contributed one ounce of silver per head to the association, for the ostensible purpose of providing mutual assistance as parents approached old age. The association had been formed during the first month of the year only to be closed down by the official arrests immediately before its second meeting, scheduled to be held on the "elder brother's" birthday on the nineteenth of the third month. Authorities uncovered the second Fumuhui in Lianchitan village, also in Zhuluo, in the eighth month. This group of 21 had formed originally on the fifth day of the fifth lunar month (*duanwujie*) and had met once again on the eighteenth day of the sixth month.

Some 60 years later, an important figure in the transmission of the Tiandihui from the mainland to Taiwan noted in his deposition that "at the outset" people joined the Tiandihui "to help finance weddings and funerals" (*TDH* 1: 110–12). In the wake of the suppression of Lin Shuangwen and the search for Tiandihui origins, Qing officials arrested twelve Tiandihui members in Zhangpu county, Zhangzhou, only to have all twelve insist that they had merely formed a pact to make contributions toward a common burial fund (*TDH* 1: 76).

Funeral societies of this sort were extremely common. As noted in the genealogical section above, mutual bereavement societies may date back to the Tang period, and proliferated during the Ming. After the Japanese acquisition of Taiwan in 1895, investigators discovered examples of burial societies that held money in trust and guaranteed terms of the agreement through contracts. Members referred to *hui* leaders as *zongli* and *luzhu*, terminology employed by other, mainstream, *hui*.[57] Burton Pasternak found several *fumuhui* in the southern Taiwanese villages he selected for ethnographic fieldwork in the 1960's.[58] Although none of the archival evidence presented here discusses the longevity of the various funeral societies, more recent examples confirm that members only contribute money to a mutual aid association of this sort when they anticipate that the relationships cementing the association will endure.

Many scholars have connected the proliferation and geographic spread of brotherhoods and secret societies with the increasing number of itinerants on the highways and byways of late imperial China.[59] The enduring nature of the brotherhood associations under discussion here illustrates that not all members of brotherhood associations and secret societies were itinerant drifters or roving bandits. Evidence from Lin Shuangwen's Tiandihui confirms this picture. The large number of arrests during and after the Lin Shuangwen rebellion allows us to paint a sociodemographic portrait of Tiandihui members: of those for whom we have information, 56 percent had living parents, 60 percent were married, and 36 percent had children. Furthermore, their average age was 37 *sui*, and their average length of residence on Taiwan more than 21 years (see Appendix A). Many of these pre-uprising members clearly had homes, families, and communities. Taken together with the information on the Iron Rulers Society, Small Knives Society, and Fumuhui, this suggests that brotherhood associations were at least a semipermanent fixture of life in certain parts of the Southeast Coast during the eighteenth century, and that those who joined were poor, but probably not desperate.

BROTHERHOOD ASSOCIATIONS AND LOCAL OFFICIALS

One reason that such formally illegal associations could endure for relatively long periods of time is that many local officials tolerated them. Ji Qiguang, who served as county magistrate of Zhuluo, Taiwan, in the mid-1680's, immediately after the establishment of Qing rule on Taiwan, noted in an undated proclamation:

In recent years it has become an evil custom for two or three young no-goods, looking for trouble and striving to stand out [i.e., for notoriety, *haoshi zhengqi*], to burn incense and pour out libations, and call one another brother [*chengge hudi*], seeking to forget differences of nobility and baseness and to aid one another in poverty and wealth. [They pledge to] remain together in sadness and in joy, and to watch out for each other in life and in death. Of course, this is not the result. In fact, with one word of disagreement, they turn on each other and kill out of vengeance. . . . Moreover, there is a clear law against the formation of such brotherhoods: the leader is to be strangled, and the followers beaten 100 strokes and exiled 3,000 *li*. Consequently, scholars and gentry [*xueshi dafu*] scorn such things, and it is most prevalent among idlers who loiter around the marketplaces [*youshou youshi*]. There is no doubt that the root cause for this is a mentality of hunger for name and power [*haoming haoshi zhi xin*]. [The formation of such pacts] is not difficult, but when it comes to actual [shared] interests, brotherhood members are as in the dark as strangers, and when one of their number falls into a well, they are quick to drop stones on him [i.e., quick to join others in profiting from another's downfall]. Still, there are many who have ruined their families and their reputations through disasters brought on through these pacts [*meng*].⁶⁰

The magistrate describes these brotherhoods in terms that suggest their openness and involvement in the family lives of association members:

Brotherhoods are the handmaiden of betrayal. If A and B join together in a brotherhood, then A's mother is B's mother, B's elder sister is A's elder sister, A's wife becomes elder aunt [*dasao*], B's wife becomes younger aunt [*dixi*]. . . . The dwellings of peddlers and tenant farmers [i.e., those likely to be attracted to such brotherhoods] lack the levels and refinements necessary to keep inner divided from outer, and in such circumstances [brotherhood members, including women] will circulate through one another's houses as if they were true flesh and blood. I fear that over time, eyes will cross paths and eyebrows speak, shoulders will brush and gestures be made, and people will cease to avoid situations that look suspicious. . . . In some cases, there will be those who climb into "mother's" bed, or who raise the curtain of "elder sister's" boudoir.⁶¹

In other words, brotherhoods destroy families and obscure bloodlines. Ji then goes on to argue that "brotherhoods are the foundation of poverty," since one would be expected to feed one's newfound "brothers" at any time, which would lead naturally to excessive borrowing and ruination; that "brotherhoods are the gateway to banditry," since whenever men got together they drank, and when they drank they gambled, when they gambled they lost money, and when they lost money they turned to banditry; and that "brotherhoods are the road to contention," since "men's hearts are as different as their faces. Even if you call each other brothers, how can you forget your ultimate differences? Whether it be a drinking quarrel or a fight over money, someone will take a few punches or swear at the other[s], and the problems will start right away." Such contention would eventually lead to larger and larger fights and final punishment at the hands of the authorities.

Although Magistrate Ji did consider the formation of brotherhoods an unsavory practice and did cite the penalties against them from the Qing code, he did not seem to believe that brotherhoods presented a particular danger to the state. He described brotherhoods instead as a casual fraternity, relatively open—certainly not secret, if one of the goals was to "stand out"—if a bit vulgar, and suggested that they produced the same low-level social disorder as gambling. He used the same cajoling logic to persuade the people not to engage in such practices that we see in interdictions of excessive feasting, festival violence, or any number of other minor but persistent social ills.

Other evidence of official tolerance suggests much the same attitude. In the Small Knives Society case mentioned above, Huang Shijian's investigations into the history of the association revealed ten years of official lack of interest in the local peddler groups. Small Knives Society members arrested in 1772, when the officials first discovered the organization, received only the relatively minor punishment of wearing the cangue, after which authorities released them, allowing them to return to their homes. Beginning from 1774, local officials repeatedly uncovered Small Knives societies consisting of three to six people. In 1775, the Qing arrested a number of Small Knives Society members in the context of a *xiedou* between members of the local Zhangzhou and Quanzhou communities, and although society members denied involvement in the feud violence, they admitted their membership in the Small Knives Society.[62] Once again, after forcing them to wear the cangue, authorities released them to the care of local security personnel. Such punishment appears to be lenient: according to a 1774 substatute, leaders of groups of less than twenty that did not subvert the age hierarchy and for which there was no evidence of blood oaths or burning of petitions were to receive 100 blows of the heavy bamboo and two months of the cangue. The leaders of the 1775 Small Knives Society appear to have been spared the bamboo. Perhaps more to the point is the fact that Qing authorities refused to consider the numerous instances of Small Knives Society activity as an example of an organized conspiracy, choosing rather to treat each as a discrete example of regrettable, but minor, misbehavior. The organization was fairly widespread, well known, and tolerated.

A 1780 case confirms that the Small Knives Society was a known feature of the local landscape. In the summer of QL 45 (1780), a group of
soldiers set out to sacrifice to a comrade-in-arms who had been killed in
fighting Taiwan's aborigines. They found that a house had been built on
the spot where their comrade had been killed (perhaps they had left a
makeshift shrine earlier) and, undeterred, laid out their sacrificial items
in front of the house and carried on with the ritual. The occupant of the
house, surprised and unsympathetic, scattered the sacrificial objects,
and a brawl ensued. In the course of the brawl, troops opened fire and
injured Lin Shui, a peddler who had been selling fruit in the immediate
vicinity, even though he had had nothing to do with the fight over the
sacrifice. There was a Lin Shui among the original eighteen Small Knives
Society members organized in 1772 by Lin Da, and it is likely that the
two Lins are the same person. In any case, the injured Lin Shui took his
complaints to the local magistrate, who intervened immediately. Lin
then organized, or reactivated, a Small Knives Society to deal with the
attempts at vengeance by the troops.[63] This surely suggests that the
Small Knives Society was more or less an accepted actor in the local society of 1780 Zhanghua. Examples of other brotherhood associations or
secret societies that brought suit confirm this picture (*TDH* 6: 342).

BROTHER ASSOCIATIONS AND LOCAL ELITES

Another reason that formally illegal associations could endure for
relatively long periods of time at the margins of polite society lies in the
relations between association members and the members of other, legal
groups. The fact that, as has been mentioned, many brotherhood association members retained their membership in local lineages, villages, presumably temple societies and other social networks, suggests that local
elites knew about, tolerated, and in some instances even made use of the
associations.

Indeed, elites not only sometimes tolerated and made use of associations; they set up their own named brotherhoods to pursue their own
private purposes. Brothers Yang Guangxun and Yang Mashi set up competing associations—the Increase Younger Brothers Society (*Tiandihui*)
and the Thunder God Society (*Leigonghui*)—to do battle over their shares
in their father's estate. Their father, Yang Wenlin, was a wealthy man
who owned considerable property in the remote Jiugonglin area of Douliumen in Zhuluo county, Taiwan, and had pursued elite status by purchasing the degree of first assistant magistrate. Yang Guangxun had also
purchased elite status, in his case a *gongsheng* degree, and his younger
brother, Yang Mashi, had acquired a *jiansheng* degree.[64] The details of
this case are discussed more fully in Chapter 2. Here the case is impor-

tant as an illustration that associations could be attached to, and even established by, elite members of local society, demonstrating just how close *hui* could be to orthodox institutions of land and family.

In other instances the links between association members and lineage or village heads are more attenuated, if still clear. The leaders of the Iron Rulers Society in Western Fujian were well-known members of local society—one had attained (probably purchased) the status of *jiansheng*, which, even if it had declined in value since the Ming, still "constituted a privileged . . . [status] among the commoners."[65] In addition, according to depositions, part of the original rationale for merging the two smaller associations in 1750 to form the larger Iron Rulers Society was to help each other in the event of fights *over property*, which is surely some indication of their position in the community. Leaders of the Iron Rulers Society were also able to rent a local temple as a temporary headquarters for their planned rebellion, and a former member who found himself ostracized by those plotting rebellion was able to sacrifice the substantial sum of twelve ounces of silver to attempt to buy his way into the ranks of the inner circle.* At the outset they had banded together in brotherhoods based on surname, lineage, and marriage ties—again suggesting their interconnections with other social networks.

The example of Lin Shuangwen is another illustration of this sort of interconnection. Whatever else Lin may have been, he was not a *wulai*, a member of the uprooted, the dispossessed. On the contrary, he was a member of the Lin lineage that dominated Daliyi, Zhanghua, Taiwan, with its three to four thousand members (LM 1984: 262–64). Both his parents were alive and in Daliyi, and Lin had at least three brothers and numerous "lineage brothers" (i.e., cousins). At the age of 26, he married a fifteen-year-old woman named Huang, and the fact of marriage should be some indication of wealth, power, or promise in this bride-poor society. (Lin's brother's wife, however, came into the family as a child bride, indicating that the family, if not destitute, was hardly prosperous.) Lin Shuangwen's wife gave birth to a son in QL 49 (1784), but the baby caught smallpox about the time of the uprising and died (*TDH* 4: 437). Lin accepted the power of the lineage elders over at least some of his activities: in the period immediately before the uprising, as Zhanghua county authorities attempted to arrest him, he obeyed the counsel of his elders and took refuge in the mountains rather than immediately lead his Tiandihui in revolt (LM 1984: 218–19, 221–22).

Another instance is the case of Lu Mao, identified in some sources as

---

* Twelve taels of silver would have bought roughly 8.5 *shi* of rice, more than three times the average annual per capita consumption in the late imperial period. This estimate is based on figures in Wang Yeh-chien 1986: 88.

a very early member of the Tiandihui, who in 1768 organized an attempted rebellion in southern Fujian based on a blood brotherhood. Surname ties clearly facilitated recruitment into the brotherhood: one of Lu's lieutenants, surnamed Cai, recruited 52 members, of whom 48 shared his surname.[66]

This evidence suggests that some brotherhoods were fixtures in the societies of the eighteenth-century Southeast Coast and were at least on some occasions tolerated by local elites and even local officials. Granted, in the fuller narratives from which I have taken this evidence, itinerant monks, wandering martial arts experts, and other stereotypical images of social marginality do appear, but locals remain as important to the brotherhood association as these drifters, and even when the drifters functioned as association leaders, many *members* were drawn from the ranks of the marginalized population of local society. The Yangs from the Tiandihui-Leigonghui case were sons of a wealthy landowner, titular members of the local elite, who formed associations to fight over property rights. The members of the Iron Rulers Society, some of whom possessed lower-level scholarly degrees, also banded together in part out of a desire to provide self-defense in the event of fights over property, and preexisting ties of marriage facilitated the expansion of the *hui*. Lin Shuangwen took refuge in a cave on the orders of his lineage leaders. Lu Mao's lieutenants recruited followers through single-surname residence patterns.

Unsurprisingly, few of these associations were secret, or shared the characteristics we have traditionally associated with secret societies. Although there is some confusion on this point, some of the documents suggest that locals who were not members of the associations chose the names for both the Iron Rulers Society and the Small Knives Society on Taiwan—which hardly qualifies as secret. In fact, locals also referred to the Small Knives Society as the Plague God Society (*wangyehui*), because members "were as great as the plague god." Many of the associations held their initiation rites or other celebratory meetings on dates that coincide with the Chinese ritual calendar, suggesting that linkages between the ritual life of the association and the broader sphere of popular religion paralleled ties between *hui* membership and the larger social order.[67]

Many of the activities engaged in by these brotherhood associations had their roots in mutual aid—a theme that appears repeatedly in depositions as well as in official commentaries on brotherhood practices. Of course, though "mutual aid" sounds harmless, it can also conceal a variety of nefarious practices, and it is not surprising, given the nature of the source material, that few of the brotherhood associations described above appear to have been completely innocent. The Father and Mother societies caught up in the Qing dragnet in the late 1720's in Taiwan seem on the surface the least criminal of those discussed here, but both associations selected "younger brothers" (*weidi*)—one bearing the surname Zhu—and presented them with gifts of a robe, a hat, a pair of shoes, and in one case, a ring. Zhu is of course the surname of the Ming dynastic house, which often carried rebellious or messianic overtones in the Qing period. At least one strain of messianism in Chinese popular culture believed that a savior would appear in the guise of a young prince—which might explain the gifts.[68] If either of these possibilities is true, then the Qing was clearly correct to be suspicious of what appeared on the surface to be a simple burial society. Furthermore, four years later in Chaozhou, northern Guangdong, Yu Mao, a cashiered military *juren*, used the cover of a Father and Mother Society as part of his plan to carry out a vengeful attack on the prefectural city—where, presumably, he had been stripped of his elite status.[69]

Many other brotherhood associations had similarly violent or criminal dimensions. The Taiwan Small Knives Society of the 1770's and 1780's, described above as a protective society of petty merchants and peddlers, also functioned as hired mercenaries during a huge ethnic feud in 1782. A Small Knives Society attached to local military units in mainland Fujian murdered the local magistrate in hopes of stopping his investigation into their activities.[70] For reasons that remain unclear, the Iron Rulers Society in 1752 began to manufacture pseudoimperial banners and seals and to spread the word that rebellion was in the offing. Lin Shuangwen's Tiandihui, although originally a mutual aid–criminal organization, wound up playing a significant part in what has been viewed as the first "Triad" rebellion in Chinese history. As this suggests, brotherhood associations frequently engaged in activities that might be called rebellious as well as criminal.

These examples could be multiplied many times over. Unsavory criminal brotherhoods linked up with Qing armies in very early Qing Fujian.[71] In the late 1760's, Li Amin set up a brotherhood association to intimidate local shopkeepers in southern Fujian into paying protection money so that they might survive a rebellion he threatened to lead.[72] Owing to the nature of the sources used to investigate Qing brotherhood associations, the vast majority will, quite naturally, fall into the Qing categories of "violent" or "criminal" (categories that in these cases are not so distant from our own); but I am not arguing that all brotherhood associations were innocent. I am only saying that not all early and mid-Qing brotherhood associations consisted of wanderers, criminals, or dissidents. Furthermore, if one can use these obviously biased sources to reconstruct the social milieu in which these associations functioned in a way that suggests their nearness to rather than distance from the main institutions of local society, then a fuller historical record would surely provide even more examples of brotherhood associations as informal institutions catering to those pushed to the margins of social life.

CHAPTER 2

Brotherhood Associations, Secret Societies, and Rebellion

THE BACKGROUND TO THE LIN SHUANGWEN UPRISING

The Heaven and Earth Society has been around for a long time.
I never entered, and don't know when it started. (TDH 5: 10)
— *Deposition of Zhuang Dajiu, chief instigator in the southern*
wing of the Lin Shuangwen rebellion.

Chapter 1 presented a variety of simple brotherhoods, named brotherhoods, and secret societies, and argued that all these brotherhood associations should be understood as informal institutions linked to the more familiar lineages and villages of the society of the Southeast Coast, even if, in many cases, these brotherhood associations were at best informal institutions in embryo. The next two chapters examine specific examples of rebellion and the role of named brotherhoods and secret societies therein. In part, this focus compensates for possible biases in the interpretation developed in Chapter 1, which attempted to look past the crime and violence of brotherhood associations and toward their close relationship to a traditional social order. In part, such an approach simply acknowledges that many brotherhoods and secret societies did indeed engage in rebellion. This chapter traces the background to the Lin Shuangwen uprising of 1787–88, the first Triad rebellion in Chinese history, examining the creation of the Heaven and Earth Society in southern Fujian, the transmission of the society to Taiwan, Lin Shuangwen's character and activities as head of his branch of the Tiandihui, and finally the specific events that culminated in rebellion.

Although the Tiandihui emerged out of the same milieu as other named brotherhoods and secret societies and appealed to members in part as a mutual aid fraternity, Tiandihui initiation rituals and written materials also employed apocalyptic and occasionally rebellious and restorationist symbols with no obvious connection to the search for "mutual aid." In addition, Yan Yan, the traveling cloth merchant who transmitted Tiandihui teachings to Taiwan—and indeed to Lin Shuangwen himself—had been initiated into the Tiandihui by someone very close to the supposed founder of the society, suggesting that he must have been familiar with Tiandihui practices, and should have conveyed their meaning accurately. Nonetheless, the apocalyptic and restorationist aspects of Tiandihui membership had very little impact on Lin Shuangwen and his followers. Before the rebellion, Lin's Tiandihui engaged in "mutual aid" in the form of crime, and there is no hint that the meanings embedded in Tiandihui rituals stirred Lin's imagination in the direction of a challenge to the Qing state. Instead, when we examine the set of events that culminated in the rebellion, we find that contingent factors, particularly the actions of other violent named brotherhoods and the heavy-handed Chinese state, played more central roles than did Lin and his society, both of which remained passive until outside events intervened.

Lin Shuangwen's uprising was one of the largest and most successful in eighteenth-century China, and it was also the first rebellion in Chinese history led by the Heaven and Earth Society, the Triads, whose pro-Ming, anti-Qing message recurs repeatedly in nineteenth-century Chinese sources.* Originating in central Taiwan in late 1787, Lin's forces went on to hold major cities on Taiwan for more than a year,† and the suppression of the rebellion numbered among the Qianlong emperor's "ten great campaigns."[1] The size of Lin's force is difficult to estimate, and degrees of mobilization varied over time, but suppression of the rebels required the transfer of 40,000 troops from outside the Southeast Coast (Taiwan, Fujian, Guangdong) as well as the mobilization of almost 50,000 local militia (*yimin*) to supplement the regular Taiwan garrison strength of 12,000.[2] Almost ten thousand Qing troops died in the course of the campaign.[3]

The scale of the damage wrought by the protracted conflict is suggested by Qing calculations that they dispensed aid to nearly 650,000 refugees displaced by the rebellion, for whom they built nearly 100,000 thatched huts.[4] Taiwan's official population count as of 1777, a decade before the rebellion, was 839,803.[5] Lin's uprising dominated the life of the island from the eleventh month of QL 51 (1787), when Lin led his first battle against Qing installations, through the second month of QL 53 (1788), when Qing authorities finally executed Lin in Beijing. A rebellion of this scale left a rich archival trail of thousands of docu-

---

* In the course of investigations that followed the Lin Shuangwen uprising, Qing officials uncovered (somewhat questionable) evidence suggesting that both the Lu Mao uprising of 1768 and the Li Amin uprising of 1770 had been led by the Tiandihui. See the archival documents reprinted in Qin and Li 1986: 30–37. Even if the Tiandihui was involved with these two earlier events, Qing officials did not learn of the existence of the Tiandihui until the Lin Shuangwen rising.

† See Appendix B for a brief chronology of the Lin Shuangwen rebellion.

ments and depositions, and the uprising offers fertile ground for research on the relationship between named brotherhoods, secret societies, and rebellion.[6]

With the exception of the Heaven and Earth Society, whose role is discussed extensively below, no single force or series of circumstances explains Lin's rebellion, and therefore the role of the Tiandihui seems all the more important. No natural disaster visited Taiwan in the prerebellion months, and the fall harvest that immediately preceded the uprising appears to have been a success.[7] The omens that figure prominently in the lore of Chinese rebellions can come in other forms, of course, and local gazetteers report that a strange and disturbing bird, a sort of multicolored eagle, perched on a tree in a village in Zhanghua county, where the rebellion began, during the fourth month, and stayed for more than twenty days. One hundred other birds gathered around, following from tree to tree, "just as soldiers surround their general." In the same month that the rebellion began, three stars fell thundering from the heavens and landed in Zhanghua.[8] It seems likely that these omens took on greater significance *after* Lin Shuangwen began his rebellion; in any case, there is little empirical evidence to suggest that unusual or unexpected hardships caused the discontent that resulted in rebellion.

Yet there was discontent. Three aspects stand out as worthy of discussion: a mixture of named brotherhood and secret society organization, which served as an axis of organization and mobilization for crime and violence of various sorts, and, just as significantly, excited the suspicion and intervention of Qing authorities; the Qing state itself on Taiwan, which must have represented to most Taiwanese a frustrating combination of ineffectual, corrupt, and unpredictably violent rule; and ethnic violence (feuds, *xiedou*) among settlers on Taiwan from three separate mainland communities, which could readily become avenues of mobilization in the context of rebellion. All these must be considered if we are to build a context in which to understand the significance of Lin Shuangwen's Heaven and Earth Society, and the relationship of the society to the rebellion he led.

The Creation of the Heaven and Earth Society

Secret societies began to appear in the Southeast Coast in the mid- to late eighteenth century, appealing to the same body of marginalized young men who were attracted to the named brotherhood but at the same time representing something distinct. Fujian Governor Dingchang's 1764 memorial, discussed at the beginning of Chapter 1, is again helpful in the distinctions it draws between harmless pilgrimage societies, religious organizations, and mutual aid groups, on the one hand, and "named associations," which "secretly manufacture symbols that facilitate recruitment" while pretending "that they are worshiping a deity" on the other.[9] Dingchang's discussion of a form of brotherhood association distinguished by secrecy, deception (i.e., they falsely claim to be worshiping the gods), and the manipulation of disturbing symbols, could easily apply to the Tiandihui, the most famous of all Chinese secret societies, which apparently emerged at roughly the same time and place. Indeed, recent research has traced the time and place of the origin of the Tiandihui to 1761 or 1762, in the Goddess of Mercy Temple, Gaoxi township, in Zhangpu county, Zhangzhou prefecture, southern Fujian. If Dingchang did not have the Tiandihui in mind when writing his memorial, he must have been thinking of a close cousin.[10]

The distinction between named brotherhoods and secret societies is a fine one. Both generally employed blood oaths to create a bond of fictive kinship among members who referred to their fraternity by a name that included the ideograph *hui*. Both offered the promise of mutual aid and protection. Both could function as masks for more nefarious purposes. The Heaven and Earth Society, as the chief and most important example of a secret society, added to these shared characteristics a set of distinct ritual practices and written materials that drew on apocalyptic, messianic, rebellious, and pro-Ming political themes.

Despite decades of study, the specific circumstances that motivated the founders of the Heaven and Earth Society remain mysterious. Of course, the Southeast Coast, and Fujian in particular, teemed with brotherhood associations, but neither socioeconomic nor political factors alone explain the creation of this particular society in southern Fujian in the 1760's. The choice by Tiandihui founders to graft apocalyptic and rebellious messages onto the social form of the named brotherhood may not have had a specific social or political cause. Many rebellions, near-rebellions, and "heterodox" associations in Chinese history grew out of the personalities of particular individuals rather than the exigencies of sociopolitical forces (although the impact of these individual visions clearly varied according to the larger social context).[11] It was natural for the founders of a society to draw on the heterodox strains that made up an important part of popular culture, including apocalyptic aspects of salvationist popular religion, transformational and protective aspects of magico-religious practices, and the prophetic dreams and sacred objects attached to legitimation beliefs. For all its apparent "creation" in the mid-eighteenth century, the Tiandihui is more accurately understood as a repackaging of elements, many of which would have been familiar to large numbers of nonelite Chinese.

The basic ritual and mythology of the Tiandihui are well known. The formation of any Tiandihui organization required burning incense and passing through a gate of swords or knives. Burning incense accompanies virtually every religious act in Chinese culture, and in this the Tiandihui differed little from other brotherhood associations or religious groups. Possibly from the beginning, many Tiandihui groups added rice buckets, colored flags, scissors, scales, rulers, ropes, and a variety of other items to the altar. On many occasions, the initiation ritual also included worship of Tiandihui deities, generally mythic figures in the history of the society, as recorded in the origin myth. By the late eighteenth and early nineteenth centuries the Tiandihui rituals could be directed also at other gods commonly worshiped in popular religion.

Initiates took an oath of brotherhood, pledged loyalty to their brothers, and heard threats of the death that would come if they revealed society secrets. Members sealed their oath by drinking chicken blood (or occasionally human blood) mixed with liquor. In addition to the oath, new members passed through a gate, generally made up of swords or knives, that symbolized the passage into a new community and the danger intendant on that passage. The head of the society, frequently (though not during the Lin Shuangwen rising) called "teacher" or "master" (*shi*), taught code words and secret gestures to permit the society members to identify each other, as well as "brothers" from other branches, while among nonmembers. Some of these passwords also appear to have been imbued with magic or sacred power.

The most common gesture was to use three fingers while smoking or drinking, accepting or passing a cup or a pipe. The most common password was "when speaking, never forget 'the origin'"; "when passing objects, never forget 'three'" (*kaikou buli ben, chushou buli san*). "The origin" refers to the practice of taking on a new surname, Hong, which members then called "the original surname." "Never forget 'three'" refers to the secret gesture employing three fingers. Other passwords used numbers to describe the construction of the Hong character, such as "five dots and twenty-one" (*wudian ershiyi*). Still other passwords, such as *muli doushi zhitianxia*, which Barend ter Haar translates as "the Zhu [surname] will rule all-under-Heaven," contain hidden references to restorationist goals, although the degree to which all members understood the implications of the passwords is unclear.[12] These passwords and hand signs were unique to the Heaven and Earth Society, but many other religious and rebellious traditions throughout Chinese history had employed similar devices for similar purposes.[13]

A founding myth, which came to be quite elaborate by the nineteenth century, accompanied the ritual and the identifying signs, and this myth provides clues to the purposes attached by some members to the Heaven and Earth Society. According to the simplest and most common versions of this myth (which is accepted by some scholars as historical fact), the founder was Wan Tixi (or Wan Tuxi), also known as monk Hong Erfang, who had wandered to Sichuan from his home in Fujian or Guangdong and returned to set up the society. This in part explains the prominence of the *hong* ideograph in the initiation ritual and password.

Other versions are less simple. One 1788 deposition, for example, recounted that two people from Sichuan, one surnamed Li and the other surnamed Zhu, had created the Heaven and Earth Society. Li and Zhu were connected with another figure named Ma Jiulong, who recruited 48 monks and practiced magic tricks to expel spirit soldiers.[14] Later, these 48 monks dispersed in separate directions to spread the society. Monk Wan started the Guangdong branch (*TDH* 1: 112).

Many depositions repeatedly link various Lis and Zhus with the founding of the society. We find references to a fifteen- or sixteen-year-old boy named Zhu, to Zhu Dingyuan, as well as Zhu Hongde, again reported to be fifteen or sixteen years old at the time of the creation of the society (in Zhangpu county, Fujian); this Zhu Hongde was "born from eating a peach of the immortals" (*TDH* 1: 87, 111). One also finds many combinations of the Li, Zhu, and Hong surnames, frequently with the "peach" motif, yielding references to Li Taohong and Li Zhuhong, among others (*TDH* 1: 112).

The use of secret passwords and hand signals, together with the frequent appearance of the surnames Li and Zhu and the references to immortality, suggests that sinister and perhaps messianic purposes had a part in the founding and initial propagation of the Tiandihui; certainly the connection between messianism and imperial surnames is well known.[15] It may be that the imperial surnames signaled only a hoped-for change of dynasty, but one of the meanings of the character *hong*, generally used as a surname in Tiandihui documents, is "flood," which can carry more genuinely apocalyptic and messianic overtones. Indeed, we find references to floods and water in the documents and depositions from the late 1780's; another password identified members as being "from the water," and a line chanted during some Tiandihui initiation ceremonies was, "The flood waters flow and fill the heavens" (*TDH* 1: 87). Furthermore, Yan Yan's mention of "spirit soldiers" draws on exorcistic themes, probably connected to Daoist eschatology, again echoing what might be called messianic themes, and the identification of the area beyond the gates of initiation as the "City of Willows" surely carried salvationist connotations in some contexts.[16]

Scattered among these apocalyptic suggestions are "political" slogans that seem to call into question the legitimacy of the ruling house. "Carry out the Way in accord with Heaven" (*shuntian xingdao*), for example, is surely linked to the Mandate of Heaven and those who hold it. Again, the commonly repeated password *muli doushi zhitianxia* suggests a political dimension to apocalyptic beliefs. In addition, the character *ming* frequently appeared in Tiandihui written materials in the form of split characters—*ri* (sun) and *yue* (month)—suggesting a veiled reference either to the Ming dynasty or to an older apocalyptic tradition centering on Prince Moonlight (or the Luminous King).[17]

Much of this will sound familiar to those who have studied nineteenth- and twentieth-century Triad rituals, but two of the later elements do not appear in this reconstruction of the early Tiandihui. First, the elaborate foundation myth (known as the *Xiluxu*) with its saga of loyal monks, treacherous ministers, and gullible emperors, which characterized the nineteenth-century Tiandihui, is present only in embryo, although this may of course be simply a question of sources.[18] Second, although there are scattered references to the Ming, there is no explicit anti-Qing sentiment, no slogan in which Ming and Qing are clearly opposed, as came to be the case later in the famous slogan, "Overthrow the Qing and support the Ming" (*fanQing-fuMing*) and its many variants.

These two points aside, the reconstruction of the early Tiandihui looks very much like the Tiandihui familiar from later on, particularly in its basic ritual forms, and if the evidence concerning the political stance of the Triad is still indeterminate, there are tantalizing hints that it did not have too far to go to assume the consistently anti-Qing posture associated with the rituals of the nineteenth-century secret societies. Indeed, as research into Triad origins continues, we may yet uncover sources to prove that anti-Qing language marked the Tiandihui from the very outset. This complex of symbols, rituals, and beliefs distinguishes secret societies such as the Tiandihui from the majority of brotherhood associations discussed in Chapter 1, even if secret societies were in form simply a variety of named brotherhood.

The Transmission of the Tiandihui to Taiwan

This account of the creation of the Tiandihui has been reconstructed largely from eighteenth-century archival materials rather than from the more plentiful nineteenth-century sources. Most of the material presented comes from depositions of Tiandihui members arrested in the late 1780's or early 1790's as Qing authorities sought out the origins of the Tiandihui, and although evidence from the 1760's, when Wan Tixi supposedly set up the Tiandihui, is scarce, the Qing did locate a number of society members who claimed to have been students of the founder or of his original students. This is thus a reasonably accurate representation of what early Tiandihui enthusiasts understood their society to be. Reliance on the accounts of enthusiasts may, of course, distort the perceptions of locals who embraced the Tiandihui for reasons that had little to do with the visions of the original founder. The Lin Shuangwen uprising illustrates just how little the apocalyptic and rebellious ideas of the Tiandihui affected Lin and his fellow *hui* members, even as they rose up against the Qing.

The Heaven and Earth Society came to Taiwan when Yan Yan, alias Yan Ruohai, crossed the straits to Taiwan from his home in Pinghe county, Zhangzhou prefecture, Fujian, in QL 48 (1783–84), three or four years before Lin's rebellion. Yan Yan was a cloth merchant and a Tiandihui member, having been initiated into the brotherhood in his village the previous year by the itinerant doctor Chen Biao, who has been credibly linked to the founding of the Tiandihui. Because Yan Yan had direct, personal contact with someone very close to the founding of the Tiandihui, we might expect him to have a fairly accurate understanding of the intentions of those founders.

After migrating to Taiwan, Yan set up shop in Zhanghua city, at the same time seeking to spread the Tiandihui. He met Lin Shuangwen in QL 49 (1784); they came to be friends, and, according to Yan's account, Lin asked to enter the society (*TDH* 1: 110–12). The fullest account of the nature of the Heaven and Earth Society in 1780's Taiwan comes from Yan Yan's confession, which paints a picture of a somewhat Spartan Tiandihui, a mixture of a mutual aid fraternity like many of the earlier brotherhood associations and a secret society, though one whose rituals and symbols seem to have figured less prominently than in some others. In response to Qing interrogators, Yan Yan deposed:

> Whenever someone wants to enter the *hui*, you have to set up an incense table, and have them swear under the sword. Then if there are difficulties, those of the same teaching (*jiao*) will all offer their help. Also, fearing that there would be too many people and that they wouldn't be able to recognize each other, we arranged that on seeing people *hui* members would stick out three fingers [as a signal]. The *hong* character was also a signal, which we called "five drops and twenty one." Those who knew this were also of the same faith. (*TDH* 1: 110–12)

On more basic subjects, Yan continued:

> The name Heaven and Earth Society comes from the fact that heaven and earth are the foundations of human life, and it means no more than to worship (*jing*) heaven and earth.[19] Originally, people entered to help fi-

nance weddings and funerals; and if there was a fight, you could help each other. Also, in the case of robbery, once the robbers heard the signals of the same teaching they would leave each other alone. And if you recruited more people, you could get compensation and thanks from these people, so a great many wanted to enter. (*TDH* 1: 110–12, 116–17)

Yan also knew the mythology of the founding of the Tiandihui; in fact, he is the source for a good deal of the reconstruction of the 1780's foundation myth presented above. He told Qing officials about Zhu, Li, and Ma Jiulong, but denied the existence of Hong Erfang, instead insisting that this imaginary figure was a symbolic reference to Li, Zhu, and monk Wan. We can assume that Yan as a missionary for the Tiandihui passed on all or most of this information, though how much of it mattered to Lin Shuangwen and his followers we cannot say. In any event, Yan did not keep in constant touch with Lin Shuangwen after initiating him into the Tiandihui, although Lin sought him out after the onset of the rebellion with an offer of an "official post." According to his deposition, Yan declined and fled to the south of the island (*TDH* 1: 110–12). Although Yan had every reason to minimize his role in the rebellion, the absence of any mention of him in the rebel depositions suggests that after initiating Lin Shuangwen he took no further part in the rebellion.

In addition to Yan's testimony, we also have a copy of an initiation oath, confiscated from one of Lin Shuangwen's "soldiers" by Qing authorities, that sheds further light on the meaning of the Tiandihui in the Taiwanese context. It reads, in part:

> With the God of the Earth and [other] venerated spirits as witnesses, the incense master [characters missing in text] prepares . . . gold and silver incense [and other ritual items] . . . and presents these to the gods. . . . We inherit the transmission of the teaching of the *mingzhu* from the Maxi temple at the Gaoxi cloister in the Fenghua pavilion, Guangdong province. Tonight we drink blood and take an oath, becoming brothers, whose hearts will never separate. We list the names of those taking the oath to the left. Originally of different surnames, we are now joined together; although sharing no common father, we are [re]born as "Hong" . . .
>
> What we transmit tonight is secret. Do not tell your parents. . . . Should anyone tell, blood will gush to the heavens, and the entire family will perish. From this day forward, with the sealing of the oath, let us empty all private grudges and hatreds into the rivers and seas, in order that we may become even more harmonious. If there be good among us let us share it; if there be errors let us correct each other. . . . Elder and younger brothers must follow the laws, and cannot . . . rely on their strength to cheat the weak, or engage in violence . . . thereby betraying our oath. . . . Let each be responsible for his actions, and avoid implicating others. (*TDH* 1: 161–62)

The reference to the "transmission of the teaching" from the Fenghua pavilion is repeated in many Tiandihui foundation myths (*TDH* 1: 90). The reference to the *mingzhu* could point to the Ming ruler, suggesting restorationist overtones, to the "Ruler of Light," suggesting interpenetration with Prince Moonlight and the messianic traditions discussed above, or could be substituted for "alliance leader" (*mengzhu*), the title that Lin Shuangwen took for himself after the rebellion.[20] In addition to these elements, clearly drawn from the Tiandihui tradition, the oath also draws on more general brotherhood practices, such as that reflected by a similar oath taken by the Tiechihui, discussed in Chapter 1. The Tiechihui oath reads, in part: "If we wish to come together to unite our hearts, this will require long study. We must not forget that it is not through wine and meat that one finds true friends (*zhiji*); nor through ignoring others' troubles. [Let us act in such a way that] we feel no shame before the ancients, and distinguish ourselves from the commonplace."[21] This connection of Lin's Tiandihui to the tradition of named brotherhoods is important, because aside from Yan's testimony and the oath, everything else we know about Lin's Tiandihui suggests that it more closely resembled a named brotherhood than a secret society, and therefore the apocalyptic and political elements of Tiandihui membership did not survive their transmission from Yan Yan to Lin Shuangwen. Whatever the sense of *mingzhu*, neither the Ming dynasty nor the apocalyptic tradition appears again in Lin's rebellion, and they are of little help in explaining the uprising.

Lin Shuangwen's Tiandihui

Lin Shuangwen's attraction to a mutual aid society is not difficult to understand. Lin was the sort of person who was often drawn to unorthodox organizations such as brotherhood associations, and he could have fitted quite easily into many of the brotherhood associations already discussed. Lin, like Yan Yan, was from Pinghe county, Zhangzhou prefecture, Fujian, and there is little doubt that ties of dialect and place of origin contributed to their friendship. Lin had migrated with his father to Zhanghua county, Taiwan, as a child in QL 38 (1773) and was 32 years old at the time of the uprising. Zhanghua county had been carved out of the frontier of northern Taiwan in 1723 in response to growing population pressure and the perceived security threat in the wake of the Zhu Yigui rebellion.[22] Lin Shuangwen's home, and the center of the later rebellion, was Daliyi, a market town on the Dadu river in central Taiwan. By the 1750's, Daliyi was a regionally important market town, serving the upland valleys, dealing chiefly with the transshipment of grain. The *yi* component of the place name Daliyi refers to a sort of bollard for tying the bamboo rafts that plied the swift currents of the Dadu river and stopped at Daliyi to trade.[23] By the 1780's, if not before, Daliyi was a stronghold of the Zhangzhou Lins, the dominant lineage in Daliyi, and a functioning lineage structure existed. One deposition notes that there were "several thousand" Lins in the Daliyi area, and a Qing memorial records that Daliyi was an exclusively Lin village.[24]

Nonetheless, Daliyi was in a turbulent area, close to the inner mountains inhabited by the "raw" (i.e., unassimilated) aborigines and subject to violent confrontations between lineages and ethnic groups.[25] Although Daliyi was not far from the Qing yamen at Zhanghua, only one road led to it, and passage was difficult, particularly during the long rainy seasons. The Lin lineage competed for authority with mercenary organizations, some of which preyed upon the ethnic feuds that had been an important part of the region's recent past. The 1782 Zhang-Quan feud (analyzed in detail in Chapter 5) involved the Lins not only with their Quanzhou neighbors but also with the Qing local authorities: toward the end of the feud, officials marched into Daliyi and arrested 95 Lins, executing the leaders and confiscating "cudgels, fowling pieces, and beheading knives."[26]

Lin Shuangwen appears to have been a local troublemaker, the sort of person authorities naturally suspected whenever anything went wrong, though we lack precise details concerning his pre-uprising career. Some sources record that Lin had worked as an arrest runner in the Zhanghua yamen as a young man.[27] Yang Zhenguo, who did work in the Zhanghua county yamen and who later joined Lin's forces, confirmed that he had once arrested Lin for robbery, and that Lin had bribed his way out of jail, Yang and Lin becoming fast friends in the process (*TDH* 1: 408–9). Fellow rebel Gao Wenlin says that Lin was a thief and a fence who also lent protection to other thieves (*TDH* 1: 252–53). Liu Huaiqing, who had served as a clerk in the criminal section of the Zhanghua county yamen prior to the rebellion and was coerced into cooperating with the rebels after their attack on Zhanghua, reported that Lin "sheltered bandits and formed gangs" (*TDH* 1: 252–53). An elder from a lineage related to the Daliyi Lins noted that Lin traded with the raw aborigines in the mountains (LM: 262–64). In his own confession, the taciturn Lin noted only that he had "pulled a cart for a living" (*LM*: 218–19).

Lin's father described his son as "forever dissatisfied with his lot (*bu'an benfen*). He hung around with no-goods and . . . robbed the villages around Daliyi" (*TDH* 4: 435–36). Lin's third younger brother, Lin Yong, used the same language, and agreed with his father that Lin, along with fellow Tiandihui members Wang Fen and Lin Pan, "robbed neighboring villages of their property" (*TDH* 5: 9–16). Lin's wife observed in her confession: "My husband has a crude and violent nature, and was never peaceful with me. The year before last when [he] wanted to rise up, I urged him several times not to, but he wouldn't listen, and took a knife and said he was going to kill me. I didn't dare say anything more" (*TDH* 4: 437). Current residents of the Daliyi area remember Lin as a local strongman (*tuhao*).[28] All together, the picture we get of Lin is that of a petty criminal and local tough.

This picture accords with another of Yan Yan's observations concerning Lin Shuangwen. Asked in the wake of the rebellion to explain his recruitment of the obviously "evil" Lin, Yan replied: "I got people to enter the society in order to increase the amount of money the *hui* had, not to make friends. When I first met Lin Shuangwen, I thought he was noble and generous rather than stingy, so I led him into the *hui*, thinking that I could make something off him" (*TDH* 1: 116). The entrepreneurial aspects of secret society membership, and particularly secret society leadership, may not have been lost on Lin Shuangwen either, although we have no evidence that he marketed the secret society as did many of the Tiandihui "teachers" we shall encounter in Chapter 4.

Of course, because the Qing bureaucracy, which believed that only evil people committed evil acts, is the source for most of this information about Lin, it is not surprising to find him described in such terms. Other descriptions of him seem to derive from popular perceptions. Those who fought with him most often depicted him as "straightforward," a characteristic frequently mentioned in combination with that of "*yiqi*," meaning "just," or "loyal," or "trustworthy"—a frontier value reinforced by themes from popular literature or local opera and central to brotherhood membership.[29] Lin Ling, one of Lin Shuangwen's original Tiandihui members, noted in his confession that "because Lin Shuangwen was straightforward and had *yiqi*, we made him elder brother" (LM: 222). Lin Shuangwen himself cited the same virtues as having led to his election as alliance leader (*mengzhu*), which he declined, appropriately, twice (*TDH* 4: 397–400). As just noted, Yan Yan found Lin Shuangwen "noble and generous" (*kangkai*)—another virtue often attributed to knights-errant and celebrated in military romances.[30] Gao Wenlin commented that Lin was very free with the money that came his way, which inspired people to follow him (*TDH* 1: 251–52).

Power did not affect Lin unduly, if the confessions of his fellow rebels can be believed; even with the early success of the rebellion and his adoption of imperial pretensions, his men still called him simply "elder brother" (LM: 276). He did not engage in acts of unusual cruelty. There are reports of his having rewarded at least one person for killing a Qing official, of his having killed one of his own "generals" in frustration after failing to take the prefectural city, and of his having threatened another officer for a poor strategic choice involving the defense of Zhuluo (*TDH* 1: 322–23; LM: 232, 291). Men under his command did engage in acts of extreme violence—such as quartering captured officials—and there were also examples of horrible ethnic violence (LM: 114). But there is no evidence of the sustained and probably pathological viciousness found in late Ming rebels such as Wang Xianzhong. Lin's logistic and strategic planning once the rebellion began showed a good deal of intelligence.

In all, Lin seems to have been a self-important local strongman, and joining the Tiandihui does not seem to have marked a turning point in his life. In fact, Lin and his society members reveal little about their motivation in joining the Heaven and Earth Society. In his own confession, Lin said only, "I had often heard that there was something called the Tiandihui in Zhangzhou and Quanzhou, which gathered together many people who took oaths and formed bands [pledging to] help each other in time of need" (LM 1984: 218–19). Gao Wenlin, an old friend of Lin Shuangwen's and an early member of the Tiandihui, noted that Lin recruited him by "saying that everyone would provide mutual aid in times of trouble, that there would be no need to fear other people cheating us, or to fear official arrest," suggesting that soldiers or yamen runners numbered among Tiandihui members. Gao's deposition also suggests that Lin may have simplified the initiation ritual, noting that "whoever entered the *hui* had to bow to the heavens and take an oath to the earth." He also noted that the secret identification gesture was for Tiandihui members to "stick out their thumbs on meeting each other as a signal"—a variation on the three-finger signal, which again suggests that Lin may have taken liberties in his transmission of the Tiandihui and that he read no magic power into the gestures and code words of the initiation ceremony (*TDH* 1: 251–52). Most other members revealed even less about the nature of the organization: Chen Pang, a porter from Dadu, is representative of a large number who joined to avoid being cheated (LM: 231). As confrontation with the state loomed in the autumn of QL 51 (1786), a number of Lin's lineage members joined, presumably to protect home and family (*LM*: 237).

Even the simplified version of the initiation rituals seems to have changed with the acceleration of recruitment during the fall and early winter. By the beginning of the twelfth month (1787), Yang Zhang learned only an identification signal when recruited in Zhuluo (LM: 274). And after the rebellion got under way in earnest, these "secret" Tiandihui identification signals were replaced by a more immediately identifiable circle of hair grown close to the topknot (LM: 218–19). At first glance, this signals an apparent contradiction between a secret society that employs what appear to be apocalyptic and restorationist symbols, and a body of sworn members of this society who make no use of these elements, even as rebellion approaches.

We know little about the activities of the Tiandihui in the prerebellion period. Qing interrogators frequently disappoint scholars with the narrowness of their questions, and in this context they were especially unambitious; they seem to have assumed that the Tiandihui had been organized solely for the purpose of rebellion, and confined their questions to names, places, and dates. Even given these narrow concerns, they were unable to construct a satisfactory history of the organization on Taiwan. Such basic questions as when the leading figures of the Tiandihui joined the society lack definite answers. Yan Yan, for example, reports having met Lin Shuangwen in QL 49 (1784), and suggests that Lin joined that same year (*TDH* 1: 110–12). Lin dates his entry into the Tiandihui some two years later, in the eighth month of QL 51 (1786), as the confrontation with the Qing state neared, but Lin's assertion is implausible because other rebels recall joining with Lin Shuangwen in both the fourth and the seventh months of that year.[31] In any case, if Lin Shuangwen did indeed join the Tiandihui in QL 49 (1784), the Qing uncovered no record of any activity directly linked to the Tiandihui until several months before the rebellion—an interim of twelve to eighteen months.

Traditional Chinese accounts of the Lin Shuangwen rebellion assume that the Tiandihui facilitated the organization of an island-wide conspiracy. Yang Tingli, the coastal defense subprefect stationed at Tainan, who ably managed the defense of the prefectural capital through much of the early period of the rebellion, wrote a book about the Lin Shuangwen rebellion in 1790 entitled *Record of Events in the Eastern Seas* (*Dongying jishi*).[32] Yang argues that all the Tiandihui leaders who emerged in the course of the rebellion had been in contact in the period before the violence broke out, thus imagining an organization stretching from Danshui in the north to Fengshan in the south.[33] The 1830 Zhanghua gazetteer repeats this same information, and also argues that there were three divisions (*fang*) of the Tiandihui in the north of Taiwan alone.[34]

Archival records do not confirm these accounts. The majority of the society members for whom we have information were from Zhanghua county—hardly surprising, since this is where Daliyi was and where the uprising began. We have some village names, but without better reference tools it is difficult to determine exactly where these villages lay and therefore to comment on arguments suggesting that secret society networks largely conformed to those of standard marketing communities.[35]

We can also trace recruitment networks—in one case all the way to Zhuluo, the county to the south—but these networks reveal nothing more than that recruitment followed predictable lines of kinship and friendship.[36]

Zhuang Datian led the "southern Tiandihui armies" once the rebellion was under way. This has frequently been taken as evidence of an island-wide secret society–organized conspiracy, but it is not clear that he was even a Tiandihui member. Zhuang was a wealthy landlord in Xiadanshui in southern Taiwan, where he owned more than 40 *mou* of rental land as well as sugarcane acreage that yielded more than two thousand catties of sugar per year. He also owned rental land in northern Taiwan. According to depositions collected in the wake of the rebellion, a junior member of his lineage, Zhuang Dajiu, brought Zhuang into the rebellion. Dajiu confessed to having met with Lin Shuangwen at Aligang in southern Taiwan in the eighth month of QL 51 (1786) to plan the rebellion. When the rebellion broke out, Lin apparently sent word to the younger Zhuang, who began making preparations to launch a complementary rising in the south. Fearing that at 23 he was too young to command respect, Zhuang implored his lineage elder to come forward as "elder brother," and Zhuang Datian—after some professed hesitation—complied (*TDH* 5: 9–10).

The Tiandihui seems to have had little, if anything, to do with the organization of the southern branch of the rebellion. When asked about the society, Lin's alleged southern contact, Zhuang Dajiu, replied, "The Tiandihui has been around for a long time, [but] I never entered, and don't know about its origins" (*TDH* 5: 10). The forces under Zhuang Datian did use Tiandihui symbolism, such as *shuntian* and the *hong* character, on their banners and in their military titles, but some members denied knowledge of what the symbolism meant. As one of those captured deposed: "Zhuang Datian wrote the *hong* slogan [*honghao*] on the banners. I am illiterate, and don't know what it means. I never entered the Tiandihui, and don't know when it began" (*TDH* 5: 16). Zhuang Datian himself deposed: "As for the Tiandihui, Lin Shuangwen sent a letter telling us all to enter. When we met, there was a signal, and if you said 'five drops and twenty-one' then everyone would know that you were a member of the *hui*. Thus since I was the [military leader], I was also the head of the *hui* [*huitou*]. There was no reason for my being called the *huitou*" (LM: 224–26).

There were other Tiandihui organizations on Taiwan in the immediate prerebellion period, which might lend credence to the idea of an island-wide Tiandihui conspiracy. In the decade following the Lin Shuangwen rising, Qing authorities arrested several dozen men in mainland southern Fujian who had joined the Tiandihui on Taiwan before Lin's rebellion (generally, early in QL 51 [1786]) and then returned to the mainland during or after the rebellion to avoid apprehension. According to their depositions, the Tiandihui to which they had belonged had no connections with Lin Shuangwen's Tiandihui, and they did not partici-pate in the rebellion. Officials arrested these men at least four years, and in some cases more than ten years, after Lin's rebellion—because of their continued involvement in crime—and it was surely to their advantage to deny involvement in the rebellion. The information they provided about the Tiandihui does tend to suggest, however, that they may have been telling the truth.

First, many of these men referred to those who initiated them into the secret society as "teachers," and all paid their teachers for the privilege of joining (*TDH* 5: 450–52). Although these are extremely common prac-tices, they were apparently not employed in Lin Shuangwen's Tiandihui. Second, many of these seem to have been very recent arrivals to Taiwan, with no access to money, power, or protection. Some had been "peddlers of salt, fish, and fruit on Taiwan." Others had been day laborers. One joined because "Taiwan was an unfamiliar place, and it was hard to find people to rely on." Another joined because "he found himself in a strange place, and worried about being cheated." In short, many of these seem to have been truly desperate, rather than simply less fortunate members of settled communities (*TDH* 5: 424–31).

Lin's Tiandihui, in contrast, appears to have consisted of a more settled clientele. To repeat information from Chapter 1, 56 percent of Tiandihui members had living parents, 60 percent were married, and 36 percent had children. Their average age was 37 *sui*, and most had been on Taiwan for more than 20 years (see Appendix A). We have incomplete information on economic class and occupation; the little information we do have suggests a predictable cross section of peasants, tenant farmers, peddlers, local strongmen, and disgruntled lower elites. Lin himself had ready support networks in the form of a family and a functioning lineage: both his parents were alive and in Daliyi, and he had at least three broth-ers and numerous cousins. It appears evident from the data from Lin's Tiandihui group that one could be poor, but not desperate, and still join the Tiandihui. Lin Shuangwen himself was not a *wulai*, a member of the uprooted, the dispossessed, and his society members had homes, fami-lies, and communities.[37]

Although the motivations of Chinese rebels are often vague, the pro-cess of rebellion is usually fairly clear. Most narratives of peasant rebel-lion include accounts of late-night meetings in secluded places, where liquor, the strength of numbers, and the absence of elders embolden young toughs to contemplate their potential glory as contenders for the throne. Many of those involved in the Lin Shuangwen rising recalled their initiation into the Tiandihui (an admission that ensured their painful death at the hands of Qing executioners), but none mentioned specific planning for rebellion.

The confessions on which the above analysis is based constitute the most complete record of the peacetime activities of any named brotherhood or secret society in eighteenth-century Southeast China. There are always hidden biases in confessions; interrogators and accused always have their own priorities. In this instance, however, the confessions were conducted under the supervision of a high military official, Fukang'an, who had been transferred to Taiwan only after the rebellion had been in progress for several months. Fukang'an had no stake in covering up initial blunders, and he was in fact determined to reveal the incompetence and corruption of those officials on Taiwan at the time of the rebellion.[38] One would expect confessions secured in such a setting to include more rather than less information about the rebellious nature of the Tiandihui and its leaders, particularly since we know that officials frequently employed torture to procure the desired information. Such was not the case.

In fact, despite the massive postrebellion effort by Qing authorities to track down and interrogate all Tiandihui members, the interrogations revealed very little about the nature of Lin Shuangwen's Tiandihui or the motivation of those that joined. One possible explanation for this is that the Heaven and Earth Society was, after all, an illegal and *secret* organization: Tiandihui leaders and followers took their secrets with them to their graves. A less romantic but more plausible explanation grows out of the findings of Chapter 1 about eighteenth-century brotherhoods in general: for most, joining the Tiandihui was not a major decision that demanded significant redirection of personal and social loyalties. Granted, associations like that of the Heaven and Earth Society were illegal—but they were also extremely common and far from secret. Lin's wife's effort to dissuade him from rebelling surely suggests that not all secret society members kept their membership a secret from family members, whatever the language of the initiation oath. Many people had joined other brotherhoods in other contexts, and the Tiandihui was just one more. In sum, I suspect that there was rather less to membership in Lin's Tiandihui than met the eye, particularly since the apocalyptic and rebellious elements of Yan Yan's Tiandihui faded in significance. In the period leading up to the rebellion, Lin Shuangwen had put together a group of marginalized young men for the purposes of mutual aid and criminal entrepreneurship. Yan Yan's secret society, with its overtones of messianism and rebellion, seems to have become a less dangerous brotherhood association in the transmission of the Tiandihui to Lin Shuangwen and his followers.

Named Brotherhoods, the State, and Rebellion

And yet, a massive rebellion occurred. Rather than apocalyptic beliefs, a fight over the division of family property set in motion the chain of events that led to the Lin Shuangwen uprising, once again illustrating the embeddedness of most brotherhood associations in the ordinary routines of social life.

FAMILY DIVISION AND "SECRET SOCIETIES"

Yang Wenlin was a wealthy man who owned considerable property in the remote Jiugonglin area of Douliumen in Zhuluo county and had pursued elite status by purchasing the degree of first assistant magistrate. Yang was also getting old and perhaps approaching senility (*TDH* 1: 168). He had two sons. The eldest, Yang Guangxun, was adopted, a common practice. Like his father, Guangxun had purchased elite status—in his case a *gongsheng* degree—but was, according to the presumably biased official accounts written after the uprising, a "troublemaker." His younger brother, Yang Mashi, was not adopted, and had acquired a *jiansheng* degree (the government documents formulaically note, nonetheless, that he, like Lin Shuangwen, was "dissatisfied with his lot"; *TDH* 1: 164). Old Yang doted on the younger son, and following the division of family property, had the elder Guangxun live several *li* away from Jiugonglin at Shiliuban, where he provided him with food and money. Yang Guangxun jealously insisted that these arrangements were unfair and inadequate, and he quarreled frequently with his father and brother over the disposition of family property (*TDH* 1: 164, 170–75).

This classic family squabble developed in an unexpected direction. Increasingly aggrieved at his treatment at the hands of his father, Yang Guangxun decided to take direct action. On QL 51.6.29 (1786), he sent men to rob his father's private quarters, but was found out by Yang Mashi. Guangxun then went on to form a private mercenary group, which he called a *hui*, to seize the autumn harvest, presumably establishing some sort of rights to the land as well as storing up provisions for an oncoming struggle. Rapid migration to Taiwan throughout the eighteenth century had done much to populate the frontier, but large amounts of reclaimed land remained unregistered with the state, so that anyone with the physical strength and daring to seize land and claim it as his own could well get away with it: the state often preferred increased tax revenues to justice.[39]

During the seventh month, Guangxun recruited some 75 people, paying each one two silver dollars in return for their services, and promising to divide further profits in the event of victory.[40] He listed the names and addresses of his men in a membership book, so that, according to his confession, he would be able to claim back his money from any member who did not render the appropriate service at the required time. Listing names and addresses suggests that he did not know these people or where they lived, and thus underscores the mercenary nature of the organization. The authorities who eventually arrested Guangxun recorded the name of his association as the "Increase Younger Brothers Society" (*Tiandihui*), "since," as officials summarized Yang Guangxun's deposition, "the aim was to increase daily the number of brothers and to engage in a victorious battle."[41] When younger brother Yang Mashi heard about Guangxun's activities, he, too, decided to form a *hui*, and recruited 24 people, paying each 500 wen of cash. Mashi called his *hui* the Thunder God Society (*Leigonghui*) because, again according to an official summary of the deposition, his brother's "evil nature assured that he would be struck by thunder" (*TDH* 1: 171).

News of the Yangs and their associations reached Qing officials on Taiwan during the intercalary seventh month, roughly four weeks after Guangxun began to put together his band. The sources paint a somewhat confusing picture of the official attempts to suppress the Yangs and their associations, unsurprising since botching this job eventuated in the much larger Lin Shuangwen rising. Postrebellion recriminations, obfuscations, and the search for scapegoats make it unlikely that we shall ever know the whole truth about the official prosecution of the Yang family feud.

Fairly prompt action seems to have been taken. On *run* 7.4, under orders from Brigade General Chai Daji and daotai Yongfu, acting Zhuluo county magistrate Dong Qiyan led his men to the Jiugonglin and Shiliuban areas and arrested fourteen of those involved, including Yang Mashi. Officials also brought in the father, Wenlin, for questioning. Acting Magistrate Dong ordered his troops to continue arrest efforts.

Three days later, sublieutenant Chen He arrested Zhang Lie, one of the members of Yang Guangxun's Increase Younger Brothers Society, and began to escort him to the Zhuluo county seat for questioning. Chen had made the arrest in early afternoon, and as evening approached, Zhuluo remained at some distance, so he and his fellow officers, together with the prisoner, bedded down in the Ni Family Inn in Douliumen.

By afternoon, Yang Guangxun had learned of the arrest, and he quickly mobilized 47 of the members of the Increase Younger Brothers Society, inciting them to take knives and clubs and free Zhang Lie. This band reached Douliumen late in the evening where they found the inn in which the official party had stopped for the night and set fire in or around it, then waited outside for the residents to come pouring out. The readiness of Yang's *hui* to challenge the state may suggest that his explanation of its foundation is incomplete, or it may simply reflect the rough-and-ready nature of life on the Taiwan frontier.

Chen He and his men emerged with weapons drawn, but it was a lopsided four against 47, and Yang's band triumphed. Three of the four soldiers were killed, and Zhang Lie fled with members of the band. The fire and the commotion had, however, roused the soldiers of the garrison post at Douliumen, who pursued the attackers and engaged them in a battle in which eight of the gang were killed and fifteen injured. Only two were captured. The documents report that it was a dark, rainy night, which made pursuit difficult (no explanation is given for the ability of the rebels to start a fire or fire their guns in such weather). The government forces did not escape without injury: Yang's band killed the household servant of the Douliumen subdistrict magistrate in the skirmish.

Reports of violence between armed *hui* members and the state prompted immediate action. Magistrate Dong returned to Douliumen from Zhuluo the following day, and higher officials and their troops arrived on the tenth, traveling overnight from Tainan, the prefectural capital. By the fifteenth, the troops had arrested 53 of those involved either in the *hui* or in the freeing of Zhang Lie. This included Yang Guangxun, whom officials arrested in Zhanghua county and delivered to Zhuluo on the fifteenth by Zhanghua county magistrate Liu Hengji. Troops searched Yang Guangxun's home and found a membership book listing the names, addresses, and dates of entry of 75 members of his Increase Younger Brothers Society but no weapons or illegal paraphernalia (such as banners or letters of deputation). Questioning revealed that there were 24 members of Yang Mashi's Leigonghui. Including the two brothers and the father, the number of those implicated came to 102.

On the twenty-ninth of the month, the Qing beheaded eighteen of these as rebels, including Yang Guangxun, and displayed their heads as a warning to their neighbors. They sentenced twenty others to imminent beheading for having participated in the action to free prisoner Zhang Lie; officials judged the relatives of these twenty to be implicated as well, and ordered their property confiscated.[42] Eight were "excused from sentencing" because "they had died of injuries." As a *jiansheng* who acted as the head of an illegal association, Yang Mashi should, by statute, have been sentenced to military exile, but the supervising officials, Chai Daji and Yongfu, felt that this case demanded severity and sentenced him to exile in Yili as a coolie. Forty-nine members of the two *hui*—25 of the Increase Younger Brothers Society who had not participated in the rescue of Zhang Lie, and 24 Leigonghui members who had not engaged in violence at all—should by law have been sentenced to imprisonment within Fujian province; but again, the supervising officials feared the possibility of further trouble and decided on the harsher sentence of military service in the malarial border areas of Yun-Gui and Liang-Guang. Father Yang Wenlin held the degree of first assistant magistrate and was in custody while the violence between his son Yang Guangxun and the state occurred. Nonetheless, the officials argued, he had proved himself unable to manage his sons in their daily affairs, permitting them to set up *hui* and fight; exile—the sentence that he merited under the principle of collective responsibility—would be insufficient to expiate his guilt. They sent him instead to the border areas of Yun-Gui and Liang-Guang "where malaria was somewhat less prevalent," to live under the observation of local officials. His property went over to the state. The degrees held by the three Yangs were, naturally enough, revoked, and they were required to make restitution for the damaged Ni Family Inn. Officials confiscated and melted down the weapons used by the criminals. Granted, five of the 102 remained unaccounted for—Zhang Lie, Lai Rong, Ye Sheng, Cai Fu, and Zhang Yuan—but on the surface the affair seemed to have been expeditiously and professionally handled by the local officials on Taiwan, who promised to make every effort to apprehend those criminals still at large. On the first day of the ninth month, the Qianlong emperor issued an edict commending all those involved (*TDH* 1: 167).

FLIGHT TO DALIYI

The connections between the Yang Guangxun case and the Lin Shuangwen uprising are more than just thematic. On 8.16, newly appointed Zhanghua county magistrate Yu Lin learned that in the Daliyi area, Lin Shuangwen had put together a named brotherhood, and that the escapees from the Yang Guangxun affair had also taken refuge in Daliyi. Zhanghua county jailer Li Erhe attempted to investigate and make arrests, but "because Daliyi was a remote place and there were a lot of people there" he was unsuccessful (*TDH* 1: 254–55). Yamen runner Yang Zhenguo—a former acquaintance of Lin Shuangwen's, it turns out— went on a similar arrest mission in the tenth month; his superiors jailed him when he failed to capture Lin (*TDH* 1: 408–9). Later that same month, authorities arrested Lin Jiaqi, a Lin lineage head from Abili village, twenty *li* from Daliyi, for having failed to meet his tax obligations. Jiaqi attempted to fulfill his obligations to the state in another manner: by volunteering to talk to Lin Shuangwen. Authorities released him from jail, and according to his testimony, he talked to Lin, his father, and his branch head, trying unsuccessfully to persuade them to turn Lin Shuangwen in (LM: 262–64).

On QL 51.11.7 (1786), Brigade General Chai Daji came to Zhanghua on inspection, and Magistrate Yu, by now clearly exasperated, asked that Chai send troops to take care of Lin. Chai was apparently not anxious to undertake the mission, and did not in fact go himself; on QL 51.11.20 (1787), Yu led troops under Major Di Shiwen and Colonel He Sheng'e and camped at Dadun, some ten *li* from Daliyi. Failing to arrest Lin, they seized villagers at random and burned their houses, hoping by such measures to compel the locals to turn over the *hui* members.

Such tactics were apparently not unusual. Some reports record that Qing troops burned five commoners' homes as officials carried out the initial arrests in the Yang Guangxun case.[43] Li Erhe, the Zhanghua jailer, reported hearsay evidence that the tactic had worked (if obviously only temporarily) in Dadun, where the troops stalked Lin Shuangwen: "I heard that they handed over five *hui* members, of whom two were beaten to death and three sent back and incarcerated in the Zhanghua county jail" (*TDH* 1: 254–55). Whatever the truth of the jailor's account, Lin Pan, a Tiandihui member, was the owner of one of the houses. This sparked Lin Shuangwen's anger (LM: 222). Lin's confession summarizes this series of events:

> In the Douliumen area, Yang Guangxun and his younger brother set up opposing societies and recruited members to enter into a quarrel over the division of family property. Someone reported their actions, and implicated us in the complaint. Consequently, the civil and military officials of Zhanghua sent their underlings to every corner to carry out arrests. These underlings used this as a pretext for extortion and arrested all sorts of people whether or not they were related to the case, so that all the villages were in an uproar. (LM: 218–19)

The rebel attack on Dadun came on 51.11.28, eight days after Zhanghua county authorities began their coercive tactics. The following day the rebels attacked Zhanghua and Lugang, and a week later they took Zhuluo.

THE TWO TIANDIHUIS, THE STATE, AND REBELLION

We can speak with some confidence on the general trajectory of the confrontation: local associations, engaged in more or less systematic robbery and violence, met up with a heavy-handed state determined to establish at least momentary control. Specific questions remain more difficult to answer.

First, were the two Tiandihuis—Lin Shuangwen's Heaven and Earth Society and Yang Guangxun's Increase Younger Brothers Society—part of one network? If so, were the activities that culminated in the rebellion part of a conspiracy to rise up against the state?

Some contemporary observers answered yes to both questions. Yang Tingli's summation of the Yang Guangxun case paints a picture of bribery, corruption, and collusion between criminals and local officials that permitted a well-organized Triad conspiracy to launch its attack on the local establishment.[44] Yang Tingli's assertions, which seem to have no extant documentary basis, have been copied by many later scholars.[45]

The Qing court, ever susceptible to conspiracy theories, also came to accept this interpretation.[46] As early as QL 51.8.10 (1786), Min-Zhe Governor-General Changqing and Fujian Governor Xu Cizeng had worried in a memorial that "the *daotai*'s reports [concerning the Yang Guangxun affair] may be untrue or incomplete " (*TDH* 1: 162). By the second month of QL 52 (1787), with the rebellion in full swing and Qing officials frantic to track down the origins of the Triads (the Qianlong emperor, for one, having only learned about their existence in the wake of the Lin Shuangwen rising), many were ready to blame the entire disaster on the negligence and dishonesty of Chai Daji and Yongfu. On QL 52.2.6 (1787), the emperor issued an angry court letter to high officials in Fujian and Guangdong:

> [Rebellions] are all the result of local officials' habitual unwillingness to carry out genuine investigations. Whenever there is trouble, all they want to do is bring the affair to an end; they don't thoroughly investigate the roots [of the problem] . . . and as a result their leniency nourishes evil.
>
> Take last year's Yang Guangxun case on Taiwan. It is clear that the name of that *hui* was the same as that of the Heaven and Earth Society which we have recently uncovered. Local officials clearly changed ["heaven and earth" to] "increase younger brothers" in order to minimize the importance of the affair, hoping to avoid punishment. . . . Let the Governor-General make investigations into whose idea it was to change the characters, so that we may carry out impeachments. (*TDH* 1: 72).

Three weeks later, Fujian-Zhejiang Governor-General Li Shiyao reported to the emperor that the confusion had been sorted out:

> As for the handling of last year's Yang Guangxun case, the so-called "Increase Younger Brothers Society" is clearly the same as the Heaven and Earth Society we are investigating now. All that happened was that someone substituted a homonym in order to make the affair seem less impor-

tant. Really clever. I have examined the original paperwork of this case in great detail, and have discovered that the "increase younger brothers" characters appear both in a joint memorial by Brigade General Chai Daji and *daotai* Yongfu, as well as a report by Taiwan prefect Sun Jingsui.

Sun Jingsui has died [killed in the initial rebel attack on Zhanghua (LM: 320–21)], so if we ask the Brigade General or the *daotai* to explain the use of the characters, they will blame it on the prefect. But the prefect sent in his report on *run* 7.17 of last year, and the Brigade General and *daotai* had already memorialized on the previous day, so they cannot claim ignorance. (*TDH* 1: 79)

Li also cast doubt on other aspects of the two officials' behavior, suggesting that the name register for Yang Guangxun's "Increase Younger Brothers Society" was a forgery: "In the dossier of this case, there is a copy of the criminals' register book . . . on which the characters 'increase younger brothers' are clearly written, but the register includes only a few dozen names, and is clearly falsely put together according to the names of those arrested [i.e., after the fact]. It is not original, and difficult to believe" (*TDH* 1: 79). We should note, however, the "forgers" also included the names of the escaped criminals in the supposedly fabricated register, suggesting that they missed a good opportunity to absolve themselves.

Later, the investigating officials spread the blame to include Zhanghua county magistrate Liu Hengji, who had allegedly been hungry for a commendation and therefore had not pursued the other parties to the Yang Guangxun case; and Fujian Provincial Judge Li Yongqi, who had gone to Taiwan in the ninth month of QL 51 (1786) to investigate the Yang Guangxun case and had not found any irregularities (in spite of having reinterrogated most of the surviving members of the affair).[47] With the passage of time, even more scurrilous reports surfaced, encouraged in part by the postrebellion official savaging of Chai Daji, whose military administration on Taiwan had apparently been lax and corrupt in the extreme, according to the results of the investigations.[48]

It is difficult to judge the truth of these accusations. On the one hand, the names of both the Increase Younger Brothers Society and the Thunder God Society do seem somewhat odd, particularly in light of the Triad rebellion that ensued. In addition, we should note that the Increase Younger Brothers Society reappears frequently in mainland Southeast China in the early nineteenth century as a variant of the Heaven and Earth Society.[49] It is not inconceivable that Lin Shuangwen, or members of his Tiandihui who hailed from Zhuluo county, were in contact with Yang Guangxun, particularly since Yang fled to Daliyi to take refuge. It is unfortunate, though not necessarily unusual, that no direct confessions seem to have survived from the Yang Guangxun case, which might have spoken to these earlier contacts. But it does seem implausible that the activities of Yang Guangxun were part of a coordinated strategy to rise up against the Qing; it seems more likely that, even if there were contacts between Lin and Yang, Yang had dedicated his *hui* to a purely personal and local grudge.

Other accusations are easier to accept. Collusion between local officials and powerful local elites, criminal or otherwise, was far from uncommon. Yang Tingli's account of the Yang Guangxun case almost suggests an official betrayal of a deal Yang and his family members had struck with local officials and troops that prompted Yang's attack on the inn in Douliumen. The postrebellion investigation into Chai Daji leaves no doubt that he was corrupt, greedy, and unconcerned with military affairs.*

On the other hand, it is clear that Chai and Yongfu were railroaded, victims of the common Qing practice of fixing the blame for complex events on a few persons who should supposedly have had the foresight to take the situation in hand. The case against them seems flawed in a number of ways. First, the charges that they altered the characters for Tiandihui from "Heaven and Earth Society" to "Increase Younger Brothers Society" and that they fabricated Yang Guangxun's membership register lose some of their force when we recall that the Lin Shuangwen rising was the first large-scale Triad uprising in Chinese history, and the first time that many officials, including the emperor, learned of its existence. Even assuming that local officials knew of the existence of Triad groups, there is little reason to believe that these Triads were any more— or less—to be feared than the countless other brotherhood associations that dotted the countryside of Southeast China. In fact, even after the Lin Shuangwen rebellion began, the Qianlong emperor completely ignored a reference to the Heaven and Earth Society in a memorial late in the twelfth month (*TDH* 1: 221). In altering and fabricating documents, Chai and Yongfu would seem to have taken a risk all out of proportion to the situation they were dealing with. In addition, if this was a falsification designed to paper over official malfeasance, it must surely go down as one of the clumsiest and most transparent on record; if the officials had made the decision to delude their superiors, why not choose a *hui*

---

* It remains unclear, however, how exceptional Chai was in this respect. The Qianlong emperor had originally been quite fond of Chai Daji, not least because of Chai's supposedly courageous and prolonged defense of Zhuluo against Lin Shuangwen's troops, which was later derided as cowardly foot-dragging. When Chai was first accused of altering the characters of Tiandihui, the emperor noted in an interlinear comment: "We are currently using this person, so this affair can wait. And even if he did it, it is [no more than] a bad habit of the Green Standards; clearly he had no intention of things going this far." See *TDH* 1: 79.

name with no relation to the "Tiandihui [Triads]," or better yet, deny *hui* involvement altogether?

Furthermore, the charges of alteration and fabrication of official documents, however serious, were in essence symbolic of the more general issue of negligence: officials presumably did their utmost to wrap up troublesome issues as quickly as possible, whatever the consequences. It is implied over and over again in the impeachment of Chai Daji that his negligence allowed Zhang Lie to escape, and that his escape somehow led to the Lin Shuangwen uprising. It is less frequently mentioned that all but five of the criminals involved in the case were apprehended and punished to the full extent (indeed, more than the full extent) of the law within a few weeks of the discovery of the existence of the two *hui*. That a number of fugitives remained on the loose was an unfortunate, but inevitable, part of Chai Daji's profession, and a cursory reading of the Veritable Records from almost any period of the Qing dynasty will reveal imperial and official concern about criminals who have escaped from somewhere, in the wake of some violent action. If the Lin Shuangwen rebellion had not followed the Yang Guangxun affair, Chai's prosecution of the latter would never have been censured for negligence. In fact, it is probably more accurate to view his handling of the affair as unduly hasty and heavy-handed.

In any case, we must be careful not to confuse the bureaucratic management of the consequences of rebellion with the local situation from which the rebellion grew. One doubts that *hui* members, or the communities in which *hui* were embedded, would have chosen the term "negligent" to describe the Qing officials and armies. Even though Yang Guangxun and Lin Shuangwen were hardly innocent, the Qing state surely seemed to them violent, venal, and unpredictable. Questioned about his motivations in rising up, Lin Shuangwen deposed as follows:

> Because the local officials, when they were arresting Tiandihui members, took no care to distinguish between good and bad people, but simply made arrests at random, we truly came to hate them. We thought about bringing suit at the [provincial] yamen, but it meant crossing the ocean—a long way—so we decided we couldn't do that. And if we went to the *daotai* or the prefect, we feared that the officials would just protect one another. . . . So we didn't bring suit, but banded together and killed the officials. (*TDH* 4: 400)

Nor is there any reason to believe that official actions in this instance were unusual. Liu Huaiqing, who had served as a clerk in the criminal section of the Zhanghua county yamen before the rebels coerced him into cooperation after their attack on Zhanghua, characterized the confrontation in the following terms:

As for magistrate Yu, he had not been at his post for very long, and even if there was nothing good about him, there was nothing particularly evil about him either. But Lin had really done nothing more than shelter robbers and criminals. He was not part of a wealthy household, and had not been an object of official extortion. The *daotai* and prefect on Taiwan did not have particularly bad reputations. Former acting Zhanghua magistrate Liu Xiangji was known to have a reputation for integrity, but he extorted money whenever he discovered cases of gambling or disputes. (*TDH* 4:346)

Liu thus suggests that state violence, which I have characterized as unpredictable, was actually not particularly unusual. Indeed, it might be more helpful to view this violence as embedded in daily social life—much like the brotherhood association. From this perspective, rebellion requires no particularly sophisticated explanation. As Lin Shuangwen himself confessed: "Once we had [killed the officials] . . . there was no choice but to take advantage of the situation and rise up. This is the truth" (*TDH* 4: 400).

In this chapter I have attempted to describe the set of events that led up to Lin's rebellion. Given that Lin's uprising is frequently cited as the first Triad rebellion in Chinese history, and then linked to rising popular discontent with the Manchu rulers, the primary findings of this chapter are striking.

First, Yan Yan's secret society, which clearly had both messianic and restorationist connotations, became a named brotherhood under the leadership of Lin Shuangwen. As we shall see in Chapter 3, neither messianism nor Ming restoration figured at all in the proclamations Lin and his men issued after the rebellion got under way, even if they did retain considerable Tiandihui symbolism. Second, the rebellion grew out of local tensions, largely inflamed by the Qing state, which, in this instance, proved to be hypersensitive to brotherhoods and secret societies. Both of the Tiandihuis discussed in this chapter appear to have been of the "embedded" variety, and it seems unlikely that the establishment of either society marked an explicit decision to rise up.

The approach taken in this chapter suggests the importance of focusing on the *popular* perceptions of the meanings attached to Tiandihui membership (or membership in any brotherhood association). Even though the apocalyptic overtones of the rituals, passwords, and oaths of the Tiandihui founders are unmistakable, Lin Shuangwen and his Tiandihui members largely ignored them, even as violence against the state loomed. This surely suggests the danger of overemphasizing the political intent attendant on secret society membership.

CHAPTER 3

Rebellions With and Without Secret Societies

ZHU YIGUI AND LIN SHUANGWEN COMPARED

After we arrived in Taiwan, we repeatedly interrogated [the Lin Shuangwen] rebels on the subject of the origins of the Tiandihui, but discovered only that they used three fingers to take pipes or drink tea, and that when speaking they never left out the "ben" character. They could not provide further details. (TDH 1: 96)

The ideas and practices associated with the Heaven and Earth Society had little to do with the events leading up to the Lin Shuangwen rebellion. The violence grew out of local conflicts, aggravated by heavy-handed practices of the Chinese state that struck Lin Shuangwen and his band of righteous toughs as unfair. The present chapter continues to explore the relationship between named brotherhoods, secret societies, and rebellion by taking a closer look at Lin's rebellion itself. During rebellion, even groups such as Lin Shuangwen's Tiandihui, which were apparently not originally rebellious, felt compelled to explain their actions, and their statements provide clues to the orientation and "ideology" of the group. It would have been logical in this context for Lin to use the symbols and language of the Tiandihui, but neither he nor his followers particularly mentioned the rebellions and rebellious messages implicit in the Tiandihui tradition, and none of those connected with apocalypse or Ming restoration. This omission is further confirmation that Lin was not drawn to the Tiandihui by these elements, and suggests that the Tiandihui tradition in effect competed with other, less specific, rebellious traditions present within Chinese popular culture, which themselves were aggravated by the hostile attitude of the Qing state toward brotherhoods and secret societies.

To illustrate further the insignificance of the Tiandihui to Lin's rebellion, the second half of this chapter compares Lin's rebellion with that of Zhu Yigui. Zhu's rebellion took place more than 60 years earlier, in 1721, in southern Taiwan, and though it did not last as long as Lin's, Zhu held the entire island for a brief period. More importantly, Zhu's rebellion occurred before the proliferation of the brotherhoods and secret societies, and the informal brotherhood (*baiba*), rather than the secret society, served as the vehicle of organization during Zhu's rebellion. The informal brotherhood had played only a minor role in the social life of the region in the prerebellion period, and apart from the dangerous connotations of the blood oath, had no immediately messianic or rebellious associations. In spite of the important differences between informal brotherhood and secret society, however, Zhu's and Lin's rebellions are more similar than different in the realms of symbolism and ideology. If anything, Zhu's rebellion, fueled by natural disasters and official malfeasance, looks to have been more "messianic" and restorationist than Lin's, which was brought on by violent Qing suppression of a supposedly restorationist secret society.

Ideology and Organization in the Lin Shuangwen Uprising

With the death of Qing officials at the hands of Lin's band, Tiandihui members became rebels, by definition. As rebels, they had to justify their actions, to themselves and to others, they had to plan for further confrontations with Qing troops, and they had to administer the areas under rebel control.

The rebels took up their role as symbolic contenders for the heavenly mandate almost immediately after capturing Zhanghua city. They established a reign period—at first "Heaven's Revolution" (*tianyun*), which they changed with the new year to "Following [the Way of] Heaven" (*shuntian*)—and issued proclamations dated accordingly (LM: 207–17). They looted the cloth stores in Zhanghua (and presumably in the other cities they attacked) and made heavy silk banners bearing this latter phrase (*TDH* 1: 252–53). Other banners, which we assume led the troops into battle, simply bore the ranks of commander, general, and so on, and all had embroidered borders (*TDH* 1: 325). Lin Shuangwen called himself "alliance leader" (*mengzhu*) and for the celebration that followed the rebel victory at Zhanghua, wore a black silk hat embroidered with two entwined golden dragons, with a fringe of gold thread worn toward the back. He wore robes taken from the yamen. His men all wore headbands of black cloth.[1] A few weeks after the initial success of the rebellion, the rebels carved seals to be used by Lin Shuangwen and by other "officials." Lin's read "Seal of the *Shuntian* Great Alliance Leader," and he used vermillion ink. (In the early period of the rebellion, before the preparation of the seals, the rebels simply wrote "sealed" (*yin*) on the documents in vermillion).[2]

Lin and those who served as his strategists, primarily Dong Xi, who died before his confession could be taken, also conscripted literate personnel to assist in the administration of their regime. Chief among these was Liu Huaiqing, who had served as a clerk in the criminal section of the Zhanghua county yamen. After the rebels took the county, they seized Liu and threatened to kill him if he did not cooperate. He agreed, and received in compensation the magistracy of the county, after which he and Dong Xi composed proclamations reflecting the transformation of Lin's Heaven and Earth Society from local named brotherhood to leader of a moral campaign against corrupt Qing officials.

Take, for example, the justification for the uprising, for violence against the state. The arbitrary arrests and extortion carried out by troops and local yamen underlings constituted the proximate cause for this violence. Lin Shuangwen himself later explained: "We had entered the Tiandihui, and later the local officials made us anxious with their arrests. We were afraid of our possible punishment, and also afraid that the troops were going to burn our houses" (*TDH* 4: 418–19). It was a legitimate grievance—official malfeasance.

Look now at the explanation for the violence in one of the proclamations issued by the Lin Shuangwen army as one division moved north following the successful initial attacks on Zhanghua and Zhuluo: on QL 51.12.8 (1787), Lin Shuangwen prefaced this proclamation by stating that its purpose was "to pacify the people's hearts and to protect [the people still engaged in] agriculture" (*yi an minxin, yi bao nongye shi*) and announced:

> Only if the officials love the people as their children do they deserve to be called the fathers and mothers of the people. Those on Taiwan today are all corrupt officials and dirty underlings who harm the souls of the people [*shengling*]. Your commander could not bear not to extirpate [such evil], and in order to save my people, I raised a righteous army, and swore before heaven that the inhumane and the unrighteous would perish under 10,000 swords. (*TDH* 1: 153)

A few weeks later Lin reinforced this justification with another proclamation: "This alliance commander set out to practice the Way in accord with Heaven because the corrupt officials and dirty underlings were paring the fat from the people. We raised the flag of righteousness to dispose of the venal officials and save the common people. We have not wrongly killed a single person or wrongly taken a single item" (*TDH* 1: 154). In their own eyes, they were no longer local toughs fighting against a corrupt force of government servants for access to local power and prestige. Lin Shuangwen and company had now become heirs to Mencius and moral critics of the entire government establishment on Taiwan, claiming to speak for all good subjects.[3] Unfortunately, there is no way of determining the extent to which the literate clerk Liu Huaiqing imposed language and moral categories on the rebels; in any case, its popularity in drama and military romance must have ensured that the posture and language of the imperial pretender be fairly well known.[4]

Lin and the rebels also constructed civil and military organizations to support their bid to supplant Qing authority. It is difficult to separate Lin's generous bestowal of rank as a reward to prestige-hungry rebels from an actual military organization that carried out commands and fought the Qing, especially since most of the ranks were fanciful, and some merely broadcast Tiandihui symbolism—*honghao dajiangjun* ("the great 'Hong' general"), for example (*TDH* 4: 110–11). Moreover, the Qing policy of arresting the leaders and forgiving the followers means that we have a group of rebels top-heavy in generals and commanders and low on lieutenants and foot soldiers. Most titles simply described the (sometimes hoped for) achievements of those in command of troops: Great South-Opening General (*kainan dajiangjun*), Great South-Pacifying General (*annan dajiangjun*), Great West-Pacifying General (*pingxi dajiangjun*), Great General Who Sweeps the North (*saobei dajiangjun*), Great Protecting General (*baojia dajiangjun*), General Loyal to the Military (*zhongwu jiangjun*), among others (*TDH* 5: 10; LM: 221, 223, 241–43, 278). Other titles emphasized what seem to have been nationalist themes: Nation-Protecting General (*huguo jiangjun*), National Commander (*guoyuanshuai*), Great Nation-Subduing General (*zhengguo dajiangjun*) (LM: 237, 241, 276). Still others have imperial connotations: Bulwark General of the State (*fuguo jiangjun*), which in Ming-Qing times was a "title of nobility conferred on males directly descended from an Emperor."[5] Another example is *jinwu jiangjun*, which referred to imperial insignia from Han times on.[6] Yet another is the Nine-Gates Provincial Military Commander (*jiumen tidu*), the nine gates being of course a common symbolic reference to the imperial capital.[7] Some titles employed Tiandihui symbolism by affixing the character *hong* at the beginning of titles otherwise indistinguishable from those just mentioned; southern leader Zhuang Datian, for example, took the title "Great *Hong* Bulwark-Generalissimo of the State" (*honghao fuguo dayuanshuai*) (LM: 224–26). It seems clear, nonetheless, that the Tiandihui symbolism did not dominate the selection of titles and that other traditions contributed also.

Lin's actions are perhaps more revealing of military organization and strategy than his choice of titles. After the failure of the first attack on the prefectural city, Lin sent trusted subordinates to Wurizhuang, Tianzhongyang, Douliumen, Yangukeng, and Nanbeitou (LM: 218–19) (see Map 2). All five of these subordinates were early recruits to the Tiandihui, whom the leadership sent to occupy strategic transportation cross-

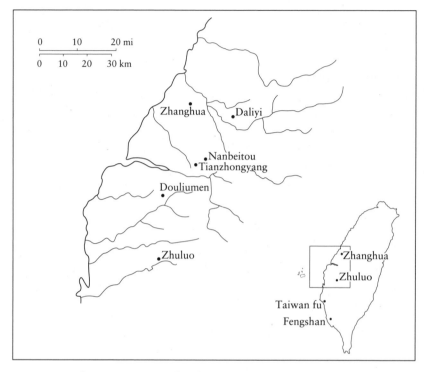

Map 2. Lin Shuangwen's initial military dispositions in central Taiwan

roads or mountain passes. (I shall discuss below how these men recruited followers and held territory; apparently, little formal command structure existed below the level of "general.") Not only did personal ties infuse Lin's military organization—which in this instance meant that Tiandihui connections were very important indeed—but also the theater of combat was small enough to allow Lin himself to exercise personal command in most instances.* Aside from a number of joint attacks on the prefectural city, Zhuang Datian's uprising in the south was only tangentially related to Lin Shuangwen and his northern rebels. Both Zhuang and Lin denied ever having met, and Lin made few attempts to influence Zhuang's strategy, although the two leaders did exchange letters to discuss military affairs (*TDH* 5: 12).

A civil organization copied traditional imperial institutions. Under Lin, who never assumed an imperial name—as did Deng Maoqi in the

---

* The importance of Lin's presence is underscored by his having used a double—a recruit who looked like him—to inspire the rebels during several battles in the fall of QL 52 (1788). See the confession of Lai Da, Lin's double, in LM 1984: 221.

fifteenth century and Zhu Yigui earlier in the eighteenth—were found the rudiments of an "Imperial Household Department," and a "Grand Secretariat." Lin Hou served as head of Lin's "Board of Revenue" (LM: 285–86). Liu Huaiqing was promised eventual appointment to the "Censorate" (*TDH* 4: 340–41). The more important local officials included a "provincial treasurer" and several "county magistrates" and "submagistrates" (LM: 32–38).

The principal functions of these local institutions were tax collection and dispute resolution. A number of Tiandihui members reported being assigned tax-collection duty, and all report assessing a duty of two *dou* per *shi* on lands under their control, destined to feed the army and the administration. Zhuang Datian's men reported a similar practice in the southern part of Taiwan (*TDH* 5: 15). Taxes were to be collected twice annually in the areas under Lin Shuangwen's control, in the first and ninth months for mountain land and in the second and eighth for paddy lands (LM: 218–19). The rebel magistrate of Zhanghua county reported: "I also wrote out receipts, and when underlings visited the various villages in the surrounding countryside to solicit money from wealthy families, those who gave money received a banner recording how much they had contributed, so that other rebels should not disturb them further. Those who did not contribute were subject to robbery and plunder" (*TDH* 4: 340–41).

This suggests that there may have been plenty of room for "illegalities" in the rebel tax collection structure—as there was in that of the Qing, after all—and Lin Shuangwen himself suggests that such abuses did in fact occur (LM: 218–19). One of the proclamations addressed just such malpractices:

> On the issue of the procurement and storage of grain, which we need for our military supplies, it is not permitted that the brothers ask for more than the quotas. We have discovered that perverse no-goods have used tax collection as a pretext to rob the various villages of grain and property. They have carried out their wanton cruelty without limit, and this is illegal in the extreme. In addition to carrying out separate arrests and investigations, we also issue this proclamation to notify the gentry and elders of the various villages of each county that if hereafter they encounter criminal thugs who dare to carry out such expropriation on the pretext that the army needs these supplies, then the villagers are permitted to band together, tie them up, and bring them to the government. They will be prosecuted according to the law, and will not be treated leniently. (*TDH* 1: 156)

The rebels clearly made some attempt to live up to their self-image and not to engage in pure robbery under the pretext of military exigency. In fact, tax "officials" did keep count of the amount of grain collected, recording between 8,000 and 10,000 *shi*, though the period in question is not clear (LM: 285–86). One supposes that in spite of such efforts at legitimacy and fairness, order sometimes gave way. Jiang Ting reported, "When we ran out of provisions, we stole and plundered for our own use" (*TDH* 4: 340–41).

Dispute resolution remained one of the major duties of county magistrates under the rebels, particularly in disputes that involved members of the rebel forces but presumably also those living in rebel-held territory:

> Question for Liu Huaiqing: Since Lin Shuangwen had you serve as Zhanghua county magistrate, you surely lived inside the yamen. Did you have yamen clerks and runners working for you? What cases did you try? When you tried cases, how did you sit in the hall? How did you beat people? When people came into court, did they present their cases while kneeling or standing? . . .
>
> Liu Huaiqing: When Lin Shuangwen took Zhanghua city, he arrested me and had me serve as Zhanghua county magistrate. At the time, the clerks and yamen runners had all fled, and the yamen offices had been looted by the rebels, so I lived in the house next to the yamen. I never sat in the hall, nor did I have clerks and runners to do my bidding. I only served as magistrate for eight days, and wrote a few proclamations that prohibited the people under Lin from fighting among themselves. This I did. But I never tried anyone, nor did I beat anyone.
>
> Later on, after Zhanghua had been retaken by the *yimin*, I fled to Daliyi, and Lin Shuangwen, again because I had served as a clerk in the criminal department, had me take care of the occasional fight or suit. When I tried cases, it was only in a regular room, without clerks or lackeys. There were only a few servants standing at the side. If someone was in the wrong, I did have them beaten. Some of these people [who had done wrong] did kneel to bring suit, but those who had done nothing wrong spoke to me while standing. There were no hall regulations [*tanggui*], not like now when you great people question us. (*TDH* 4: 350–52)

So far as possible, the rebels did make some attempt to regularize civil life and to clarify the obligations between "state" and people.

In addition to the secular arm of Lin's government, Lin also set up a council of elders at Daliyi, staffed by some of his own lineage elders. Lin Rao, one of those who had convinced Lin to hide himself in the mountains rather than join the uprising at the beginning of the rebellion, testified: "Once [Lin] rose up, I worked for him. Our general title was 'the elders,' and we took care of the seals of the Head Commandery [*zongzhi shuaifu qianyin*]. All the officials had to follow our arrangements. Whenever Lin Shuangwen went out to fight, I took care of everything that had to be done at Daliyi" (LM: 221–22). No one else notes the power of this "Head Commandery," and one suspects that Lin Shuangwen invented a function for his lineage elders, who chose in this instance to serve their kinsman rather than carry out their duties as mediators in the orthodox Confucian order.

ETHNICITY AND THE REBELLION

Although Lin's ideology and organization helped to shape the rebellion, ethnic divisions, which in eighteenth-century Taiwan referred to Han communities grouped by native origin, fueled much of the violence. Most Taiwanese identified themselves as Zhangzhou people, Quanzhou people, or Hakkas.* Beginning from the 1780's, tensions in Taiwanese society erupted into what Harry J. Lamley has called a "severe phase of subethnic strife" that affected the island in waves through the 1860's.[8] Prior to the 1780's, Taiwan had been characterized by both frequent violence and ethnic social organization, but not consistently by ethnic violence within the Han community. Ethnic considerations had of course played a role in migration and settlement patterns, and, as certain incidents during Taiwan's frequent rebellions indicate, violence did on occasion follow ethnic lines. Before the 1780's, however, the relative sparseness of settlement and the common challenges of wresting and reclaiming farmland from understandably hostile aborigines also in many instances led to cross-ethnic *cooperation*.[9] But in the last two decades of the eighteenth century this relative cooperation gave way to recurring episodes of bloody ethnic violence, called *xiedou*, generally translated as "feuds." When these feuds flared up, Zhangzhou people, Quanzhou people, and Hakkas, many of whom were unrelated by ties of kinship, residence, or marketing—could be mobilized *simply on the basis of ethnicity*.[10]

With this broad-based mobilization, "feuds" could be extremely destructive; in one 1782 feud, in which Lin Shuangwen's lineage and community were centrally involved, roughly four hundred villages suffered damages, thousands of people fled their homes to seek protection from more powerful neighbors, hundreds of deaths resulted, and the state executed almost three hundred.[11] Such violence, which could erupt and spread with frightening speed, meant that many communities remained in a semipermanent state of mobilization. Rumors, sometimes intentionally circulated by mercenaries or toughs seeking to profit from

* There was of course considerable violence between the Han and aboriginal communities on Taiwan, a topic not treated in this volume. See Shepherd 1993 for an excellent treatment of this and other topics relating to Han-aborigine relations in Taiwan.

feud violence, could prompt villages to invest temporary leadership in mercenary strongmen who organized for both defensive and offensive violence.

During this prerebellion period in which ethnic divisions and enmities were common, Lin's Tiandihui did not discriminate against Quanzhou people—a significant fact often obscured by the later division, during the rebellion, into Zhangzhou rebels and Quanzhou and Hakka *yimin*. At least three of Lin Shuangwen's original Tiandihui members were from Quanzhou (thirteen joined together with Lin, but we have no information on the ethnicity of five of these). One explanation of the cross-ethnic nature of Lin's Tiandihui might be Lin's criminal activities, which made such contacts useful. In any case, the cross-ethnic nature of Lin Shuangwen's Tiandihui confirms that this particular secret society lay across, not within, some of the major social boundaries of late eighteenth-century Taiwan.

Efforts to recruit Quanzhou people increased in the fall of QL 51 (1786) and continued in the period immediately following the Tiandihui attack on Dadun and Zhanghua. However, interethnic hostility proved to be more powerful than either the Tiandihui "cause" or general popular animosity toward the Qing state. Lin's efforts to forge a panethnic alliance failed, and much of the violence of the rebellion pitted Zhangzhou rebel against Quanzhou (and to a lesser extent Hakka) *yimin*. In this sense, ethnicity was central to both the success and the failure of the rebellion. Lin could not have raised forces island-wide without the mobilizing power of ethnic anger, and the Qing fight against Lin and his rebels would have been even more protracted without the aid of the similarly motivated *yimin*.

After taking Zhanghua city, the rebels made it a point to recruit Liu Zhixian, a clerk of Quanzhou origins who worked in the Zhanghua yamen. In Liu's words, "Since I had long served as a yamen underling in Taiwan, and could gather together Quanzhou people, they wanted me to enter the band" (LM: 230–31). Other recruitment efforts reflected similar desires. Liu sent someone to recruit Li Qi, a Quanzhou man from Zhuluo county, because he had heard that Li "had achieved some merit in mediating an early Zhang-Quan *xiedou*" (LM: 278). Guo Jian, a Quanzhou man, was charged with tax collection in the Beitou area (LM: 241). Liu Tiance, a Guangdong native, agreed to collect taxes in the Beishiwei area of Zhuluo (LM: 278). Lin Shuangwen also recruited Lai Ao, another Guangdong native from Nantou, Zhanghua, for his fighting abilities (LM: 276). Chen Mei, a Quanzhou man from Bengang, was also part of Lin's inner circle, although this may have been on account of Chen's fortune-telling abilities rather than his ties to the broader Quanzhou community (LM: 223–24; *TDH* 4: 397–400).

Much the same pattern is identifiable in the southern uprising led by Zhuang Datian, who, like Lin Shuangwen, was a Zhangzhou man from Pinghe county. One of his commanders, Zhuang Xishe, was a Quanzhou person who did eventually surrender to the Qing and seek redemption as a *yimin* leader. Both Huang Cheng and Xu Guanglai were Quanzhou men recruited by Zhuang Datian to collect grain taxes from the local Quanzhou population (LM: 246; *TDH* 5: 15). There is no question that the leadership of both wings of the rebellion sought to recruit participants from all ethnic groups in hopes of avoiding ethnic tensions.

Further proof of these intentions lies in the proclamations issued by Lin Shuangwen's government. In a document dated QL 51.12.8 (1787), Lin noted that he had "heard that some of the little brothers your commander left holding the [Danshui] government offices have been fighting with Hakkas. This should not be." He went on to say that when the army returned to the area, investigations would be made to determine the truth of these rumors. If the investigations found errors on the part of rebel troops, then restitution was to be made two times over: "If we have burned a hut we will rebuild in tile" (*TDH* 1: 153). A later proclamation was even more explicit:

> I have heard recently that the generals and branch leaders (*gutou*) of the various brigades have been unable to restrain their soldiers, and have allowed them to wantonly kill the various outside [i.e., non-Zhangzhou] *yimin* out of private grudges . . . so that the people's minds have begun to sway in fear. This is certainly not the way to pacify the country. In addition to ordering the generals of each brigade to keep control over their troops, I am also issuing this proclamation forbidding [such behavior].
>
> Thus I order the soldiers as follows: on reading this proclamation, let the soldiers return to their units, and let the people be secure in their occupations. As for those who were forced into joining the *yimin*, let them repent of their actions and return to the fold. Fujianese, Hakkas, [other?] Chinese, and aborigines are all part of the common people, and all deserve our sympathies. You must not keep on making excuses to arrest and terrorize, and if you do continue and do not obey, once you are found out . . . we will behead you and display your heads to the masses in accordance with military law. (*TDH* 1: 154)

These proclamations prove the intentions of the leadership of the rebellion to prevent undirected private violence. But the same evidence also illustrates that the best intentions did not always produce the desired results. There was simply no time and no mechanism to recruit adequate numbers of foot soldiers and convince them not to use their position to engage in ethnic vengeance or entrepreneurship. Recruitment for major campaigns presumably presented little problem: en route, one promised booty to the cooperative and threatened violence to the noncompliant. Recruitment during long periods of relative inactivity must have been more difficult. In at least one instance, Lin managed, through coercion, to recruit a wealthy landlord, who brought his money and his contacts with him (LM: 249–50). One suspects, however, that most recruitment followed the following pattern:

> Deposition of Lai Ying: I am from Pinghe county, Zhangzhou, and am forty-nine years old. . . . I run a medicine shop in Sanfenpu. In the twelfth month of last year [QL 51 (1787)], I joined Lin Shuangwen, who put me in charge of [the village of Sanfenpu], with 100 men under me. . . . Lin made me "Great North-Suppressing General" [*zhenbei dajiangjun*]. . . .
> Question: Did you recruit those 100 men? Why did he give them to you?
> Lai: No, Lin Shuangwen gave them to me. . . . I don't have any particular skills, just crude strength. (LM: 277; *TDH* 4: 431–32)

Lin surely had little choice but to seek out local toughs, flatter their egos with extravagant titles, and trust them to be loyal and obedient.

Another confession gives the flavor of recruitment in areas at some distance from the central command:

> On 12.12 of last year [QL 51 (1787)], Shen An and Chen Yuan, fellow villagers whom I had always known, came and told me that they had already thrown their lots in with Lin Shuangwen and were now leaders. They tried to get me to enter the band and be a leader too, and help them fight. At first I was unwilling, but Shen An said they would burn my house, so I had no choice but to go along. We had more than one hundred men, and camped on the mountain, planning to loot villages. On 12.13, more than 300 Quanzhou *yimin* came to get us. I grabbed a bamboo spear and followed Shen An to the front to fight. We were defeated, and our 100 men fled. (LM: 266–67)

Many Quanzhou villages that joined the rebellion must have followed the example of Huang Fu, a Quanzhou Tiandihui member who used those connections to build a 1,000-man defense corps that "held all four roads [into his village]." Huang noted that even when one of Lin Shuangwen's men called for his assistance, "I didn't dare go out and fight, but just gathered everyone together to resist [Qing government and *yimin* attack]" (LM: 275; *TDH* 4: 428–29). The intentional sealing off of this Quanzhou village shows how dangerous the countryside under rebel control could be. Limited evidence suggests that in spite of Lin Shuangwen's best efforts, rebel success depended on empowering local strongmen in their local areas, a situation similar to what we observe in the context of the ethnic *xiedou* in Taiwan. Ethnic tension helped to sustain the rebellion.

Ethnic division also explains the failure of the rebellion. The coastal areas were Quanzhou strongholds, which the rebels were never able to take, and they therefore could not slow or interrupt troop transfers from the mainland. Before the arrival of Fukang'an and his troops, the rebels' main opponents were ethnically organized bodies of *yimin*, a good many of whom were drifters or displaced refugees who agreed to serve in the army in return for a daily rice ration. At the end of QL 52.3 (1787), for example, when the northern and southern rebel forces converged for a joint attack on the prefectural city, the Green Standard officers led some 10,000 *yimin* out to fight. At the end of one day's battles, the exhausted and hungry force rushed back into the city and staged a near-riot. The wealthy, unable to distinguish the *yimin* from the rebels, made preparations to flee to the coast.[12] Other groups formed more spontaneously in response to the *xiedou*-like nature of the rebellion, and the acts of cruelty in which they engaged only served to increase ethnic polarization. Hakka and Quanzhou *yimin* who captured Tiandihui leader Wang Fen in northern Zhanghua cut off his head, hands, and feet and delivered them in a bucket of lime to the Green Standard command (*TDH* 1: 351–52). When government and *yimin* forces retook Zhanghua city on QL 51.12.12 (1787), the *yimin* were so violent that they alienated the fence-sitters and forced those who had been coerced into cooperation by the rebels back into the rebel camp.[13] Other instances repeated the same pattern.[14]

Although local details of rebel organization are scarce, nothing I have seen convinces me that the rebel leadership succeeded in its attempt to forge a panethnic alliance against the Qing state on Taiwan. To most of the participants in the events, the uprising was more feud than rebellion, indicating that ethnicity was a more powerful axis of organization than the Heaven and Earth Society.

THE ROLE OF THE TIANDIHUI IN THE REBELLION

For the purposes of this volume, the central question in the transformation of the Tiandihui from local self-help named brotherhood to pretender to the throne is the importance of the symbolism and practices of the Tiandihui during the rebellion. How did the Tiandihui relate to the Mencian rhetoric of the rebel proclamations? Is there anything about the rebellion to suggest that the Tiandihui provided an "ideology" of rebellion? Of governmental practice? Did the rebels even continue to recruit members to the Tiandihui after the rebellion began?

Large-scale recruitment to join the Tiandihui seems to have stopped with the beginning of armed violence, although we do have confessions from two members who joined after the rebellion was under way, and the initiation oath translated above was apparently confiscated from "a soldier," suggesting that Tiandihui rituals remained useful in some contexts (LM: 243, 267–68). One suspects nonetheless that the solidarity gained in rising up against the state might have been stronger than that produced by a blood oath.

Tiandihui symbolism marked many aspects of the rebellion. Lin's chosen title—"alliance leader" (*mengzhu*)—resonates with the terminology of brotherhoods and associations (although Zhu Yigui used the same term). Rebels added the *hong* character to the ranks of some of the generals, as noted above. Perhaps more importantly, rebels retained the language and some of the egalitarian practices associated with brotherhoods. Lin did not adopt a kingly title, and his men continued to refer to him as "elder brother" even after the initial successes of the rebellion. Proclamations frequently employed fraternal terminology: Lin noted having "heard that some of the *little brothers* your commander left holding the [Danshui] government offices have been fighting with Hakkas" (*TDH* 1: 153; emphasis added). The same language also appears in letters of deputation, enjoining commanders to lead "the brothers of the banner" (LM: 60–61). Liu Huaiqing noted a lack of formality in legal practices that might derive from the Tiandihui embrace of brotherhood—or might simply reflect their relative lack of education. The proclamations, composed by a former yamen clerk, do express what came to be typical Tiandihui language in their suggestions that the rebels were following "Heaven's Way."

For the most part, however, the Tiandihui added little to distinguish Lin Shuangwen's rebellion from many others in China's long history of peasant rebellions. Lin's men apparently abandoned Tiandihui signs of identification such as the three-fingered signal in favor of a circle of hair grown close to the topknot, which would have been harder (and more dangerous) for a *yimin* to imitate (LM: 218–19). The civil government Lin set up seems almost laughable in its attempts to copy Qing institutions, down to the "Imperial Household Department." Because the Tiandihui brought men together outside the authority structures under which they lived most of their lives, it was a natural launching pad for a number of activities, which in this case eventuated in rebellion. By cementing close personal ties, Lin's "secret society" could also provide the nucleus of leaders or generals. But there is virtually no evidence that the apocalyptic–messianic or the restorationist elements of the Tiandihui described by Yan Yan and the society founders inspired Lin Shuangwen or those who fought under him. Of course, consciousness is complex, and some rebels may have entertained the hope that cosmic forces in the form of floods, or saviors in the form of young men bearing imperial surnames, might intervene on their behalf. Others may have dreamed of the return of the Ming. On the other hand, the only reference in this well-documented rebellion to otherworldly imagination or to the Ming dynasty is that of Jin Niang, a female aboriginal shaman recruited by southern leader Zhuang Datian, who sometimes invoked the spirit of former "king" Zheng Chenggong as Zhuang's men went into battle (LM: 272–73). The combination of ethnic hostility, armed brotherhood associations, and a violent state more readily explain the Lin Shuangwen uprising than the Heaven and Earth Society.

Rebellion Without Secret Societies: Zhu Yigui

The relative insignificance of Tiandihui "ideology" to Lin Shuang-wen's rebellion becomes even clearer when we compare Lin's uprising with that of Zhu Yigui. The Zhu Yigui rebellion of 1721 was the first large-scale rebellion in Taiwanese history, and the first large-scale disturbance in the Southeast Coast after the establishment of Qing rule. This uprising predates the proliferation of brotherhood associations in the mid- and late eighteenth century (see Table 1 above), and provides a clear contrast with that led by Lin Shuangwen. In spite of the absence of brotherhood and secret society language and "ideology," many aspects of the two rebellions are very similar, and if anything, Zhu's rebellion appears more restorationist and perhaps even more messianic than Lin's.

THE ZHU YIGUI REBELLION

A combination of natural and man-made disasters set the immediate backdrop to the Zhu Yigui uprising. An earthquake struck southern Taiwan in the late fall of 1720, with aftershocks in the early winter. The earthquakes and tidal waves left many dead and destroyed large numbers of homes.[15] On top of this disaster, the winter of 1720–21 was unusually cold; crops were damaged, and people had to buy extra fuel. In southern Taiwan—Zhu was from Fengshan county, south of present-day Tainan—many were destitute, and their immediate response was to form ad hoc brotherhoods (*baiba*) and stage operas seeking divine assistance.[16]

Man-made problems added to those brought by nature. Higher authorities transferred Fengshan county magistrate Li Piyu in the fall of 1720, and while waiting for the arrival of the newly appointed magistrate, prefect Wang Zhen allowed Wang's son to manage the affairs of the county. In the period preceding the earthquake, this son imposed a series of ill-advised surcharges on oxen, sugar-grinding shops, and rattan collection, and demanded commutation of grain tax payments at a rate below market value—in actuality, another form of surcharge.* He also arrested two to three hundred people for cutting wood and bamboo in the mountainous areas. Wood would have been necessary to rebuild the houses destroyed during the earthquake. Bamboo was probably used to make thatch, but sharpened bamboo was also the poor man's weapon in this part of China. The temporary magistrate released those who bribed him, and, after the earthquakes and tidal waves, apprehended several dozen people for forming ad hoc brotherhoods "without reason" (*wugu baiba*). A playwright setting the stage of rebellion could hardly have improved on this near-classic mixture of portentous natural disasters and official insensitivity.

The mobilization that led eventually to the Zhu Yigui uprising grew out of the *baiba* response in the Taiwan countryside. Two of these pacts—namely, those led by Zhu Yigui and Du Junying—came together in the early stages of the uprising. Zhu Yigui's surname, which he shared with that of the deposed Ming ruling house, thrust him into the forefront and ensured that his name be associated with the rebellion. However, Du Junying formed his pact at least five days before Zhu's, on KX 60.3.10 (1721).

Du was a Guangdong native from Haiyang county in Chaozhou prefecture—an area where the local dialect was similar to those of Southern Fujian—who had crossed the straits to Taiwan in 1707 at the age of 41. He was 55 years old at the time of the uprising. After arriving in Taiwan, he worked as a tenant farmer as well as a rent-prompter for a local notable; Du appears to have been in control of other tenants instead of a simple tenant farmer himself.

In late 1720, a local interpreter (*tongshi*) reported to the prefect that Du had cut wood in mountainous land belonging to the interpreter, and Du fled to avoid arrest.† Early in the third month of KX 60 (1721), an old friend sought Du out with the information that the acting county magistrate was abusing the people, and suggested that since Du was already in hiding, he act as alliance leader (*mengzhu*) in the plan to rise up and seize the prefectural granary and treasury. Du agreed. They recruited 50 people and on KX 60.3.10 (1721) met to swear brotherhood. They then

---

* The rate was 0.72 taels per *shi*. According to Wang Shiaing 1958: 16, the average price for the late Kangxi period was 1.2 to 1.3 taels per *shi*.

† The function of these "interpreters" transcended mere linguistic duties. They acted as tax farmers as well as land brokers in deals involving Han and aborigines, and many of them amassed considerable wealth and power. See Shepherd 1993: 114–23, for their role in the early period of Qing settlement, and 248–52 for their role as Han settlement expanded.

sharpened bamboo to use as spears and made banners bearing the expression "*Qingtian duoguo*"—which is either a pun or a mistaken use of the character *qing*. *Qingtian* (without the water radical) means "an honorable official," and adding the water radical might suggest that the Manchu dynasty had "stolen the country" (*duoguo*).

Similar events brought Zhu Yigui into contact with the brotherhoods five days later. According to Lan Dingyuan's account in his *Ping Tai jilüe*, Zhu had been a troublemaker in his home of Changtai county, Zhangzhou, before coming to Taiwan in 1713 or 1714. In Taiwan, he worked for a time as an underling in the yamen of the Taiwan *daotai*, but he soon quit, or was fired. He then rented land and worked as a tenant in Damujiang village, some 35 *li* to the northeast of the prefectural city. Later still, he moved to Luohanmen village, some 65 *li* east of Taiwan city, where he raised geese for a living. He was 33 at the time of the rebellion.

On KX 60.4.19 (1721), 52 people met in rebel Huang Dian's village (Huang was an old friend of Zhu Yigui's), swore brotherhood, and began immediate plans for revolt. They manufactured banners reading "Great Commander Zhu," "Incite the Good People," and "Revival of the Great Ming"; they sharpened bamboo poles to serve as spears; and they recruited more adherents, who overnight came to number more than one thousand. It was this later meeting that Zhu was selected as leader because of his surname.[17]

Violence began immediately. On the very night of Zhu's selection as leader, his band raised the flag and attacked the garrison post at Gangshan some 30 *li* away from the prefectural city. Two days later, on KX 60.4.21 (1721), messengers came to Zhu Yigui from Du Junying, reporting that Du had organized the disgruntled Guangdong farm laborers from the surrounding area and now proposed joint action to take the prefectural city.[18] Between KX 60.4.21 and 5.1 (1721), when the rebels took the prefectural city, they recruited further adherents by means of persuasion and coercion—promises of rank, money, and grain against the threat of death—and engaged in a number of looting raids on local garrison posts to arm their growing numbers. Banners flew throughout southern Taiwan as Fengshan county fell on KX 60.4.27 (1721) and the prefectural city itself on KX 60.5.1 (1721). As the rebels closed in on and then took Tainan, virtually the entire civil and military government of Taiwan fled to the mainland, leaving only a diehard rear guard on the Penghu islands offshore.

After the fall of the prefectural city, the rebels' influence moved north. Within a week, all Taiwan belonged to the rebels, who now numbered in the hundreds of thousands, if traditional sources are to be believed.[19] Zhu

Yigui set himself up as "Righteous King" (*Yiwang*) in the former *daotai's* yamen, announced his "perpetual peace" (*yonghe*) reign period, and attempted to further solidify his power by handing out official ranks, money, and grain. There were attempts to set up the rudiments of a civil government—former yamen clerks were forced to staff the traditional "six boards" of the government offices—but there is little evidence that Zhu's "government" actually functioned. An internecine struggle with Du Junying, which required further military action, disrupted whatever plans Zhu may have had in that direction. There were also *yimin* responses to Zhu's rebellion, based at least in part on preexisting ethnic conflicts, that required further engagements in Danshui and Zhuluo.[20]

In any case, Zhu's power was short-lived. By the first week of the sixth month, the Qing mounted a substantial force that attacked and defeated Zhu's armies at Luermen, Tainan's closest harbor. This attack plus the promise of amnesty to all who turned themselves in broke the back of Zhu's power. The reign of "eternal peace" lasted little more than six weeks, although minor incidents prompted in part by official arrest attempts continued for several months.[21]

THE REBELLION INTERPRETED

It is not difficult to arrive at a superficially convincing explanation of the Zhu Yigui rebellion. The combination of natural disasters and official malfeasance created a large pool of poor and angry men in southern Taiwan, a region that at the best of times was rowdy and difficult to control. One measure of the depth of disaffection is the ethnic cooperation that marked the early period of the rebellion. The Fujianese Zhu and Guangdongese Du combined their forces against Qing representatives on Taiwan, and of the 24 confessions (out of a total of 64) that mention ethnicity, 14 were Fujianese, 5 Guangdongese, and 5 identified Taiwan as their native place.[22] Of course, the ethnic differences between Zhangzhou and Chaozhou were not great; Manbao, the Manchu governor-general of Fujian-Zhejiang throughout the rebellion and its suppression, noted that migrants "from Chaoyang, Haiyang, Jieyang, and Raoping [counties] in Chaozhou [prefecture] speak a language mutually intelligible with that of Zhangzhou and Quanzhou [prefectures]."[23] In addition, ethnic differences at this point in Taiwan's history were not as crucial as they came to be later in the century, when ethnic feuding became common, but neither were such differences insubstantial. The eventual struggle between Zhu Yigui and Du Junying broke down along ethnic lines, as did the organization of *yimin* to fight the rebels. Hakka communities made up the most famous *yimin* group, organizing "13 large villages and 64 small villages, uniting [migrants] from the [Guangdong and Fujian] counties of Zhenping, Chengxiang, Pingyuan, Yongding, Wuping, Dapu and Shanghang in a group of more than 12,000 . . . [that] raised the flag of the great Qing."[24]

Misery and anger undoubtedly motivated most of those who joined the initial uprising. Others were coerced by the rebels, or were lured by promises of great wealth.* In addition, some confessions provide evidence of organization and participation on the basis of residence: some village heads claim to have felt compelled to join the rebellion because the safety of their villages would have been imperiled otherwise. Ethnicity also remained an important axis of organization, in spite of the multiethnic nature of the early rebellion. Brotherhoods, the ad hoc tools used to cement the earliest organizers of the rebellion, lost much of their significance once the rebellion was under way (as did Lin Shuangwen's Tiandihui). One possibly important difference may indicate a distinction between Zhu Yigui's brotherhood and Lin Shuangwen's Tiandihui. Of the Zhu Yigui depositions that revealed information about family members, 60 percent had no living relatives; 15 percent had living parents, brothers, or children, but had no wife; 25 percent were married.[25] Similar computations for Lin Shuangwen indicate a more settled group, although these figures may not be truly comparable because the smaller number of depositions in the Zhu Yigui rebellion and the lack of secret society participation make it harder to separate those who participated in the original brotherhoods from those who joined the rebellion after it began. The Zhu Yigui figures may be for all "rebels," whereas the Lin Shuangwen figures are for Tiandihui members, leaving out many who joined the rebellion after it began. Nonetheless, it appears that Taiwan in the 1780's *was* a more populous, settled society than Taiwan in the 1720's, and this may suggest that Lin's Tiandihui, as an informal institution, appealed to those at the margins of settled society, whereas Zhu's brotherhood, set up spontaneously during a period of great hardship, appealed to the genuinely desperate.

The iconography and "ideology" of Zhu's rebellion drew on traditional rebel themes. Zhu Yigui noted in his confession that he rose up because "the people could not bear the vexations visited on them by the officials."[26] One of his banner inscriptions read "Incite the Good People." It seems clear that he meant to attack the moral failings of (inadequately) paternal officialdom rather than trumpet the egalitarian, "leveling"

---

* An incomplete sample of 51 participants in the rebellion shows that they received money amounting to 4,081 taels of silver—a substantial reward, since in the late eighteenth century, the entire annual administrative budget for the prefecture of Taiwan, including salaries and expenses for all civil officials and their yamen staffs, came to 4,699 taels of silver; see the *Taiwan fuzhi* 1696, j. 7: 16a.

themes that had been a staple of Chinese rebellions since the Tang.[27] To this Mencian emphasis were added what look to be Ming restorationist slogans as well as symbols of legitimacy derived from a variety of traditions. At first glance, the restorationism seems obvious from the explicit mention of the Ming on the banners used by the rebels and from the selection of Zhu himself as "generalissimo" (*dayuanshuai*). Given the historical connection between Taiwan's colonization and the pro-Ming stance of Zheng Chenggong, one can naturally assume that Zhu's uprising expressed a simple desire to oust the Qing and return to Ming rule.

At the same time, we cannot dismiss the possibility that Zhu and his fellow rebels drew on messianic traditions rather than on (or in addition to) fond memories of the Ming. As noted above, one prominent Chinese messianic tradition centered on the coming of savior figures, frequently descended from certain surnames having dynastic connections (Liu, Li, Zhao, Zhu), whose imminent rule was signaled by portents.[28] Such incidents were common in the Qing. Three that preceded the Zhu Yigui rising—one in 1677 in Tongan, Fujian, one in 1696 in Zhuluo, Taiwan, one in the first decade of the eighteenth century in Jiangnan—also revolved around a figure bearing the Zhu surname.[29] In these incidents, messianism could presumably overlap with Ming restorationist sentiment.

Other Qing incidents, however, involved other surnames: Li Mei was the chief figure in an Enping, Guangdong rebellion in 1729; Li Kaihua, a fictional character who appears under a number of names, figured in several rebellions;[30] Lu Mao claimed to have located Zhao Liangming, a descendant of the Song ruling house, in his attempted rebellion in 1767 in Zhangpu, Fujian.[31] An extraordinary Ming example also merits inclusion: in 1564, in Yongding (Western Fujian), a man surnamed Liu sought to foment rebellion on the strength of his descent from the first Han emperor.[32] Moreover, in many instances—as in the Tiandihui experience discussed above—several dynastic surnames appear together. This surely suggests that the connection between dynastic change, signaled by omens and by the appearance of people claiming physical descent from past rulers, and allegiance to a particular historical dynasty, is not a simple matter. A logical inference would seem to be that the charisma associated with physical descent from a dynastic house betokened the change of dynasties, but not necessarily the restoration of a particular earlier dynasty.

From this perspective, it is more difficult to determine the nature of the ideology behind Zhu's rebellion. Did Zhu's charismatic surname dictate the pro-Ming slogans? Or did pro-Ming sentiment dictate the choice of Zhu as leader? With the exception of the banners, there is no explicit expression of pro-Ming sentiment in rebel confessions or other accounts of the mass action. And apart from the possible pun on the "'honorable' officials" who had "stolen the country," we find no anti-Manchu themes, which might be considered one expression of endorsement for the fallen Ming. The rebels appear not to have employed nationalist, ethnocentric slogans, such as *"huanwo jiangshan"* ("return our rivers and mountains"), in circulation since the Song. Both officials and rebels of course wanted to play down any pro-Ming, nationalist aspect of the rebellion, but if officials were determined to cover up such details, why even mention the banners that referred to the Ming?

Other evidence also seems to argue against a strictly restorationist interpretation. Although the titles handed out by "Righteous King" Zhu Yigui to his followers emphasize either antiquity, or nobility, or both, they do not reproduce specifically Ming dynasty terminology. For example, *Guogong*—Duke of State—was an extremely popular title in the Zhu Yigui rebellion. *Gong* itself, of course, dates back to the feudal Zhou period; *guogong* referred to the "third highest of nine titles of nobility" in the Sui through Yuan period, "normally conferred on the heirs (usually eldest sons) of Commandery Princes."[33] *Dudu*, another title frequently employed by the rebels, was the title designating the "man given overall command of the empire's military forces" from the later Han through the Song dynasties. The Ming continued this title, although it now described a less powerful position. Presumably, the rebels selected the title for its pre-Ming associations.[34] With the exception of *jiangjun* (general), all the titles shared these overtones of antiquity and nobility. Zhu and his men were not scholars, and we should not overinterpret their choice of titles; nonetheless, the rebels' imaginations were not limited to the Ming experience, even if the precise connections between other traditions and these appeals to antiquity and nobility remain unclear.[35]

Also, of course, messianic and "political" concerns can overlap; any would-be rebel, visionary or cynic, would surely be aware of popular beliefs concerning the timing and legitimacy of uprisings and would seek to tailor his actions to those beliefs in order to win the allegiance of both gods and people. Zhu Yigui's confession makes reference to the natural disasters and the popular entreaties of the gods to ease their distress, but in the context of his leadership notes simply that "my 'Zhu' surname could be used to broadcast that I was a descendant of the Ming." The ruling dynasty frequently chose to believe that rebel leaders were mere hucksters who fooled the good but simple peasants into following the selfish whims of the ringleaders, and the cynical tone of Zhu's "confession" accords with what the Qing wanted to hear. Some twentieth-century legends concerning Zhu Yigui ascribe portentous dreams and magical abilities to him, but whether Zhu saw himself as a charismatic messiah is unknown.[36]

The *zhafu* that Zhu and his men distributed during the rebellion are similarly ambiguous. In a "secular" context, we translate *zhafu* as "letters of deputation" that bear "commissions" from an emperor or imperial contender, proving that those who bear these letters are in the employ of the issuer. They often bear a rank, as well as the seal of the issuer.[37] In the context of popular beliefs, however, *zhafu* were frequently purchased as protection against a coming apocalypse. In the Li Mei rebellion, the leaders sold certificates to provide protection against the disasters of plagues and demons. We do not know how Zhu's *zhafu*, which generally bore a rank or title, were intended or understood. Most rebels do not mention popular religious concerns in their depositions, and instead explain their motivations by reference to greed, self-protection, or coercion.

In sum, it is difficult to determine whether Zhu Yigui justified his rebellion through Ming restorationism or rebellious charisma associated with the name of a ruling house, or through some combination of the two. The popular meanings attached to Zhu and his uprising are even more inaccessible. Nonetheless, what stands out is that evidence of both Ming restorationism and rebellious charisma are stronger in the Zhu Yigui rebellion than in Lin Shuangwen's.

The chief difference in the process of mobilization in the Lin Shuangwen and Zhu Yigui rebellions was that Lin Shuangwen was the leader of a secret society that not only had identifiable messianic and rebellious overtones but also had existed for some time prior to the rebellion. By contrast, Zhu Yigui organized what came to be called his rebellion through a number of ad hoc brotherhoods that sprang up in response to the natural and human disasters and, aside from the blood oath, had no specific symbolism or ideology connecting them with rebellion or messianism.

In other ways, however, the two mass actions were very similar. Both sounded traditional rebel themes, drawing on a mixture of Confucian and "greenwood" traditions,[38] and neither consistently exploited nationalistic or anti-Manchu sentiments. Both set up governments modeled after the imperial court, and neither suggested the need for basic changes in anything other than government personnel. Both used the language of brotherhood, leaders Du Junying and Lin Shuangwen being known as "alliance leader" (*mengzhu*). Both wore black.

There were differences, of course, and some of these differences can be attributed to the role of the Heaven and Earth Society in Lin Shuangwen's rebellion. The use of the *hong* character in Lin Shuangwen's banners, slogans, and titles clearly drew on the Tiandihui tradition, as did also the frequent use of such terms as *shuntian* and *tianyun* as reign titles. Lin and his men seem to have used brotherhood language more frequently than did Zhu, and Lin's decision not to take on an imperial name might have something to do with the egalitarian strains in "brotherhood ideology."

On the complicated question of restorationism, messianism, and rebellion, Zhu Yigui made repeated use of the "*ming*" ideograph and was himself selected because of his surname, suggesting some mixture of pro-Ming and messianic elements. In the case of Lin Shuangwen's Tiandihui, both the pro-Ming and messianic themes, identifiable in the founding myth and the initiation ritual, apparently had little part in the justification for rebellion as reflected in rebel proclamations and depositions. The fact that Lin Shuangwen and his rebels did not make greater use of Tiandihui symbolism and "ideology," did not exploit messianic, apocalyptic, or even pro-Ming political themes, in spite of an undoubted exposure to at least some of these themes on the part of Tiandihui members who came in contact with Yan Yan, illustrates that there was sufficient justification for rebellion in Chinese popular culture quite apart from the seemingly incendiary symbolism of the Tiandihui.

Indeed, a vast literature treats rebellions in Chinese history.[39] One recent volume has stressed the "rational" character of Ming rebellions.[40] Another important study of the tempestuous Six Dynasties period emphasizes the "functional" nature of rebellions in focusing elite attention on systemic problems.[41] Other interpretations note the general consistency of rebel ideologies over the centuries.[42] Chinese Marxist historians have of course gone to great lengths to marshal evidence illustrating Mao Zedong's contention that peasant rebellions constituted the "motive force" in China's long history. This literature provides ample evidence of various sources of inspiration for rebellion, from natural disasters, to concerns about illegitimate succession, to beliefs in the changeability of the Mandate of Heaven, to apocalyptic images of the future.

The focus of this volume is on brotherhood associations rather than rebellions, although it has proved necessary to study rebellions in order to understand associations. The Lin Shuangwen and Zhu Yigui uprisings suggest that the level of conflict in Taiwan was high, that outbursts of collective violence were common, and rationales for rebellion were readily available within Chinese popular culture. In the context of these two major rebellions, the evidence suggests that brotherhood associations are not a very convincing explanatory variable, and that rebellions owed more to the long history of uprisings in China than to the organizational capacity or the symbolic power of the brotherhood or secret society.

Secret Societies
and Popular Religion

THE TIANDIHUI IN THE WESTERN
FUJIAN – EASTERN JIANGXI REGION
IN THE JIAQING-DAOGUANG PERIOD

*These heterodox societies [xiejiao] make false claims about the
world to come, in order to cheat you. But let me ask: which of
you has seen a previous life or a future life? Of course Buddhism
has always taught the doctrine of karma, which is nothing more
than a means to encourage goodness; and chanting the scriptures
and avoiding meat are only ways to calm the mind and approach
the good. Respecting the gods is no more than not daring to do
evil. Naturally, these gods and buddhas should be respected, but
the "gods and buddhas" of the secret societies should be
despised. . . . These buddhas are not true buddhas, and heaven
will not accept them, just as the holy son of heaven will not accept greedy officials and evil underlings. . . . All of you must reflect, and not be seduced.*

— *Wang Run, Provincial Director of Education, Fujian, JQ 21
(1816) (TDH 6: 220)*

*Since Li Laowu knew the rules of secret society formation
[huigui] . . . they bought a chicken and some wine [in preparation for the initiation]. Each member wrote out his birth time
[i.e., horoscope], and burned it in the fire. They set up an altar
and a spirit tablet, in the middle of which they wrote* Taishang
laojun. . . . *They also wrote down [invented characters for]
"heaven," "earth," and "Hong" [the Tiandihui founder's sur-
name]. While Tao Shengsan and the others knelt . . . Li Laowu,
with disheveled hair and bare feet, held a water bowl in his left
hand and wrote the "tian-di-hong" talisman with his right, all
the while intoning that if anyone betrayed the oath, he would
not die a good death. (TDH 6: 359)*

Even though there was no teleological relationship between secret societies and rebellion, whatever Qing officials may have thought,
brotherhood associations could serve as convenient organizational ve-
hicles for many types of unsanctioned activities, and secret societies
could transmit potentially incendiary symbols of revolt. But as the discussion of Zhu Yigui's uprising illustrated, the icons and ideology of re-

bellion were not confined to secret societies, nor was the organization of rebellions limited to named brotherhoods.

In the wake of the suppression of Lin Shuangwen, a number of rebellions employing Tiandihui symbolism and organization did occur. These rebellions, representative examples of which are sketched below, resulted from the confluence of two forces: the Qing dragnet, which sought out Tiandihui members throughout Southeast China, and the influence of the Heaven and Earth Society itself, which grew in the popular mind as a result of Lin Shuangwen's protracted battle against the forces of the state. Continuing revolts of course brought continuing repression, in a cycle familiar from the history of White Lotus uprisings.[1] A natural result of this cycle was the spread of the Tiandihui out of its original Southeast China home to other areas of South China and, eventually, to Southeast Asia and Chinatowns throughout the world. In fact, the Lin Shuangwen rebellion and its suppression may have brought about the transformation of an obscure, local tradition into an organization that became a significant part of the social life of many Chinese during the nineteenth and twentieth centuries. To some extent, this "transformation" might also help to account for the frequent involvement of secret societies in rebellious activities throughout the nineteenth century, although socioeconomic and political factors clearly figure in this explanation as well.[2]

Given the violence of the Lin Shuangwen uprising and its suppression, it must have been the rare resident of Southeast China in the early nineteenth century who knew nothing about the heterodox connotations and dangerous implications of Tiandihui membership. Indeed, one would expect Tiandihui membership in post-1800 Southeast China to be confined largely to those who wished to organize rebellion against the Qing. It is thus surprising to discover that as the Tiandihui spread out of its original core area, it took on local coloration rather than becoming consistently rebellious. On Taiwan, in the immediate aftermath of the Lin Shuangwen uprising, the Tiandihui did indeed function as a vehicle for rebellion, and there was also a small number of similar rebellions in mainland Southeast China. In Guangdong, most Tiandihui groups pursued criminal activities, chiefly robbery and banditry.[3] In the western Fujian–eastern Jiangxi area, the Tiandihui intermingled with a variety of forms of popular religion and functioned as a body of religious practices, in which Tiandihui "teachers" sold talismans and charms to ensure good health and protection against disaster.

The juxtaposition of this "transformative" decade of violence with the religious Tiandihui of the western Fujian–eastern Jiangxi region again draws attention to *popular* meanings attached to the Tiandihui, for the continuing popularity of a nonrebellious Tiandihui in the face of persistent and brutal Qing suppression is striking. At the very least, it confirms once again that rebellion was not the only meaning attached to the tradition, as there is good evidence that in western Fujian and eastern Jiangxi, religious elements were the core of the meanings members attached to the Tiandihui. These elements, borrowed from what one scholar calls the "shamanistic substructure" of Chinese popular religious culture, appear to have empowered the marginalized young men who made up the membership of most Tiandihui organizations, at least in their own minds, and perhaps in the minds of nonmembers as well, much as invulnerability rituals or *qigong* practices did (and do) in other contexts.[4] This religious embellishment could easily coexist with (and in many cases in fact drew on) traditions of blood-oath brotherhood, or of apocalyptic rebellion, and it may even help to explain why groups searching for little more than mutual aid chose to employ rituals and symbols that were guaranteed to provoke the angry reaction of the Qing state. This is not to say that Tiandihui groups were engaged in religion *instead of* mutual aid, blood-oath brotherhoods, or "apocalyptic" rebellion. Rather, the ties linking mutual aid, blood oaths, and rebellion become easier to understand if we acknowledge the religious elements at the heart of the regional Tiandihui.

Witch Hunts, Rebellions, and the Spread of the Tiandihui: The State and the Tiandihui, 1788–1800

The Tiandihui as a whole suffered an unenviable fate during the violent decade between the suppression of the Lin Shuangwen rebellion and the end of the eighteenth century. The suppression of the rebellion itself was violent. In addition to the rebels who lost their lives during the course of the uprising, the Qing executed more than 300 of those arrested, and it scoured large areas of the Southeast Coast for relatives of the rebels who were guilty by association (*TDH* 1: 99). Moreover, the Qing made a great effort to seek out the origins of the secret society, conducting house-to-house searches in some parts of the southern Fujian–northern Guangdong area. These efforts, which resemble the witch hunts described in Philip Kuhn's *Soulstealers*, provoked many of the eighteen Tiandihui-led rebellions and near-rebellions that erupted during this period.

These rebellions were met with what should have been decisive force on the part of the Qing; the state executed and exiled hundreds, possibly thousands, in this violent decade, and many of those executed were sliced to death, beheaded, or strangled in the marketplaces of their home areas, their heads subsequently displayed as a warning to those who might be tempted to form a brotherhood association or oppose the state. The fathers and elder brothers of many of those executed were also beaten, cangued, and exiled as an admonition to those in positions of social responsibility not to take those responsibilities lightly.

A detailed narrative of this decade would be long and tedious, but a brief summary is necessary to an understanding of the long-term history of the Tiandihui and, perhaps, that of named brotherhoods and secret societies in general, and to the subtleties of the connections between the Tiandihui and popular religion. The Qing attempts to stamp out "the very practice of *hui* formation" were so brutal that they might well have pushed many brotherhood associations in the direction of dissent and rebellion (*TDH* 1: 99). Throughout this decade, during which the Qing suppressed the Lin Shuangwen rebellion, and searched for the origins of the Tiandihui, dealing at the same time with major and minor uprisings, antagonism between the state and secret societies steadily increased.

THE SUPPRESSION OF THE LIN SHUANGWEN UPRISING

Lin Shuangwen and Zhuang Datian had captured most of central and southern Taiwan during the first two weeks of the rebellion, but Qing forces quickly retook the Zhulou county seat. During most of the rebellion, Qing forces remained under siege at Zhuluo, and sparred with Zhuang Datian's troops in Fengshan and Tainan in the south. The Qing held the coastal areas, thus keeping supply lines open, but for several months were unable to concentrate their forces and deal decisively with the rebels. This long standoff moved toward a rapid denouement with the arrival of Commander Fukang'an in Taiwan in the eleventh month of QL 52. Within a week, the rebel siege of Zhuluo was broken; within three weeks, Fukang'an had taken Douliumen, an important pass between central and southern Taiwan. Before the end of the month, the rebel stronghold at Daliyi had fallen, and although Lin himself was not captured until early the next year, the rebellion was effectively over with the fall of Daliyi (see Map 3 and Appendix B).

Fukang'an also took charge of the reconstruction of Taiwan. In one memorial written in the weeks after the suppression of the rebellion, he showed an astute understanding of the nature of local society, arguing that not all Tiandihui members were necessarily rebels. He cited examples of two who had turned their backs on their society associations and redeemed themselves by serving as *yimin* and fighting the rebels (TDH 1: 98). In a similarly generous vein, he also noted:

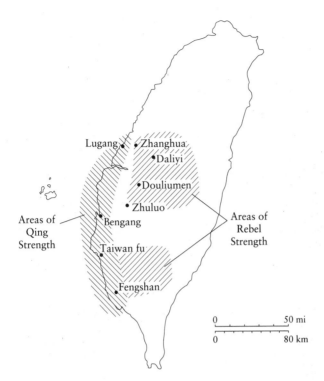

Map 3. Confrontation between rebels and Qing troops, Taiwan sites

The people will be awestruck after our great efforts to return Taiwan to order, and neither *yimin* nor villagers who entered the Tiandihui will dare go back to their evil habits. Given that the minds of the people have only just returned to tranquillity, if we carry out further investigations [into Tiandihui membership], it might be easy to raise suspicions and fears. Moreover, Tiandihui members are not distinguished by any particular appearance, nor is there any [reliable] proof [of their membership]. If we create a pretext for the spread of rumors, we will do the area no good. (*TDH* 1: 98)

All the state should do, Fukang'an argued, was pursue the leaders. The apprehension of former Tiandihui members was not worth the wrongful accusations and extortion such investigations might cause, particularly in view of Taiwan's recent history of ethnic violence.

Later in the same document, however, Fukang'an signaled that this apparent leniency had significant limits. Once the leaders of the rebellious Tiandihui had been apprehended and Taiwan returned to order, Fu wrote, "We must charge local officials to forever ban [the Tiandihui]. Any case of brotherhood or *hui* formation, even if the Tiandihui name is not used, must still be heavily punished in order to illustrate the laws. . . . It is not just that we must proscribe banding together for the purpose of robbery; it is the very practice [lit. 'name'] of *hui* formation that we must stamp out" (*TDH* 1: 99). He added that the capture of the escaped criminals—that is, the leaders of the rebellion—was essential for the pacification of the area. He proposed using troops and locals knowledgeable about the area to guard all important passes, as well as employing friendly aborigines to scour the mountainous areas for rebels still hiding there. Although this would have been less disruptive than village-by-village searches, one suspects that possibilities for abuse remained.

In addition, Fukang'an had already, within a few weeks of the suppression of the rebellion, executed some 312 "rebel leaders," and there is no doubt that more executions followed (*TDH* 1: 98). In the fourth month of QL 53 (1788), Fukang'an reported already having arrested over one hundred relatives of rebels who were guilty by virtue of collective responsibility (*TDH* 1: 100). Other documents make clear that the search for such relatives extended to the mainland Southeast Coast, and in the case of rebel leader, involved demolishing their ancestors' graves and castrating younger members of the family so as to make impossible the further propagation of such evil bloodlines (*TDH* 1: 79; 4: 399; 5: 30–31, 45). The state also confiscated large amounts of rebel property.[5]

In addition, not trusting *any* Taiwanese—rebels or *yimin*—Fukang'an ordered the confiscation of all weapons on the island. By the fourth month of QL 53 (1788), he reported the confiscation of almost 8,500 knives, spears, and guns, which were turned over to the Taiwan prefect to be recast as agricultural tools. He also "issued edicts to smithies and merchants not to manufacture any more [weapons]."[6]

THE SEARCH FOR TIANDIHUI ORIGINS

The search for the origins of the Tiandihui began while the Lin Shuangwen uprising was still in progress. Somewhat curiously, the uprising had been under way for several weeks before the emperor even learned of the involvement of the Tiandihui, and in the early period of the rebellion he seemed relatively unconcerned, noting on 51.12.27 (1787): "The rebels are a ragtag bunch. Our troops in Zhuluo killed more than two thousand of them, and the rest will surely disperse when they learn of this" (*TDH* 1: 186). At the end of the twelfth month, the emperor's chief concern was that the rebellion should not spread to the mainland, and he warned mainland officials not to stir up the locals with unnecessarily frenzied troop movements (*TDH* 1: 186–87). But when, early in the new year, arrests revealed Lin Shuangwen's membership in the Tiandihui and provided skeletal information about the foundation myth of the society (although the Qing did not understand the information in "mythic" terms), the emperor grew worried, particularly in view of the mounting rebel victories. Tracking down the founders of the Heaven and Earth Society and their coconspirators became a near-obsession.

Information revealed in early arrests looked promising. Qing officials learned that the Tiandihui had come to Taiwan via someone named Yan Yan (who had not yet been apprehended), who had identified two founders of the society while recruiting new members: Monk Hong Erfang, who lived in Fenghua Pavilion, Houxi township, Guangdong; and a fifteen- or sixteen-year-old surnamed Zhu, whose place of residence was unknown (*TDH* 1: 64). The emperor dismissed the importance of Zhu, who seemed too young to have played any important part in so massive an affair as the Lin Shuangwen rising, and charged Liang-Guang Viceroy Sun Shiyi with the task of hunting down Hong, who could presumably then direct officials to Zhu (*TDH* 1: 65–66). Thus began a region-wide search for the founders of the Tiandihui.

The original target area, northern Guangdong, was quickly broadened to include southern Fujian, and viceroys and governors of both provinces oversaw repeated, and frustrating, efforts to track down Hong Erfang and his mysterious young accomplice. The search was suspended early in QL 52.4 (1787), and only reinitiated in QL 53.3 (1788), after the capture of Lin Shuangwen, but by the spring of QL 53, officials had succeeded in arresting more than 90 admitted or suspected members of the Tiandihui, most of whom underwent repeated interrogation and torture without revealing the whereabouts of the elusive Hong and Zhu (*TDH* 1: 121, 130–31).

Some Qing officials must have wondered if the search for the origins of the Tiandihui was worth the trouble. Many of those arrested seemed quite ordinary. Xu Axie, Lai Aen, and Lin Ajun, for example, were all arrested in Raoping county, Chaozhou, in early QL 52 (1787) because they "looked suspicious," and all three confessed to having joined the Tiandihui out of desperation. They had been robbed while traveling in southern Fujian, and then informed by acquaintances there (who turned out to be in league with the robbers) that if they joined the Tiandihui, they could secure the return of the items that had been stolen from them, and could also avoid future problems by using Tiandihui hand signals and passwords (*TDH* 1: 68–72). The three provided the names of those who had initiated them into the society, but when Qing officials eagerly tracked down these "ringleaders" they were told that Xu, Lai, and Lin had quarreled with them over debts. According to their stories, there was no question of secret societies and conspiracies; the three were simply trying to save themselves and deflect official attention to those against whom they bore a grudge (*TDH* 1: 88–90).

Other arrests proved similarly disappointing. In early QL 52 (1787), the Fujian governor arrested twelve Tiandihui members in Zhangpu county, Zhangzhou, only to have all twelve insist that they had merely formed a pact to make contributions toward a common burial fund (*TDH* 1: 76). Another memorial boasted of the arrest of 29 Tiandihui members, only to reveal subsequently that all 29 were from southern Fujian and were aboard ship en route to Indonesia when they were blown ashore in Guangdong. The official thought this was highly suspicious, since Lin Shuangwen was also from southern Fujian and was engaged in a rebellion in Taiwan, but it is not clear if the charges of Tiandihui membership had any more substance than this (*TDH* 1: 83–84). In the spring of QL 53 (1788), Liang-Guang Viceroy Sun Shiyi admitted that most of those he had arrested had been very poor people seeking mutual aid in their home regions, who had never been to Taiwan or engaged in rebellious activities. He insisted, nonetheless, that "they had all propagated [Tiandihui] methods, which incited the minds of the people, and they should be sentenced to distant exile, in order to make manifest the punishments" (*TDH* 1: 95).

Admittedly, alongside these frustrations were hints that officials were on the right track. Even Xu, Lai, and Lin, who appeared otherwise insignificant, knew lines of Tiandihui lore—including the key phrases *muli doushi* and *shuntian*—which suggested that they had been in contact with someone well versed in society lore. Xu also suggested that the society had been founded in QL 32 (1767), which gave the emperor fits when he entertained the thought that officials in the Southeast Coast had been engaged in a two-decade-long cover-up (*TDH* 1: 68–72). Lin Shiyao, viceroy of Fujian-Zhejiang, also found written evidence that Hong and Zhu were the society founders (*TDH* 1: 90). Other arrested Tiandihui members identified contacts that also looked promising: Lin Gongyu, arrested in Chaozhou, Guangdong, in QL 52.2 (1787) spoke of Zhu Hongde and Hong Litao, the latter supposedly a monk from Zhangpu who had taken his vows at the Fulian temple in Longqi, Zhangzhou (*TDH* 1: 90–91). Lin also repeated the *muli doushi* slogan and added other verses (*TDH* 1: 87). And though the Qing dragnet did not immediately snag the key figures in the conspiracy, enough people were arrested to suggest that the Tiandihui was a regionally important phenomenon that merited official attention even if arrest efforts consistently yielded only minor figures.

These hopeful signs led to official actions that suggest the atmosphere of a witch hunt. In the early months of QL 52 (1787), although the emperor's attention was increasingly drawn to the rebellion and away from the search for Tiandihui origins, he continued to insist in frequent edicts that local officials on the mainland locate Hong and Zhu. After all, he argued, the officials knew Hong's address: Fenghua Pavilion, Houxi, Guangdong. Liang-Guang Viceroy Sun Shiyi responded that there was no Fenghua Pavilion in either Huizhou or Chaozhou prefecture, but that he had heard that in Suixiangbao in Jiayingzhou, there was a pavilion behind a temple that housed a Monk Hong and someone surnamed Zhu. Sun sent underlings to make inquiries, only to learn that there was no Suixiangbao, nor was there any such temple in any other *bao*. Still, the magistrate of Jiayingzhou had learned that there were three monks, Honglang and Hongke, and a seventeen- or eighteen-year-old youth named Ligao, whose lay surname was Zhu, all living together in the Lingfeng temple some 30 *li* from the *zhou* capital. The magistrate sent men to the temple and discovered seven people, among whom were indeed the three monks. They found no evidence of illegal writings, however, and furthermore the information revealed in the depositions of those arrested, so far as it concerned people and places, was all local and readily verified. Local security personnel vouched for all seven, who were nonetheless incarcerated (*TDH* 1: 90–91).

These were not isolated incidents. The magistrate reported that there was a monk at the Nanshan temple whose lay surname was Hong, and who had a son also serving as a monk in the Huanglong cloister in Chaoyang. The Chaoyang county magistrate arrested this son and brought him to the prefecture for questioning (*TDH* 1: 90–91). Viceroy Sun further reported that there were large numbers of Hongs and Zhus in the Chaoyang area, most of whom were salt workers, and the rest farmers, suggesting the extensive investigations local officials must have undertaken (*TDH* 1: 90–91). A year later, when further arrests produced the names of Zhao Mingde, Chen Pi, and Chen Dong, all supposedly from northern Guangdong, Sun reported that the prefect of Chaozhou had made house-to-house investigations and had discovered that there were more than 500 Zhaos in Guyuan *jia*, but no Zhao Mingde. There were one or two Zhaos in Yuangao and Dama *jia*, but both were simple peasants. In Baoan *bao*, however, the prefect learned that there were three Zhao brothers, who had left some ten years ago and had not returned. Their impoverished mother had remained in Baoan, and the authorities hauled her in for questioning. As for Chen Pi and Chen Dong, the prefect noted that there were many Chens in the area, and that a house-by-house search was not practical, so he instead consulted all local elders, who denied knowledge of either person (*TDH* 1: 128). Nor did apparent innocence excuse those arrested from punishment. The emperor asserted that "even if [the Hongs and Zhus investigated in Jiaying-zhou in early QL 52 (1787)] are not the correct criminals [i.e., the Hong and Zhu identified as Tiandihui founders], we cannot allow them to remain in China proper [*neidi*], and must instead sentence them to bonded servitude in exile" (*TDH* 1: 101).

Only with the arrest of Yan Yan in 53.3 (1788) did Qing officials begin to uncover the kind of information they were looking for. As noted in Chapter 2, Yan deposed that the Tiandihui was created by two people, Zhu Dingyuan and one surnamed Li, and that it had come from Sichuan long ago. In addition, there was a Ma Jiulong who had gathered together 48 monks to practice techniques of driving out spirit soldiers. Many of these 48 later died or dispersed, and Monk Wan, also known as Tuxi, started the branch of the Tiandihui in Guangdong. Yan also provided further information concerning Zhao Mingde, Chen Pi, and Chen Biao, who had come to Zhaoan, Zhangzhou, from Huizhou, Guangdong, to proselytize, and "Dog Face" Zhang (lit., "broken face dog"—*polian' gou*—but supplemental descriptions make clear that the reference is to an unpleasant physical appearance), at whose home Zhao and the others often stayed while in Zhaoan. Chen Pi had supposedly traveled to Taiwan to spread the secret society, but had long since returned to the mainland. Yan himself had been recruited by Chen Biao in QL 48 (1783) in Pinghe county, while Chen was posing as a doctor. Chen Biao was the only one Yan claimed to have met, and his information about the other people mentioned all came through Chen (*TDH* 1: 96–98).

Although Yan's information did not completely accord with that revealed in previous depositions, his "authority" as the acknowledged transmitter of the Tiandihui to Lin Shuangwen assured that he would be taken seriously, and the names he provided proved extremely useful. After frenzied sweeps of the countryside, Liu Shiyao succeeded in the fifth month of QL 53 (1788) in arresting Dog Face Zhang, who provided further information concerning the whereabouts of Zhao Mingde, Chen Pi, and Chen Dong (*TDH* 1: 104–5). Late in the year, Guangdong Governor Tulupu reported the arrest of Chen Pi, who confessed that Tixi, the monk who transmitted the secret society, was from Guanyin Pavilion in Gaoxi township, Zhangpu county; Chen Biao was from Yunliao township, Pinghe county; and Zhao Mingde from the outskirts of Yunshao city in Zhangpu (*TDH* 1: 137). Within the next few weeks, Qing authorities tracked down and arrested Chen Biao and Monk Xingyi, who was eventually identified as the son of Monk Tixi (*TDH* 1: 138–40).

Repeated interrogations, using torture, of Chen Biao and Xingyi allowed Qing officials to piece together a version of the early history of the Tiandihui. The founder of the society was Zheng Kai, who had taken vows and become a monk, after which he was known as Tixi, or Tiqi, or Tuxi, or Monk Hong. According to the founder's son, *"hong"* had been his childhood name, and *"er"* of *"erfang"* his generational designation (*TDH* 1: 138). No explanation was given for the *"fang"* or *"erfang,"* possibly because *erfang* means "second branch," which suggested linkages between Tixi and other "branches" elsewhere, something for which these confessions provided no evidence. Yan Yan's reference to Monk Wan was explained by the fact that *hong* and *wan* are homophones in Zhangpu dialect.[7] Tixi founded the Tiandihui in QL 27 (1762) at the Guanyin temple in Gaoxi, Zhangpu (the same place he eventually died, and was buried). He invented and spread the "society secrets" (*huijue*), which included the "five drops and twenty-one" identifying numerical code, the *hong* character, *shuntian*, and *muli doushi zhitianxia*.

Under repeated torture, and in response to specific (an American lawyer would certainly say "leading") questions, Chen Biao and Xingyi further revealed that Tixi had also been the ringleader behind two planned rebellions that had occurred much earlier in southern Fujian. In QL 32 (1767), Lu Mao, who had joined the Tiandihui through Tixi in QL 27 (1762), organized a band of over 300, planning to attack the Zhangpu county seat under the supposed leadership of a descendant of the Song dynasty, Zhao Liangming.[8] In QL 35 (1770), Li Amin, also a Tiandihui member, rallied followers from Zhangpu around a Ming descendant, Zhu Zhenxiang, and planned yet another rising. Both these plans fell through, but both, according to Chen Biao and Xingyi, had been the work of the Tiandihui, obviously a source of regional instability for some time.[9]

With the failure of the two attempted uprisings, Tixi and Chen Biao decided to lie low. In QL 44 (1779), Tixi, who apparently remained quietly in his Guanyin temple throughout this period, took ill. On his deathbed, he taught the society secrets to his son, Zheng Ji, "hoping to provide him with the means to make a living." The poverty-stricken son also inherited his father's temple land, thus becoming a monk and taking the name Xingyi. He confessed to having passed on the secrets to one laborer who worked on the temple, but even Qing officials admitted that Xingyi was not an important link in the transmission of the society (presumably because they could not connect him with entrepreneurship or violence). In QL 47 (1782), Chen Biao, feeling that enough time had passed, began once again to market society membership, selling entrance into the society to lineage members and neighbors. Yan Yan was one of those who joined, and through Yan Yan the society found its way to Taiwan, where Lin Shuangwen used it to organize a massive rebellion.[10]

The emperor—and with him, the rest of Qing officialdom—appears to have been satisfied with these explanations, although as the Tiandihui continued to spread in the 1790's, the Qing continued to try to track down further references to various "Hongs" and "Zhus" (*TDH* 5: 472–74). They had traced a chain of transmission to an identifiable "evil person" whose depravity had brought about the founding of the secret society. Chen Biao's greed had ensured its survival and transmission. Officials were thus happy to overlook the many unanswered questions left by the investigation: the young Zhu, identified by several names in many depositions, was never found. Indeed, many names produced in the course of interrogations were never matched up with actual people. Yan Yan's reference to Sichuan was never clarified, nor were his comments concerning Ma Jiulong and the other monks who spread the Tiandihui.[11] Officials were also surprisingly uncurious about the details of Zheng Kai's–Tixi's life; although they did perform a "blood drip" test to determine that the remains of Tixi matched Xingyi's blood type, they did not question neighbors, local security personnel, or other relatives. Granted, Tixi had supposedly been dead for a decade, but he had also supposedly spent several years at the Guanyin Pavilion. Surely *someone* might remember him. Officials evinced the same lack of curiosity about the details of Chen Biao's life.

In addition, most of the information on which the Qing officials based their reconstruction of the origins of the Tiandihui came solely from the "confessions" of Chen Biao and Xingyi. A close reading of the documents describing these interrogations reveals that Qing officials were convinced that these two provided the clearest links with the supposed Tiandihui founder, and were therefore determined to exploit these sources of information to the fullest, despite the criminals' "shiftiness."[12] In some instances, it appears that Qing officials put words in the mouths of the two. For example, the information that the Lu Mao and Li Amin uprisings had been led by the Tiandihui comes largely from these interrogations, and officials were obviously convinced of the Tiandihui role in these planned uprisings *before* beginning their questioning of Chen Biao and Xingyi. Both near-rebellions could, of course, have been the work of the Tiandihui.[13] However, more than 300 were arrested in the Lu Mao affair, and it is difficult to imagine that someone would not have revealed the central role of the Tiandihui, if only to lessen his own punishment. One might note also that connecting Lu Mao and Li Amin to Tixi and the Tiandihui made the entire explanation of Tiandihui origins look more convincing. Otherwise, all Qing officials had to offer was a dead monk, with no personal history other than that he lived for a long time in the same temple.

Still, some person or other must have founded the Tiandihui—or at least there must have been someone to have made such a claim—and it may indeed have been Zheng Kai. Many modern scholars accept most of the Qing interpretation, which strikes me as at best only partially true, particularly in view of the well-known Qing propensity for conspiracy theories and the willingness on the part of local officials to construct interpretations to please the emperor. Barend ter Haar, who is more familiar with popular traditions of prophecy and apocalypse than were most Qing officials, has done a more convincing job of tracing the origins of the Tiandihui to other messianic and rebellious traditions, although his goal is not to locate the specific place and time of the actual "founding" of the society.[14]

For the purposes of this chapter, it is perhaps more appropriate to focus on the social effects of the Qing search for Tiandihui origins than on the credibility of the Qing findings and arguments. In the same memorial where Fujian-Zhejiang Viceroy Wula'na and Fujian Governor Xu Sizeng reported the results of the interrogations of Chen Biao and Xingyi, they also noted that "between one and two hundred criminals from Fujian have already been sent to Beijing, or to Guangdong, and have been executed or exiled. More than twenty more have been arrested and are currently being processed."[15] If we estimate that 150 were arrested in Fujian, and add to that the conservative estimate that 100 were arrested in Guangdong, we have at least 250 people arrested, interrogated, tortured, exiled, and possibly executed, from most of the counties of southern Fujian and northern Guangdong. In many instances the Qing adopted a broad interpretation of "guilt."

Many of the arrests made by Qing officials suggest that prior to the Lin Shuangwen uprising and the search for Tiandihui origins, the Tiandihui was a relatively obscure local tradition, connected to small-scale mutual aid practices, which even in the context of the Lin Shuangwen rebellion played only a supporting role. The number of arrests made, and the way in which many arrests were made, suggest that the Tiandihui could never again be an obscure, local tradition.

TIANDIHUI REBELLIONS IN THE WAKE
OF THE LIN SHUANGWEN UPRISING

The Tiandihui-led rebellions and near-rebellions that occurred in the wake of the suppression of Lin Shuangwen also mark the "transformation" of a local tradition into an organization with at least regional prominence. Beginning in QL 54 (1789), roughly one year after the suppression of Lin Shuangwen's rebellion, there were rebellions, secret society activities that invited Qing repression, or executions and exiles of secret society members, every year until the end of the century, as Table 2 and Map 4 indicate. An examination of these cases reveals that during this period, an identifiable set of practices associated with the Tiandihui became connected to rebellion. In some instances, direct connections to Lin Shuangwen prompted further secret society activity. In others, the messianic or millenarian ideas identified as part of early Tiandihui history figured prominently. In still other cases, the power or charisma associated with the Tiandihui, but not the ideas or symbols connected with its foundation myth or initiation rituals, seems to have been central to continued secret society activity. And in the background of all of these cases stood the Qing state, which made concerted efforts throughout this period to stamp out the Tiandihui and its analogues.

Lin Shuangwen–connected violence. A number of examples of Tiandihui-related violence and rebellion in the wake of the Lin Shuangwen rebellion stemmed directly from Lin and his rebellion. One such was the Zhang Maqiu rebellion of QL 52.12 (1787), which occurred in Zhangpu, Zhangzhou, southern Fujian, while the Lin Shuangwen uprising was still raging. Zhang, a local gambler and thief, took advantage of the preoccupation of local authorities with Lin Shuangwen to organize an attack on the Zhangpu county seat, on the assumption that even if he and his men failed, they could always flee to Taiwan and join Lin. To boost his credibility, he claimed Tiandihui membership (in fact, he asserted that his father and uncle had been Tiandihui members too), and manufactured banners bearing the *shuntian* slogan. Zhang claimed that Lu

TABLE 2
Tiandihui-Related Activities (Robbery, Feuds, Near-Rebellions,
Rebellions) in Southeast China, 1788–1800

Li Shui, QL 52.7 (1787), Longqi, Zhangzhou, Fujian (*TDH* 5: 424–27, 429–30, 432–35)
Zhang Maqiu, QL 52.10 (1787), Zhangpu, Zhangzhou, Fujian (*TDH* 5: 363–75)
Huang Jiangzhu, QL 54.3 (1789), Longqi, Zhangzhou, Fujian (robbery) (*TDH* 5: 424–50)
Zhang Biao–Xie Zhi, QL 55.9 (1790), Nantou, Zhanghua, Taiwan (*TDH* 5: 375–404)
Chen Lao–Su Ye, QL 57.5 (1792), Jinjiang, Quanzhou, Fujian (*TDH* 5: 450–82)
Zheng Guangcai, QL 59.6 (1794), Fengshan, Taiwan (*TDH* 6: 73–78)
Chen Guang'ai, QL 60.2 (1795), Fengshan, Taiwan (*TDH* 6: 1–10)
Chen Zhouquan, QL 60.3 (1795), Zhanghua, Taiwan (*TDH* 6: 11–68)
Yang Zhao, JQ 3.1 (1798), Danshui, Taiwan (*TDH* 6: 78–86)
Jiu Daqian, JQ 3.5 (1798), Yangjiang county, Zhaoqing prefecture, Guangdong (*TDH* 6: 416–21)
Xu Zhang, JQ 3.7 (1798), Jiayi, Taiwan (*TDH* 6: 86–90)
Wang Jiang, JQ 3.10 (1798), Fengshan, Taiwan (*TDH* 6: 90–95)
Luo Mingyang, JQ 4.10 (1799), Pucheng, Fujian (*TDH* 6: 141–44)
Pan Lang, JQ 4.11 (1799), Nan'an, Fujian (*TDH* 6: 144–46)
Xiaodaohui, JQ 5.3 (1800), Jiayi, Taiwan (*TDH* 5: 95–130)
Fuo Xing, JQ 5.6 (1800), Putian, Fujian (*TDH* 6: 146–48)

Map 4. Secret society–related violence in the 1790's

Mao had used *shuntian* banners in his planned uprising in Zhangpu in QL 33 (1768), and that Lin Shuangwen called himself the *shuntian* general; he even asserted, falsely, that his banners had been sent to him by Lin Shuangwen. He also at various points during the planning and execution of his failed rebellion promised that large numbers of Lin Shuangwen's forces were on the point of arriving to support him (*TDH* 5: 367–73).

Other incidents reveal different sorts of ties. Qing officials arrested a number of men who had joined the Tiandihui on Taiwan in the period before the Lin Shuangwen rebellion and then fled back to the mainland after the rebellion got under way.[16] All these claimed, understandably, that they had not been part of Lin Shuangwen's Tiandihui and had only kept up or revived their Tiandihui ties in order to carry out robberies. Under the circumstances of the recent major Tiandihui-led rebellion, it is not surprising that local officials subjected all those arrested to intensive interrogation and torture, during the course of which their former, as well as current, Tiandihui networks came to light. Moreover, many of these man seem to have been desperate outsiders, without meaningful ties to any settled community, and it is easy to imagine that in the Qing search for the origins of the Tiandihui and the remnants of the Lin Shuangwen rebellion, both popular and official attention might focus on just such desperate people.

Tiandihui ideas: messianic (?) rebellion. In other cases, the messianic or millenarian ideas of the early Tiandihui tradition seem to have played a significant role. The best example of this is Chen Zhouquan, who had extensive connections with the Tiandihui, and led a short-lived rebellion on Taiwan in 1795.

Chen was originally from Tongan county, Quanzhou prefecture, in southern Fujian, but he grew up in Taiwan. He returned to Tongan in QL 57 (1792), after the Lin Shuangwen uprising, and joined a mainland Tiandihui led by Chen Sulao and Su Ye (*TDH* 5: 450–82). Both these leaders, and quite possibly Chen Zhouquan himself, had been members of the Tiandihui on Taiwan (although, according to their confessions, not directly connected with either Lin Shuangwen or Zhuang Datian) and had joined the rebellion when Lin Shuangwen raised his banner. After Lin was apprehended and the uprising quashed, Chen Sulao and Su Ye took refuge in Taiwan's dense inner mountains. In the spring of QL 57 (1792), they returned to the coastal areas of Taiwan, managed to talk their way aboard a boat, and returned to the mainland.

Chen Sulao and Su Ye reestablished the Tiandihui on the mainland chiefly as a vehicle for robbery, but it is clear that they also shared in the ritual and symbolic tradition associated with the early Tiandihui. They taught the three-finger identification sign, had initiates burn incense, take an oath, and pass through a gate of swords. To recruit new members, they spread the word that Zhu Jiutao (Nine Peaches Zhu), also known as Hong Sanfang (Third Branch Hong), of Gaoxi, in Shicheng, Guangdong, had set up a named brotherhood, and suggested that their association was in some way linked to his.

As their numbers grew (the Qing eventually arrested more than 200), Chen and Su worried that the three-finger sign might be inadequate, so they issued membership certificates as well. These certificates, printed on sheets of yellow paper, bore newly invented characters for "heaven" and "earth," created out of fear that Qing armies were in hot pursuit (although the characters were still apparently pronounced "*tian*" and "*di*").* Accompanying these newly created characters was the slogan

---

* "Heaven" combined the character *qing*—green or black—on the left with the character *qi*—cosmic breath—on the right; "earth" had *hei*—black—on the left and the same *qi* on the right.

"*shunguo yuanfen*," which according to the interpretations of Qing officials combined two meanings: *shunguo*, following [the Way of] the nation," was copied from Lin Shuangwen's reign period, *shuntian*, "following [the Way of] Heaven; and *yuanfen*, which expressed the idea that Chen and Su represented a "branch" (*fen*) of the "original" (*yuan*). Directly below the invented characters was the image of what appears to be a peach, and thus connected to Nine Peaches Zhu (*TDH* 5: 452). They also penned a verse based on the ideas of heaven, earth, and change:

> When the heavens turn to water, the water
> becomes immortal.
> When the earth turns to fire, everything mixes
> with water.
> When the hexagram takes on the *tian-di* form,
> Tens of thousands of changes will ensue. (*TDH* 5: 452)

Although the precise meaning of the verse, which served as a supplemental password, is never explained, it is not hard to find apocalyptic overtones in its references to heaven, earth, immortality, and change, particularly since the hexagram referred to must be Pi (number twelve), which has the *qian* ("heaven") trigram on top and the *kun* ("earth") trigram on the bottom, and describes a decidedly negative situation.[17]

Qing authorities arrested over 200 of those associated with Chen Sulao and Su Ye in the late summer of QL 57 (1792), at which point Chen Zhouquan fled back to Taiwan, where he worked as a sugar peddler in the southern county of Fengshan. During the first month of QL 60 (1795), he joined a society led by Chen Guang'ai (this *hui* appears to have been ritually identical to the Tiandihui, but no name is specified in the documents) and the following month participated in an abortive rebellion that fizzled out after an attack on a local garrison post (*TDH* 6: 1–10).

With the failure of the Chen Guang'ai rebellion, Chen Zhouquan fled north to Zhanghua county. In the third month of the year, a famine affecting both Taiwan and the mainland forced up rice prices, and starving people in Zhanghua competed for the increasingly expensive grain with wealthy mainland merchants, whose ships were docked at Lugang. Chen Zhouquan established yet another Tiandihui and led a substantial revolt of 1,200 men beginning in the third month (*TDH* 6: 41–42).

This revolt made extensive use of messianic and Tiandihui symbolism. On seizing Zhanghua city, the rebels issued an edict in the name of "Zhu, leader of the great alliance" to the effect that "my brothers and I today seize the heavens and the country." They chose as their reign period *Tianyun*—Heaven's Revolution—which had also been the first choice of Lin Shuangwen (*TDH* 6: 11). Yao Ying, who served in Taiwan in the late 1810's but wrote about Chen's rebellion considerably after the fact (1830, and with no clear documentary basis), records even more information in his account of the rising, noting that Chen had also made reference to Nine Peaches Zhu, and included images of peaches on seals the rebels had carved, claiming that he was arriving from the mainland with thousands of ships, and that all members of Chen's band called themselves "Zhu."[18] Archival records confirm that Chen did spread the rumor that ships were arriving from the mainland on a particular day and that this was in fact a *jiazi* day on the traditional lunar calendar, frequently linked to millenarian prophecies.[19] Qing military officials were also taken in by the rumor; the emperor later castigated one of his generals for firing on ships in the Lu'ermen harbor (close to the prefectural capital of Tainan), pointing out that they were probably innocent merchants (*TDH* 6: 27).

Although this series of Tiandihui activities linked to Chen Sulao, Su Ye, and Chen Zhouquan provides the clearest examples of the use by Tiandihui members of apocalyptic imagery, it was by no means the sole example. A 1796 register discovered in Nanping county, Fujian, contained a reference to "Li Zhuhong," "Li" and "Zhu" both being dynastic surnames with messianic connotations, and "*hong*," of course, being one of the chief code references to the Tiandihui (*TDH* 1: 149). The emperor observed (in the context of the Chen Zhouquan case) that "when the evil Taiwanese rise up, they often falsely rely on the Zhu surname," suggesting that he had noted this practice on more than one occasion (*TDH* 6: 18). Other evidence combines possibly messianic sentiments with what look to be clear political statements. Zhan Qingzhen, a Tiandihui member from Chaozhou, Guangdong, caught in the search for Tiandihui origins and exiled to Xinjiang, sent a letter to his relatives in 1791 that contained a separate piece of paper on which was written:

> Band together as ten-thousand and support the Ming [under?] Li Taohong;
> Follow Heaven and submit to the Ming so that harmony may result. (*TDH* 5: 413)

Although the motivation of those who employed these terms and symbols is never clearly spelled out in confessions, the violent atmosphere of the decade that followed Lin Shuangwen may well have led some Tiandihui members to take the apocalyptic implications of Tiandihui symbolism seriously.

The idea of the Tiandihui: charisma. In other cases, the very idea of forming a Tiandihui, as opposed to the particular ideas and symbols associated with the Tiandihui, explains some of the violence and rebellion of the decade. In the second half of this chapter, I argue that religious beliefs and practices explain the attraction of the society in early nineteenth-century western Fujian and eastern Jiangxi, where the Tiandihui was believed to provide a kind of magical protection to those who practiced its rituals and charms. In the cases discussed in the present section, it was apparently a similar power, a charismatic attraction, associated in the popular mind with the Tiandihui that accounted for the spread of the tradition. In some cases, of course, this attraction drew on apocalyptic or rebellious associations, but there is ample evidence that the Tiandihui was popular among some people who did not initially know how to set up the society or what the contents of society rituals or initiation ceremonies might be. In these cases, the idea that the Tiandihui was an association to be feared, or perhaps one that possessed supernatural powers, seems to have been paramount to those who sought to found their own branches of the society.

One good example is the Zhang Biao-Xie Zhi case. Zhang Biao was a Zhanghou man who lived in the Nantou area of Zhanghua, Taiwan, and had frequent conflicts with members of the local Quanzhou community. In the summer of QL 55 (1790), Zhang decided to form a named brotherhood and recruit people to defend against possible violence by Quanzhou people. He seems not to have had any specific plans for this brotherhood until he told an old friend, Xie Zhi, of his intentions, and Xie counseled him to set up a Heaven and Earth Society. Zhang readily agreed, and asked Xie how one went about it. Xie had learned of the society's initiation rituals from someone who had fled in the wake of the suppression of Lin Shuangwen. The instructions that Xie passed onto Zhang for the establishment of the society differed only in very minor details from the familiar set of practices, and for our purposes, the important points are: first, that the Tiandihui was seen as preferable to a nonspecific named brotherhood; and second, that it was important to know the technical details related to the proper founding of the society (*TDH* 5: 375–404).

Another instance illustrates these themes even more clearly. Chen Tan sold betel nut for a living in Zhanghua county, Taiwan, and was good friends with Wu Guangcai and Wu Ji. In the third month of QL 57 (1792), the two Wus came to Chen's hut and complained of their poverty. Chen replied: "if you want to live well, there's no choice but to recruit people to form a *hui* and steal. . . . And if you're going to set up a *hui*, only the Tiandihui will recruit lots of people. If you assemble a lot of people, then you can resist when the troops appear." Unfortunately, none of those present knew how to go about setting up a Tiandihui. Wu Guangcai subsequently sought out former members of Zhang Biao's Tiandihui, who had taken refuge in Taiwan's inner mountains, and invited them to teach the willing students the proper methods (*TDH* 5: 393–95). These examples could be multiplied, and the evidence suggests that in some cases, the Tiandihui appealed to certain types within the population of Southeast China as a more powerful and more useful version of the brotherhood association than an unnamed brotherhood or a named brotherhood without the promise of Tiandihui efficacy.[20]

Changes in the name of the Tiandihui suggest a similar association in the popular mind between the particular rituals associated with the Tiandihui and supernatural power of some sort. As illustrated by the Chen Sulao-Su Ye case above, where invented characters substituted for the dangerous "Tiandihui," similar or identical rituals and practices spread under different names. Zheng Guangcai, who ran a protection racket in southern Taiwan in QL 59 (1794), decided that a "mutual aid" organization such as the Tiandihui would be helpful to solidify his racket, but because he feared that the Tiandihui name would attract official attention, he called his *hui* the Small Knives Society (*Xiaodaohui*) (*TDH* 6: 73–78). Yang Qi made a similar decision in Danshui county, northern Taiwan, several years later, in JQ 3 (1798). He sought to empower his gang of local toughs through the establishment of a *hui* and, like Zheng Guangcai, chose the name Small Knives Society (*TDH* 6: 78–86). Xu Zhang founded a Xiaodaohui in Jiayi county, central Taiwan, in JQ 3–4 (1798–99), for similar reasons (*TDH* 6: 86–90). The larger Xiaodaohui, which organized an attempted rebellion in Jiayi county, central Taiwan, in JQ 5, simply took what appear to be Tiandihui traditions as their own; the documents record neither questions nor explanations of their choice of *hui* name (though this may in any case have been its own tradition by this point) (*TDH* 6: 95–130).

Again, these examples could be multiplied; indeed, one of the characteristics of the Tiandihui in the early nineteenth century is the proliferation of names.[21] Although we can find slight (presumably unintentional) changes in the Tiandihui tradition that accompanied these name changes, there is no question that the intention in every case was to borrow Tiandihui rituals and practices as directly as possible. This intention surely suggests that importance was attached to just these particular rituals. Indeed, the continued practice of establishing *any* named brotherhood, particularly given the well-known Qing antipathy, has to be considered testimony that some variety of occult power was attached to the very practice.

Qing suppression of Tiandihui activities. The impression that some variety of charismatic charm had much to do with the continuing popularity of *hui* formation in the decade following the Lin Shuangwen uprising is strengthened when we consider the Qing efforts to suppress the

Tiandihui and its analogues during this period. Part of the Qing efforts involved new laws. Harsh penalties toward brotherhoods and secret societies had been part of Qing law almost from the beginning of the dynasty, and the Qing experience with Lin Shuangwen provoked renewed official discussions and eventually a new, even harsher, law. I have already noted Fukang'an's comment in the immediate aftermath of the military defeat of Lin Shuangwen's armies that not only the Tiandihui but the very practice of *hui* formation had to be eradicated. Other officials faced with continuing Tiandihui-related violence voiced similar opinions. Charged with the duty of interrogating those arrested in the Zhang Biao–Xie Zhi case, Fujian Naval Admiral Hadang'a opined: "These secret society criminals stick to their confessions and do not tell the truth. They endure torture and are willing to die. . . . They are no different from Christians or Moslems." "In future *hui* cases," he declared, "let all those who willingly join be beheaded, and all those who claim to have been coerced, but who have historically not been good people, be strangled, dispensing with [the currently prescribed] punishment of exile to Xingjiang, thus avoiding their spreading the disaster elsewhere" (*TDH* 5: 395–96). The emperor agreed, and charged the Board of Punishment to note that "for *hui* cases on Taiwan, which resemble [the Zhang Biao affair] in their importance, always add one degree to the punishment" (*TDH* 5: 380–81). Such sentiments culminated in the new substatute of 1792 in which the leaders and willing followers of Tiandihui bands on Taiwan were sentenced to immediate decapitation and those who claimed to have been coerced into joining the Tiandihui to strangulation. Although this law was originally meant to be temporary, the endurance and spread of the Tiandihui ensured its continued utility, and in 1811 the same substatute was revised to include both Fujian and Guangdong.[22]

Such legal changes of course reflect the moral reasoning of the Qing state as well as the strategic measures it employed to deal with activities defined as criminal. Whether nonelite society was aware of such changes is another matter (although in one early nineteenth-century case, Tiandihui "leaders" confessed that they learned how to set up a Tiandihui by reading Qing proclamations against the society; *TDH* 6: 362). A more powerful statement of the brutality of the Qing suppression of secret societies in the decade following Lin Shuangwen is the sheer number of secret society members executed or exiled. Between 1788, when Fukang'an put down the Lin Shuangwen uprising, and 1800, at least 1,117 were executed, and 387 exiled. These figures underestimate the number of deaths, perhaps by a factor of two or three; I have derived the estimates from individual documents recounting the numbers of executions and exiles, and when we are fortunate enough to have access to memorials that give total figures for a particular case, they are invariably much higher than the sum arrived at by adding the amounts given in individual documents (presumably because our records are incomplete). In addition, the majority of these executions were carried out on the spot, in the marketplaces of the areas in which the society members lived. The heads of the executed were subsequently displayed to the public. The fathers and brothers of many society members were beaten, cangued, or exiled. Even the emperor, receiving reports that the Fujian-Zhejiang governor-general had summarily executed 158 people connected with the Chen Sulao–Su Ye case, noted, "We of course cannot but prosecute according to the law, but to [summarily] execute by slicing [and through other methods] more than 150 seems rather a lot, and my heart feels deeply troubled" (*TDH* 5: 464–65). Even if we accept only these conservative estimates for executions and exiles carried out over the twelve-year period 1788–1800, the numbers still mean that, on average, more than ten people were either executed or exiled *each month*, mostly from the areas of Taiwan and southern Fujian. And this does not include those killed during uprisings.

The Tiandihui and Popular Religion

Although the Qing had always been hostile to brotherhood associations, the violence of the last decade of the eighteenth century surely represented an extreme. From the suppression of Lin Shuangwen, through the search for Tiandihui origins, and the quelling of the smaller rebellions that occurred in the wake of Lin's uprising, the Qing consistently took the side of harshness and brutality. Looking at this decade from the perspective of those who belonged to named brotherhoods and secret societies, some of the rebellions seem to reflect the intensification of state opposition and a consequent popular antagonism toward the state. This is particularly true of rebellions that grew directly out of Lin Shuangwen's uprising and of those that drew on apocalyptic themes. Indeed, one would expect the violence of this decade to have put an end to the occasional toleration of brotherhood associations by local officials and to have brought out the latent rebelliousness and messianism of the Tiandihui. In other words, the violence of the 1790's could perhaps have set the stage for the frequent anti-Manchu agitations of the Triads and other secret societies in the nineteenth century.

It may well be that the dawn of the nineteenth century was a decisive watershed period, although further research will be necessary to write the larger history of Qing secret societies. Nevertheless, we should not ignore evidence, even from this period, that does *not* link secret societies directly to the posture of the Qing state. Here I refer to the cases such as the Zhang Biao and Chen Tan affairs where the Tiandihui seems to have bestowed charismatic power on those groups who adopted its rituals and symbols. The second section of this chapter deepens the exploration of this theme by examining the Tiandihui in the western Fujian–eastern Jiangxi region in the Jiaqing-Daoguang period. The religious nature of the Tiandihui in this region and period suggests that the Qing attempt to stamp out all brotherhood associations did not succeed in completely politicizing the Heaven and Earth Society. Whatever the long-term effects of the decade of violence, local people continued to attach local meanings to the Tiandihui.

THE SPREAD OF THE TIANDIHUI IN
THE JIAQING-DAOGUANG PERIOD

The Tiandihui reached the western Fujian–eastern Jiangxi region because the suppression of Lin Shuangwen and the Qing search for society origins forced the Tiandihui to abandon its original core area in Taiwan, southern Fujian, and northern Guangdong. Most of the eighteen incidents of *hui* activity in the decade of the 1790's (most of which was Tiandihui activity) remained centered in the Taiwan–Southeast Coast region, but already in this decade we find four instances of *hui* activity located outside this original center: one in Guangxi, one in the Guangzhou region of Guangdong (Nanhai county), and two outside the Minnan area of Fujian (in Fuding and Pucheng counties). The spread of the Tiandihui is even easier to trace in subsequent decades: of the 34 incidents of *hui* activity in the first decade of the nineteenth century, only five were in the original area of the Southeast Coast. Eight were in other parts of Guangdong (six in Huizhou prefecture, adjacent to Chaozhou), nine in other parts of Fujian, seven in Jiangxi, and five in Guangxi. In the 1810's, of the 51 total incidents, only two were in the original area, while nineteen were in other parts of Fujian,* five were in other parts of Guangdong, six were in Jiangxi, ten in Guangxi, three in Yunnan, three in Hunan, and two in Guizhou.[23] The decade of the 1820's witnessed five incidents of Tiandihui activity in Jiangxi, one in Guangxi, one in Hunan, one in Taiwan, and one in an unspecified part of Fujian.[24] Of the 21 total incidents in the 1830's, nine took place in Jiangxi, four in Yunnan, two in Guangdong, two in western Fujian, three in Guizhou, and one in Hunan.[25] By the early 1830's, we find memorials that assert that all Fujianese secret societies come from Jiangxi, which is certainly a reversal of the original direction of flow—or perhaps simply an example of how short historical memories can be (*TDH* 6: 229). (See Map 5.)

---

* The location of one incident is given only as "Fujian."

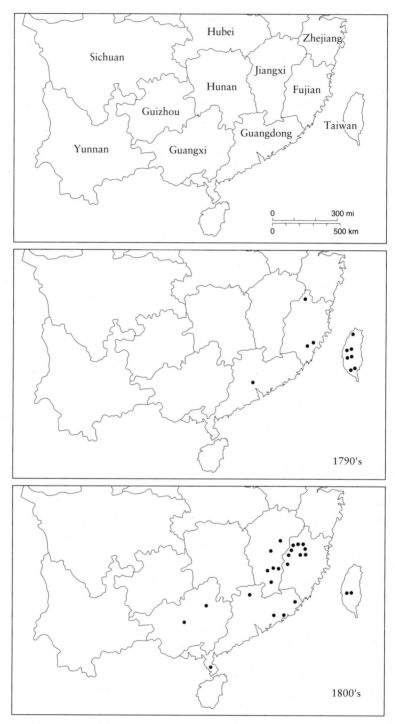

Map 5. The spread of the Tiandihui, 1800–1830

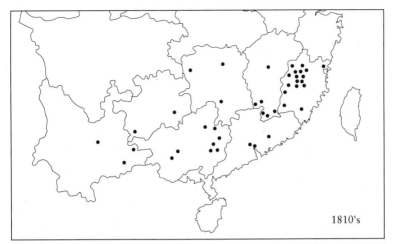

1810's

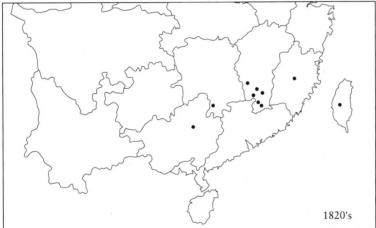

1820's

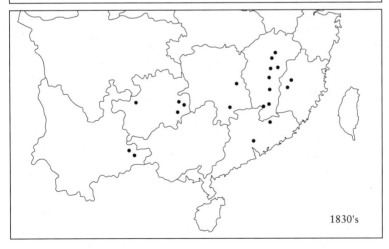

1830's

Unsurprisingly, the first wave of this spread consisted of Tiandihui members fleeing persecution, and using their knowledge of Tiandihui ritual to attract followers so that they could extract money from them and thereby support and protect themselves. The documents from the decade 1790–1800 are full of people from Zhangzhou, Quanzhou, Taiwan, and Chaozhou, moving through new areas and proselytizing.

As time went on, however, the Tiandihui ceased to be a wholly "foreign" import and developed local roots. Taking the three provinces of Fujian, Guangdong, and Guangxi over the entire Jiaqing-Daoguang period, arrested *hui* leaders established the *hui* for which they were eventually arrested in their home county in 46 out of 80 instances, or 57 percent of the time. This is even clearer if we exclude Guangxi from our calculations: 63 percent of *hui* in Fujian and almost 61 percent in Guangdong were started by leaders in their home counties.[26] Of course, even if 60 percent were started by locals, this still means that 40 percent were set up by outsiders, and we certainly find ample numbers of cases like that in 1803 in Yongding, Western Fujian, where a tea peddler from Zhangzhou sought *hui* membership because "as a loner outside his native place, he worried about being cheated" (*TDH* 6: 158–59). In addition, many of those who set up *hui* in their own counties did so after having traveled fairly extensively, at least within the region under discussion. Nonetheless, we need to revise the impression that the Tiandihui was a phenomenon consistently associated with outsiders.

As the Tiandihui spread from its original center, it took on different orientations in different areas during the Jiaqing-Daoguang era, even while maintaining a recognizable continuity in symbols and rituals. In Taiwan and coastal southern Fujian in the immediate postrebellion period, the Tiandihui served to mobilize people for further rebellions or for criminal violence, and in these instances, Tiandihui links with messianism, and, perhaps even with pro-Ming sentiment, were much clearer than in the Lin Shuangwen rising. In much of Guangdong, by contrast, the Tiandihui became a vehicle for what appears to be "simple" robbery.[27]

In the region under discussion for the remainder of this chapter— western Fujian and eastern Jiangxi—the Tiandihui functioned largely as a vehicle for a body of religious practices, which I ultimately interpret as a form of magical inducement useful to the marginalized men who continued to constitute the core of Tiandihui membership. Tiandihui members in the western Fujian–eastern Jiangxi region did engage in robbery, and Tiandihui members in Guangdong were not completely unfamiliar with rebellion, but there remain recognizable differences in the surface orientation of the Tiandihui in these various areas.[28] A comprehensive history of the Tiandihui in the early nineteenth century might well reveal that the religious aspects under examination here characterized the tradition as a whole, to greater or lesser degrees. I focus on the western Fujian–eastern Jiangxi region because these religious aspects appear with great frequency and clarity.

POPULAR RELIGIOUS ELEMENTS IN TIANDIHUI PRACTICES

The religious flavor of most of the Tiandihui groups in the western Fujian–eastern Jiangxi region is hard to ignore, but at the same time difficult to interpret. Qing officials were on the whole not interested in the religious aspects of the Heaven and Earth Society, and the religious evidence from the region is once again embedded in narratives of crime, violence, arrest, and persecution. Officials recorded depositions in which religious practices figure importantly, and they confiscated manuals and other written documents testifying to the frequent overlap between the Tiandihui and other varieties of popular religion. Yet they asked few questions about these practices, and they did not systematically seek out information about them in the same way that they sought out society ringleaders or society networks. As a result, the abundant information on these practices exists largely as a set of disembodied texts. One has to proceed by first cataloguing the evidence linking the regional Tiandihui to popular religion.

The first body of evidence consists of the religious practices shared by both the regional Tiandihui and other religious traditions. For example, many of the objects placed on the altars used in Tiandihui initiation ceremonies, and presumably in other ceremonies, are still a part of the festivals and ceremonies of contemporary Chinese popular religion in Taiwan and elsewhere. The most common object used in Tiandihui ceremonies was the rice bushel (*midou, mitong*), but a variety of objects accompanied the bushel, placed either inside or alongside: five-colored flags, seven-star lamps, mirrors, rulers, knives, scales, and ropes, among others (*TDH* 6: 187, 189, 225, 232, 332, 336).

Many anthropologists and other students of contemporary Chinese religion have noted the presence of similar or identical objects in religious ceremonies. In a recent discussion of the procession festivals of local Taiwanese cults, Stephen Feuchtwang mentions the dipper, the five-colored flags, and the gods' seals, swords, flags, and tablets.[29] John Lagerwey notes similarly that Daoist altars in contemporary Taiwan include "a red bucket filled with rice, a purifying agent, and other objects such as a ruler, a scale, a sword, a mirror, a pair of scissors, and a saucer with oil and a wick."[30] Kenneth Dean's work has confirmed that similar objects continue to be used in ritual ceremonies in mainland Fujian.[31]

The deities worshiped in the course of Tiandihui rituals provide further evidence of the overlap between the practices of the Tiandihui and those of popular religion. Unsurprisingly, the figures of most frequent worship were those of Wan Tixi and the other mythic figures in society history (*TDH* 6: 187). In other instances, worship of Guanyin and the Earth God accompanied Tiandihui initiation ceremonies, and in still others, the notion that Tiandihui rituals were carried out in the presence of divine spirits—presumably the spirits of the local gods—was indicated by a red cloth on which was written "let the gods descend" (*qingshen*).[32] In a few cases, too, the figure of Laozi himself, "the divine founder of Taoism and the third member of its triad," is mentioned in the course of Tiandihui ceremonies.[33] In one 1813 case from Jiangxi, the characters *Taishang Laojun* occupied the central place of worship in a Tiandihui initiation ceremony, and the characters "*tian*, *di*, and *hong*" were to one side.[34] The well-known Daoist deity Yuhuang shangdi appears in one set of confiscated writings (*TDH* 6: 304), and in yet another case, a Tiandihui member who used a seal carved with the inscription *Taishang Laojun* to attempt to heal the sick was found to be in possession of written materials that included the phrase *shuntian xingdao* (*TDH* 6: 203–5).

Much of the language used in contemporary Daoist ceremonies and written documents on Taiwan resonates with that of the eighteenth- and early-nineteenth-century Tiandihui. John Lagerwey notes that Daoist priests in Taiwan fight "the battle of the gods, on behalf of the gods. The traditional phrase used to describe this, found in virtually every liturgical manual, is 'to carry out transformations in the place of heaven' [*daitian xinghua*]."[35] Not only is the phrase *daitian xingdao* found in one of the manuals confiscated by Qing authorities, but *daitian xinghua* can be read as a minor variation of *shuntian xingdao*, a phrase frequently connected with Tiandihui rebellions (*TDH* 6: 189). Indeed, Lagerwey also mentions the existence of the *Shuntiangong*—the "Palace of Compliance with Heaven"—on Taiwan, confirming that the phrase has lived on in a Daoist context.[36] The phrase "heaven's revolution" (*tianyun*), found in earlier Tiandihui rebellions (both Lin Shuangwen and Chen Zhouquan) as well as in material from the western Fujian–eastern Jiangxi region, has also survived; Lagerwey cites a document written in 1980 that employs the phrase.[37]

The continued use of this language points to an even more general area of commonality between the Tiandihui and contemporary Daoism (and, of course, other varieties of Chinese popular religion): the use of written documents and some variety of "bureaucratic procedure" to communicate with the gods. One of the characteristics of the early nineteenth-century Tiandihui was, as noted earlier, the proliferation of written documents, generally containing the foundation myth of the society as well as detailed descriptions of proper initiation ceremonies, and many of these ceremonies invoked the presence of divinities. Lagerwey's careful narrative analysis of the performances of a Daoist master in modern Taiwan clearly illustrates the aspects of that tradition that might be called "bureaucratic communication."[38] Kristopher Schipper makes a similar point: the "sacrifice of writs is fundamental in Daoist ritual, where it occupies the same central place as the bloody sacrifices in other religions."[39]

In addition to the ritual objects, deities, and language that connect the regional Tiandihui to the realm of popular religion, we also find frequent mention of practices that would once have been labeled "magical" or "occult" but are now fully accepted as belonging to the realm of popular religion. The following description of one Tiandihui leader and his associates suggests the general atmosphere surrounding the society in this region and period:

> As a child, [Li Laowu] learned tailoring and silversmithing. He later changed to the practice of medicine and worked as a doctor in Fujian, selling a magic elixir [*shenqu*]. [His friend] Tao Shengsan managed burials [*yingzang dili*], and also possessed the charm books of the long-dead Fujianese Chen Shaoyun, which dealt with planchette writing, exorcism, prayers, and curing illness. His younger brother Tao Yuesan had also studied geomancy [*dili*], medicine, and the martial arts.
>
> Li circulated the story that his teacher, Monk Hong, was currently . . . in Fujian [Li and his friends were in Shangrao, Jiangxi, although Li was originally from Fujian], and possessed powerful magic. He had no need for knives or swords; he could kill people by spitting on them with water from a magic bowl. He also had a fire ball that could burn people to death.[40]

In some instances, such power was connected to practices of mutual aid. In one Tiandihui, members who were cheated were to burn three holes in white paper with incense, which would produce mutual assistance (*TDH* 6: 188). In another, those who were cheated were to rub red powder on a particular coin and stamp the imprint of the coin on a letter, which was then to be mailed together with a chicken feather to a fellow *hui* member, who was duty-bound to respond (*TDH* 6: 225).

More often, these practices took the form of "charms" or "talismans" (*fu*) recorded in manuals, or in "charm registers" (*fubu*).[41] In 1814 in Western Fujian, officials confiscated "red cloth charms, charm seals, wooden seals . . . [and] lists of charms" as a part of their investigation into Tiandihui activities (*TDH* 6: 193). A Tiandihui member arrested in Ninghua in 1806 was found to be carrying "seals and a charm manual" on his person (*TDH* 6: 288). A Tiandihui member in Shangrao, Jiangxi, "wrote the '*tian*,' '*di*,' and '*hong*' characters in talismanic style, saying that they were secret Tiandihui codes" (*TDH* 6: 359). Wu Chenbao received "two bundles of charms, one of cloth and one of yellow and white paper," from a Tiandihui member (*TDH* 6: 195). These examples could be multiplied, and it is clear that such talismans were a necessary element of at least the regional Tiandihui.

Not all references to these talismans indicate the purposes they served, but some do. In one instance, charms were to be kept on the member's person so as "to avoid disasters and misfortunes" (*TDH* 6: 199). In another instance, the Tiandihui teacher promised that the charms "would keep people from being cheated" (*TDH* 6: 195). Curses, the reverse aspect of talismans, appear in these Tiandihui cases also, although less frequently. Tiandihui leader Li Laowu "with his left hand holding a water bowl and his right hand writing the '*tian-di-hong*' talisman, intoned the words that those who turned their back on the brotherhood oath would not die a good death" (*TDH* 6: 359). In at least two cases, the phrase *shuntian xingdao*, which we generally interpret as a challenge to the legitimacy of the ruling house, was used as part of a charm (*TDH* 6: 186, 195). Some Tiandihui members, however, discarded documents that bore the phrase *shuntian*, clearly indicating that they recognized its dangerous implications (*TDH* 6: 186).

Other talismans spoke to the issue of physical safety in the event of rebellion. One Tiandihui leader "used eight pieces of red paper to write eight charms, saying that the charms could ward off swords and soldiers" (*TDH* 6: 360). Another Tiandihui member arrested in 1806 in Shaowu, western Fujian, deposed as follows, in the context of a rebellion to be discussed below:

> [My teacher] told me that when the soldiers rose up, I should take the first charm and stick it on the big gate, so that it would be known that I was of the same teaching [*jiao*], and I would not be killed or injured. The second talisman was painted on a cloth turban. When the rebellion came, I was to make a silver placard and attach [the third charm] to my waist as a sign. We were to make a banner of four characters, although I only remember the two characters "*shuntian*." We were to write the same characters on a handbasket of gold thread, and hang that at the big [village?] gate at night. Couplets were to be pasted on the door, and the mouth-water charm [*shuikou fu*] was to be pasted on the village streets. (*TDH* 6: 285)

In another instance, a Tiandihui leader demanding money from a prospective member for protection against a coming uprising told the prospective member to return to his home and "put a brass mirror on his roof beam, and use seven sheets of red paper, on which were to be written the five elements and the eight trigrams, which were to be pasted onto the mirror. He was also to use strips of tin to compose the characters "*tianyun kainian*" [the opening years of the period of Heaven's Revolution], and put these on the roof beam too. This would ward off [spirit?] soldiers" (*TDH* 6: 361). Again, these examples could be multiplied, and given the agnosticism of Qing officials, who considered such practices "vulgar," the degree to which the materials on the Tiandihui of this region and period are suffused with such practices is striking.

There is also clear evidence that the lay Buddhist tradition conventionally described by the term "White Lotus" and the Tiandihui tradition, brought to the region by flight from government suppression, were in some instances seen as roughly equivalent sets of practices and meanings. The documents reveal "teachers" who mastered both traditions, as well as intermixture of the ideas and symbols of the two traditions.

Lay Buddhism had a long history in this region, under a number of different names. Lian Lichang, in his *Fujian mimi shehui* (Secret Societies in Fujian), discusses the beliefs and activities of the Jin'gangchan, Bailianzong (Bailiancai, Bailianhui), Bailianjiao, Dashengjiao, Dashengmen, Yizimen, Guanyinjiao, Longhuahui, and Laoguanzhaijiao.[42] The history of these religions is too complicated for extended treatment at this point, but Lian makes clear that varieties of lay Buddhism had been practiced in Fujian since at least the Yuan dynasty, and that the common characteristics of most of these religious traditions included vegetarianism, chanting, and some belief in the future Buddha, Maitreya.

In addition, several rebellions in Ming-Qing Fujian were attributed by officials to White Lotus or White Lotus–like organizations, suggesting millenarian connections. In the wake of a Laoguanzhai-led mass action in 1748, Qing officials investigated the Western Fujian region and found more than 60 lodges associated with the faith. In 1782, Qing officials arrested yet more people associated with lay Buddhism (in this case the Dasheng-Luojiao) on the Fujian-Zhejiang border.[43] In the wake of the massive White Lotus–led rebellions of the late Qianlong–early Jiaqing period, imperial orders mandated the destruction of all halls or temples associated with vegetarianism.[44] Archival evidence concerning the Tiandihui in this period and region clearly reveals the intermingling of the two traditions; indeed, the only rebellions (or attempted rebellions) that I am aware of in this region and period appear to have drawn on a mixture of lay Buddhist and Tiandihui symbolism.

One example of this intermingling is the career of Li Lingkui. Originally from Jianning, Fujian, Li had purchased a degree and ran a paper shop in Nanchang, Jiangxi. In QL 47 (1782), Li bought a number of scriptures (*Dashengjing, Dajiejing, Enbenjing*) from Wu Zixiang, who was worshiped by his followers as the tenth patriarch in the Qinglianjiao (Black Lotus Teaching) tradition. The Qinglianjiao developed as a combination of the teachings of the Dashengjiao (Great Vehicle Teaching) and Luojiao (Luo Teaching), and became its own recognizable tradition in the latter part of the Qianlong reign period through the work of Wu Zixiang. Other leaders of the tradition gave it different names: Wu's disciple, and eleventh patriarch He Ruo, called it the Laoyejiao (Old Master Teaching), and his disciple Wang Tianzu called it the Laomujiao (Old Mother Teaching).[45]

Lin Lingkui bought the Qinglianjiao scriptures to assist him in warding off disasters and hardships. Over the years, he copied and sold more than ten volumes of the scriptures, earning more than 50 Mexican silver dollars. Later on, he also entered the Tiandihui, hoping to avoid harassment in his travels. Having entered and learned the secrets of the Tiandihui, he added the latter to his repertoire and began to initiate students into the Tiandihui also.

Concerned about the possibility of arrest, Lin called his Tiandihui the Yangpanhui (Open Vessel Society), and his lay Buddhist practice the Yinpanhui (Hidden Vessel Society). He sold the hand signals and slogans of the Tiandihui tradition, at least part of which was in written form, for two Mexican silver dollars, and the scriptures attached to the lay Buddhist practices for 20.4 ounces of silver (and since the full set of scriptures was quite expensive, he also sold a shortened version of the set for 10.2 ounces).* Over time, he sold more than twenty memberships in the Yangpanhui-Tiandihui (earning more than 40 Mexican silver dollars), and enough Yinpanhui memberships to earn more than 200 ounces of silver (*TDH* 6: 246).

Although Li himself seems to have had distinct motives for acquiring the Buddhist scriptures and for joining the Tiandihui, other evidence suggests that the two traditions, because they spoke to the same needs in the same language, could be somewhat interchangeable. One of Li's students who bought the scriptures and learned the skills set himself up as a teacher, offering the same choice of Yangpanhui versus Yinpanhui; when someone came to him asking for the scriptures attached to the lay Buddhist Yinpanhui, the student, discovering that his client lacked money, directed him to enter the less expensive Yangpanhui Tiandihui instead (*TDH* 6: 251). But not everyone, apparently, saw lay Buddhism and the Tiandihui as interchangeable. Another of Li's students, who had

---

* This appears to be a fairly large sum of money. Naquin 1976: 281–82 notes that in north China in the 1810's, a bond servant in a prince's household earned 4 taels per month, and the purchase price for a *mou* of land in northern Zhili was 1.8 taels. Zhou and Shao 1993: 104 report that a village teacher's annual income was 10–20 Mexican dollars.

also become a teacher, was approached by a sick person who hoped to be cured through a vegetarian diet and chanting. When the teacher told the sick person that those scriptures were still being copied and tried to placate him with a pamphlet of Tiandihui incantations, promising to provide the Buddhist scriptures when they were ready, the sick man was distressed to discover rebellious terminology in his pamphlet, and presumably rejected the teacher's advice (*TDH* 6: 171).

In JQ 8 (1803), Li Lingkui began to plan an uprising, based on his stated belief that he was the reincarnation of a latter-Tang prince. He taught his followers a four-line verse, which was to serve as their password:

> A stick of incense falls from the empty sky,
> Half *yin* and half *yang*.
> If *yin* and *yang* can come together,
> I will sit in the imperial court at the *yin-mao* hour.
> (*TDH* 6: 259)

Most of Li's recorded statements, and the actions of many of his followers, seem to draw on rather general traditions of messianism and rebellion and are not confined to either the lay Buddhist tradition or the Tiandihui, although the references to *yin* and *yang* in the above password may well be to the Yinpanhui and Yangpanhui.

Some of Li's followers, however, did draw on both traditions. In the seventh month of JQ 8 (1803), Li was arrested and executed in Fujian. One of his disciples, Liao Ganzhao, sought out Wang Tianzu, the eleventh patriarch of the Qinglianjiao, who had also claimed to be the reincarnation of the Maitreya Buddha, hoping to avenge Li's death through a rebellion based on both Li and Wang (*TDH* 6: 277). Another follower, Du Shiming, sought to initiate a similar movement by broadcasting a version of Tiandihui mythology: in JQ 10 (1805), Du began to recruit his own followers with the story that in the western districts of Chongren county, Jiangxi, there was a 32-year-old descendant of the former Ming dynasty named Zhu Hongzhu. At present, Zhu was working outside Fengjinshan ("forbidden mountain") at the wood workshop of the He family, helping to make wooden ladles. Du insisted that all Tiandihui members (described in the deposition as "those who drank [lit., ate] Tiandihui wine") from Guangdong, Fujian, Jiangxi, and Shandong were supporting Zhu. He made further mention of Wan Dage (elder brother Wan), located in Shandong, where (Tiandihui? Wan's?) power was very strong. Du promised that in the next year on the nineteenth of the second month, the rebellion would begin from Shandong, and the other places would rise up on the same day (*TDH* 6: 284).

The following year, Du did finally recruit 25 men, and recorded their names together with a contract on a piece of white silk. On the contract, he wrote, "All the brothers have pledged themselves to the banner of Wan Dage, marked with Hong," and all signed their names, taking the surname Hong and the generational name Jin (gold). Shortly thereafter, Du walked into a trap, and he was arrested in Ninghua on the twenty-sixth. He was carrying on his person the contract, the seals (*tuji*), and a charm manual (*TDH* 6: 283–89).

Although much remains obscure about these incidents, they seem to confirm that both the Tiandihui and the lay Buddhist tradition were roughly equivalent forms of popular religion, at least in the minds of the teachers who conveyed the scriptures and practices associated with the religion, and also in the minds of those who sought the teachers out and paid for instruction. One could of course argue that neither Li Lingkui nor Du Shiming was a "genuine" Tiandihui member who took Tiandihui "ideas" seriously and participated significantly in the molding of the tradition; nonetheless, even if Li and Du were outside the mainstream of Tiandihui activity, and, as the Qing officials wished to believe, cynically exploited the Tiandihui for their own entrepreneurial purposes, they seem to have found willing converts ready to believe in the charismatic power of both traditions, and willing to contemplate rebellion based on either a Tang dynasty prince or on Elder Brother Wan.

This is the only example of rebellion from this region and period, and most cases provide more evidence of religion—and petty violence—than of apocalypse or rebellion. In addition, the documents from this region contain numerous examples of religious practices that do not fit readily into the (admittedly artificial) categories I have used here. In one instance, for example, Tiandihui materials linked dream prognostication to Wan Tixi and the creation of the Tiandihui tradition.[46] Magic seals and fortune-tellers make their appearances (*TDH* 6: 201, 204). Several documents contain references to bridges used in Tiandihui initiation ceremonies, possibly a borrowing from the celestial bridge (*tianqiao*) employed in Daoist ceremonies, or from messianic traditions where saviors lead the elect "across a bridge into the Magic City."[47] One Tiandihui leader changed the name of the society to the Renyi Sanxianhui (Humane and Righteous Society of the Three Immortals) because three immortals inhabited the local temple that served as society headquarters (*TDH* 6: 187). Another group called itself the Baixianghui ("Worship Incense Society") (*TDH* 6: 189). All these examples confirm the interpenetration of secret societies with a variety of magical and religious practices.

THE TIANDIHUI AS POPULAR RELIGION

Although this evidence proves that religious elements were an integral part of the practices of the Tiandihui of the western Fujian–eastern

Jiangxi region, and not just window dressing to conceal rebellious intent, questions still remain. If society members understood the Tiandihui primarily as a repository of religious techniques, what motivated them to join the Tiandihui instead of (or in addition to) other religious organizations such as local cults or sects, which were, after all, the source of most of Tiandihui "magic," and furthermore not consistently subject to the anger of the state?

Most religious organizations in China, at both state and local levels, have been interpreted as performing integrative functions, providing the shared values and beliefs that enabled villages, market communities, and even the premodern empire to cohere—such as it did. The integrative functions of Confucianism, either as a religious-philosophical tradition, or as a set of ritual practices, need hardly be mentioned. Many practices of popular religion, from temple cults to ancestor worship to spirit mediumship, are also seen as "system affirming" in various ways.[48] Even "sectarian" religions performed integrative functions. Susan Naquin's work on the White Lotus and David Kelley's on the Luojiao illustrate that these religious traditions spoke to the poor, the itinerant, those whose needs were not served by lineages, villages, or more orthodox temple communities, even while the beliefs of these and other "sects" contained apocalyptic implications which on occasion resulted in millenarian rebellion.[49]

It is unclear what kind of "integrative" functions Tiandihui groups might have performed. Because many Tiandihui groups in this region and period engaged in crime and violence against their surrounding communities, the religious rituals of a predatory group can hardly have done much to heighten the cohesion of villages or temple communities (except of course by unifying them against predatory attack). It is true that many Tiandihui members were outsiders, unattached to local communities or local religious cults, and hence were creating new "communities" in need of ritual representation and integration. But for every "outsider" in the documents, we also find masters and members with identifiable ties to local lineages and communities. For example, one Tiandihui organization chose as its name the "Home Protecting Society" (*Baojiahui*).[50] The "outsider" answer is at best only partial.

One interpretation stresses the immediate utility of the supernatural protection supposedly provided by Tiandihui rituals. Though most Tiandihui members in this region and period were marginalized in the sense accorded this term throughout this volume, they may have sought the protection of Tiandihui rituals either because they were not centrally included in more familiar religious practices or because their marginal status made their lives particularly dangerous, thus increasing the appeal of any type of protection.

To some extent, this emphasis on the utility of Tiandihui rituals shines through even in depositions discussing "mutual aid," which is what most Tiandihui members claimed to be seeking when questioned by Qing authorities. Both modern scholars and Qing officials have tended to view the pursuit of mutual aid as a "secular" activity, or at least one that does not require much contact with the spirit world. Some Tiandihui members entertained very different ideas on this subject, as illustrated by the frequent mention of magic together with the subject of mutual aid. In one Tiandihui, members were given "a bronze coin on a string, which served as proof of membership. If a member was cheated, he was to rub red powder on the coin and stamp the imprint of the coin on a letter, which he would then mail together with a chicken feather" (*TDH* 6: 225). One suspects that these elaborate preparations had supernatural overtones.[51]

Charms, too, seem to have been part of the pursuit of mutual aid. In some instances, the connection is quite clear, as in the case where a new recruit entrusted with a charm manual by his master recruited ten more people to enter the society, promising that the charms would keep them from being cheated (*TDH* 6: 194). In other instances, although charms are not described as contributing directly to the pursuit of mutual aid, they are employed in contexts in which mutual aid is a clear focus. Even when charms did not figure in mutual aid, they remained a form of protective magic. Recall the Tiandihui member who possessed a "martial arts charm book to measure the ability of new members, as well as the Heaven-earth and yin-yang soldier charms, thunder soldiers, and thunder generals, among others," and another who had "charm books . . . dealing with planchette writing, exorcism, prayers, and curing illness" (*TDH* 6: 353, 359). Charms of one sort or another are mentioned in many if not most of the cases from this region and period.

The ritual items found on the altars during Tiandihui initiation ceremonies lend themselves to similar interpretations. One Daoist priest in contemporary Taiwan provides what might be called folkloric explanations for a number of the objects found on the altar—the mirror representing purity of heart; the scale suggesting that all will be weighed in hell according to merit; scissors (and swords) symbolizing the commitment to combat evil; and the ruler connoting rectitude in behavior.[52] Barend Ter Haar finds exorcistic as well as folkloric meanings in the same objects. This interpretation may be more useful for our present purposes:

> The sword is an exorcist's primary attribute in combatting evil demons [and also symbol of dynastic legitimacy, or challenge to same]; the mirror was hung on the rooftops of houses to ward off evil demons . . . the footrule is the carpenter's secret attribute and serves to measure auspicious

numbers of inches. . . . In modern exorcist rituals on Taiwan, scissors, ruler, and mirror are commonly used together as instruments in driving out demons. Colored flags are a necessary attribute in any Daoist ritual, representing the Five Camps, where the Soldiers of Darkness reside. These spirit soldiers assist the exorcist (Daoist priest, shaman, puppeteer, etc.) in combatting evil demons.[53]

In this interpretation, the initiation rituals of the Tiandihui, which emphasize the distinction between the inner world of the society and the outer world of nonmembers, and the danger intendant on the passage from the outer to the inner world, appear less as functional devices to heighten organizational solidarity and more as dramatizations of the achievement of protection and security as members learned the secrets of religious protection from masters.

Furthermore, if Tiandihui masters and members understood the society in terms of protective supernatural power, they may well have seen themselves as being granted some of this power. Obvious confirmation of this speculation would lie in spirit possession, which Jean DeBernardi has found in equivalents of the Tiandihui in contemporary Malaysia.[54] I have as yet found no evidence of such practices linked to the Tiandihui of early nineteenth-century western Fujian and eastern Jiangxi.[55] In the case of the Tiandihui, the charisma may have been attached to brotherhoods and blood oaths, both of which possessed historical, symbolic, and heterodox overtones, instead of invulnerability rituals. Tiandihui oaths often invoked a whole history of mythic figures and deities whom members were to worship in what can only be called a religious ceremony; and the use of blood (or blood substitutes) in the course of emotionally charged ceremonies surely also had religious overtones, as suggested by Mark Lewis's study of blood oaths in a much earlier period. It may well be that our tendency to view secret societies as Chinese versions of Robin Hood's band (which can of course be true in some instances) has blinded us to the religious dimensions of sworn brotherhoods in China.

In addition, attention to the religious core of the Tiandihui may well help us to understand the apocalyptic or messianic elements that frequently appear in Tiandihui writings. As noted in Chapter 2, apocalyptic references are scattered throughout Tiandihui handbooks and depositions from the very beginning of Tiandihui history, and these elements were repeated in various Tiandihui-led rebellions throughout the latter part of the eighteenth century. However, at no point do we find evidence that Tiandihui masters or members genuinely contemplated the end of the world as they knew it. In stark contrast to materials generated by the White Lotus tradition, we find no discussion of salvation, of the elect, of a future world vastly different from that of the present. There is little reason to believe that the apocalyptic images in Tiandihui manuals and depositions were linked to a full-fledged reimagination of time, space, and social relations. This in turn poses questions about the nature of Tiandihui "messianism," defined by Anna Seidel as "the expectation of an era of peace brought about by a supernatural deliverer from political disorders and social hardship."[56]

We may be able to solve this riddle by reference to the realms of popular religion from which I have argued the Tiandihui drew many of its rituals and symbols. Although most research on nonsectarian Chinese popular religion has emphasized the integrative or "system-affirming" nature of these practices, recent scholarship has connected these same practices to images of military violence and even of the apocalypse. This latter interpretation is based once again on popular perceptions of the cosmos and its management, which differ considerably not only from imperial, Confucian views but also from the perceptions of Daoist priests and other religious specialists. For example, whereas Daoist priests understand the *jiao*, or "rite of cosmic renewal," as a means of bringing the supernatural forces governing a local area back into balance, members of the local community may understand the same ceremony as an effort to exorcise the ghosts and demons who have gained improper control over local forces. Moreover, the forces understood to exorcise the demons—the spirit soldiers attached to local deities—are themselves believed to be very close to demonic status. And the fact that soldiers are required to banish the demons suggests the violent, military nature of the popular understanding of the forces at work in the universe.

Many members of local Chinese societies thus see the world as a "demonic cosmos . . . one in which malign and defensive forces fill the universe at all levels."[57] The widely practiced twice-monthly burning of incense is directed at the recently dead and at the spirit soldiers of the local gods. These forces are believed to be powerful and potentially evil. They can be held in check by local deities such as the earth gods, but the twice-monthly burning of incense again suggests the perilousness of the situation. Indeed, some Taiwanese apparently connect "spirit soldiers" to the 108 "baleful stars," some of which are themselves frequent objects of exorcistic rites, as well as to the forces of benign local deities. To quote Stephan Feuchtwang:

> At the procession festivals of local cults . . . the military imperium is performed in ritual practice. On the altar table in front of the main god . . . there is the god's seal, inscribed with the sign of a conferred rank. To its left is a tub . . . in which are five flags each in the color of its quarter, including the center. To the right is a stand for the god's knife or sword. By it is the god's flag. . . . The seal, the tub, the stand and the tablet accom-

pany the statue of the god when it is taken out in a ceremonial sedan chair for procession to signify his control of spirit soldiers and to dispel plague demons and malevolent spirits. In this procession, a spirit medium may in addition to the statue be possessed and represent the spirit of the god. In the course of special processions at times of plague or other infestation, the flags of the five camps are placed at points in the center . . . and the four extremities of the territory. This is called "disposing the soldiers" . . . which are addressed in the twice-monthly feeding of the troops.[58]

It bears repeating that the same objects Feuchtwang mentions in his discussion also appeared in Tiandihui initiation rituals.

Of course, we cannot say with certainty that Tiandihui masters and members shared this understanding of the cosmos, but the shamanic and exorcistic overtones of many Tiandihui practices surely suggest some overlap. And if Tiandihui masters and members did indeed conceive of the world in demonic terms, then their notion of an apocalypse may have been constructed around ideas of demonic power and cosmic imbalance, images of a world in which there was no ultimate salvation but only exorcistic interventions of limited effect, and in which protectors and demons were hard to distinguish.

In any case, it is indisputable that many aspects of brotherhood and secret society behavior beyond the period and region discussed in this chapter become more comprehensible when we focus on the religious aspects of society membership. For example, the Small Knives Society (*Xiaodaohui*), a fairly widespread secret society in some parts of Taiwan in the 1780's, was also known as the Wangyehui, or Plague God Society, referring to Taiwan's famous god who guarded against pestilence.[59] Qing authorities asked local Taiwanese about the two names, and were told simply that society members were "as big/great [*da*] as the plague god." Such a response makes sense only if society membership was thought to have supernatural characteristics. Another example is even more telling. As already noted, one of the ways Tiandihui members sought to avoid Qing persecution in the late eighteenth and early nineteenth centuries was to change the name of their society. One of the most frequent changes was from Heaven and Earth Society to Increase Younger Brothers Society. Both these names are pronounced "*tiandihui*" in Mandarin, which suggests that the change to Increase Younger Brothers Society would not have been very effective in fooling Qing officials, even if the ideographs for "*tian*" and "*di*" were different. One explanation for this curious practice is that the very *sound* of the society's name may have had religious significance.

Moreover, Chapter 1 illustrated that Chinese could easily set up organizations to pursue mutual aid without employing the rituals and symbols of secret societies. China has a long history of mutual aid societies, generally called *hui* or *she*, and generally attached to lineage or community structures. These societies posed little danger to the state, and were indeed encouraged by the authorities in many instances. Examples of these societies, such as rotating credit societies and crop-watching societies, were widespread during the Ming-Qing period, even as secret societies were created and spread. Thus when members of Qing secret societies claimed to be searching for mutual aid, we must suspect either that mutual aid had a particular meaning in this context, or that the secret societies offered special means of achieving the purposes of mutual aid, means that outweighed the obvious risks of society membership.

The two halves of this chapter illustrate both the power and the weakness of the late imperial Chinese state. Brutal suppression of the Lin Shuangwen uprising was to be expected; few states treat rebellion cavalierly. Qing efforts to seek out the founders of the Tiandihui, and Qing executions of Tiandihui members during the decade of the 1790's, signal a readiness to employ considerable force against local society for reasons of state. The "decade of suppression" stands as further evidence of the violent side of Confucian autocracy.

By the same token, Qing pretensions to absolute power were no more than that. First, Lin Shuangwen's rebellion and its suppression brought the Tiandihui, together with its apocalyptic and rebellious implications, to the attention of large numbers of people who would have remained otherwise ignorant of its existence. The Qing may not have been the Tiandihui's midwife, but it was certainly the secret society's publicist. Second, the emergence of the religious Tiandihui of the western Fujian–eastern Jiangxi region underscores the ability of local society to create and practice its own set of meanings, even in the face of state persecution. The religious aspects of these regional practices had been present in Tiandihui rituals and written documents from the very beginning, and are not unrelated to "dissent" and rebellion. Nonetheless, Tiandihui members in early nineteenth-century western Fujian and eastern Jiangxi adopted these practices because they were perceived to be powerful, not because they facilitated dissent and opposition.

CHAPTER 5

Marginality and Ideology

QING REPRESENTATIONS OF
BROTHERHOOD ASSOCIATIONS
AND SECRET SOCIETIES

People who swear blood brotherhood and burn petitions are certainly not good subjects, which is why the prohibition against such activities is so severe, and why it is included in the treason [moupan] section [of the Code]. Such people should be viewed as rebels [luanmin]. . . . If, however, there are commoners who form brotherhoods out of a sense of common purpose, and do not engage in illegal activities, then this is not covered by the prohibitions. . . . The bond of friendship is included in the five cardinal relationships, and if law-abiding citizens form brotherhoods out of friendship and structure them according to age, then this is not prohibited.

— Qing Code, cited in Xue Yunsheng, Duli cunyi, 1905

To this point, this study has argued that the histories of brotherhood associations and rebellions should be written separately, even if they came together on numerous occasions. It is clear nonetheless that Qing authorities did not accept this fact, and it is worth asking why not. This chapter thus takes up the important question of the nature of Qing *representations* of brotherhood associations and secret societies, the lenses through which Qing officials filtered their observations of the practices of these nonelite associations. I examine this question from a number of perspectives, not all of which yield the same conclusion.

Although Qing laws regarding brotherhood associations and secret societies underwent certain changes from the beginning of the dynasty through the early nineteenth century, these laws were in general very harsh, the death penalty being prescribed in many cases. Qing laws contained more than three times as many capital offenses as Ming laws and might thus be seen as harsher across the board, but most of these capital offenses involved crimes in which lives were lost, whereas the death penalty was prescribed even for many *nonviolent* brotherhood associations and secret societies.[1] Documents containing a definitive justification of this hostility have not yet been uncovered, but at some level the Qing clearly feared the perceived rebelliousness of many brotherhood associations and secret societies, as well as the heterodoxy of the blood oath.[2]

At the same time, the Qing made a persistent effort to distinguish among various types of brotherhood associations, and to make the punishment fit the crime. This suggests that whatever their fear of rebellion and heterodoxy, Qing lawmakers and officials recognized that not all activities of brotherhood associations and secret societies fell neatly into those categories. Looking past the autocratic paranoia that inspired many of the laws, it is evident that the Qing also realized that they were faced with a new, and to them distasteful, social institution that was unfortunately too widespread to suppress completely and too varied in its forms and activities to control by means of a single set of punishments.

The second perspective explored in this chapter deals with the implementation of the laws. In this context, it appears that the balance and occasional leniency of the written law often gave way in the heat of implementation to harshness and the well-known strategy of "killing the rooster to frighten the monkey." There are of course examples of prudence and even leniency in the sentencing and handling of those involved in brotherhoods and secret societies, but the many examples of harshness surely set the tone in a more authoritative way. These two perspectives—the formal law and the implementation of the law—are essentially complementary: even if the Qing at some level realized that brotherhood associations and secret societies could not be reduced to heterodox rebels, the desire for control triumphed over the pose of benevolent, paternal evenhandedness.

A third perspective compares Qing laws dealing with brotherhood associations with laws treating feuds (*xiedou*). Such a comparison is useful because we lack a full account of the body of Qing law and its implementation against which we could measure specific laws treating brotherhood associations. Furthermore, both brotherhood associations and feuds were matters frequently encountered by officials stationed in Southeast China. Qing officials discussing the problems of governing the region often linked feuds and secret societies in the way that contemporary American commentators link crime and drug abuse in their discussions of the problems of the inner city. Indeed, the language of Qing discussions of feuds and secret societies allows one to conclude that secret society violence and *xiedou* were far more similar than has conventionally been believed. Some feuds were classic vendettas between powerful lineages, and some secret societies were made up of alienated drifters with no ties to any social group outside the association; yet some Qing documents identify junior members of lineages and villages as the instigators of feud violence. These young men, marginalized in the same sense as were members of brotherhood associations, are depicted as having exploited the *xiedou* process for their own benefit, in order to gain prestige, power, and wealth. Indeed, the frequent appearance of secret societies in *xiedou* incidents underscores the similarity between the entrepreneurial violence engaged in by many secret societies and the cynical exploitation of the feud by junior lineage members. It is probably not surprising that Qing officials frequently presented *xiedou* and secret societies as similar responses to the mobile, competitive atmosphere of the late imperial Southeast Coast.

This perspective is useful for a number of reasons. First, research along these lines forces us to realize that Qing officials encountered named brotherhoods and secret societies more frequently as crime than as heterodoxy.* In addition, although Qing officials used similar language to describe both feuds and secret societies, they interpreted the two kinds of violence in very different ways. They were frequently content to reduce associational behavior to nothing more than calculating entrepreneurship, even when the evidence they gathered supported other interpretations, and even though the Code prescribed harsh penalties for illegal associations. Officials were also quick to intervene in suspected brotherhood association or secret society activities, even if these activities were relatively innocuous, and far less destructive than some *xiedou*. Qing legal discussions of *xiedou* omitted the entrepreneurial aspects, even when their own observations regarding *xiedou* supported such an interpretation. Instead, Qing officials frequently emphasized the connection of *xiedou* violence to lineages, villages, and ethnic groups, linking *xiedou* to what they understood as the central social institutions of rural China. To them, *xiedou* violence was "private" violence, and therefore normal and in some ways acceptable.[3] They rarely intervened in *xiedou* but instead left them to be resolved by lineage elders, village leaders, and local gentry.

The Qing interpretation of brotherhood associations and feuds thus represented an ideological choice to support an imagined hierarchical Confucian order against the freer, more mobile, more fragmented society evolving during the late imperial period. From this perspective, the conventional characterization of the Qing as unusually hostile to nonelite associations may lose some of its force. There were more of these associations than in previous dynasties, and governmental "concern" was probably called for. It is difficult indeed to imagine a positive Con-

---

* Although I have done no calculations, my strong impression is that the vast majority of cases in the *Tiandihui* collection involve petty crime rather than heterodoxy.

fucian sanction for the poorly connected, marginalized young men who made up brotherhoods and secret societies.

Brotherhood Associations and Secret Societies in the Qing Code, 1650–1812

Many scholars have noted an exaggerated Qing hostility toward non-elite institutions and have connected this hostility to ethnic fears.[4] This hostility (if not its ethnic basis) shines through clearly in Qing laws treating brotherhood associations and secret societies: the Qing Code was the first to include laws directed specifically against brotherhoods, named brotherhoods, and secret societies, and many of these laws prescribed extremely harsh penalties. At the same time, the history and complexity of these laws, though confirming the Qing preoccupation with control, show the extent to which thoughtful Qing lawmakers attempted to come to terms with a new social phenomenon. The discussions that are reflected in the changing emphases in the laws dealing with brotherhood associations and secret societies through the early nineteenth century revolved around the proper definition and categorization of various forms of brotherhood associations, and the need for defining the punishments to fit the crime. Properly interpreted, the laws reveal extreme Qing distrust of brotherhood associations and secret societies, but also an effort to sort out which types of brotherhood association were dangerous and which types were an unfortunate but unavoidable aspect of popular culture.[5]

Although the Qing adopted the Ming Code early in the dynasty, they quickly added new language and penalties directed specifically at brotherhood associations. Before the seventeenth century ended, the Code contained a threefold definition of brotherhood associations and secret societies that was to characterize Qing laws through the early nineteenth century. The first Qing regulation against brotherhoods, recorded only in a later edition of the *Huidian* and dated only as "early Qing,"[6] defined brotherhoods as organizations made up of persons bearing different surnames. Members of these simple brotherhoods, presumably guilty of violating kinship norms, were to receive the relatively light punishment of 100 lashes of the whip.[7] In SZ 18 (1661), Qing authorities devised a new regulation connecting brotherhoods with blood oaths and petitions that were burned to communicate with the spirit world. Although we lack information about the circumstances that prompted this change, Qing officials and lawmakers obviously interpreted these practices as akin to heterodoxy, and the new regulation prescribed imminent execution for all those involved. A decade later, a KX 10 (1671) substatute introduced yet another definition, depicting the formation of brotherhoods as a rebellious act. It was at this point that substatutes treating brotherhoods were moved from the category of "miscellaneous offenses" (*zafan*) to that of "plotting rebellion" (*moupan*). According to this substatute, leaders of rebellious brotherhoods were to be executed by strangulation after the assizes, and followers were to receive 100 blows of the heavy bamboo and life exile at a distance of 3,000 *li*.[8]

Even without knowing the full history of these revisions, it is difficult not to imagine a discussion of the nature of the brotherhood and what to do about it. By the 1670's, the definition had come to include three basic characterizations: the simple brotherhood, the (heterodox) blood-oath brotherhood, and the rebellious brotherhood (which generally included a blood oath). Subsequent laws built on these three definitions, not by arguing about which characterization was more accurate but by drafting increasingly complex legislation to attempt to deal with all types of brotherhood associations and secret societies. In essence, Qing officials and lawmakers were trying to work out the nature of brotherhood associations and their relationship to local society and politics while at the same time preserving at least the appearance of fairness, distinguishing serious crimes from regrettable misdemeanors.

The trend toward complexity began very early. In KX 7 (1668), seven years after the initial depiction of brotherhood associations as heterodox blood brotherhoods, a new substatute introduced important modifications. First, punishment for blood brotherhoods was reduced from imminent execution to execution after the assizes. Second, a clause was inserted treating simple brotherhoods, which were still to be punished by 100 lashes of the whip. Obviously, Qing officials had combined the two earliest regulations dealing with brotherhoods so that not all members of brotherhood associations would be threatened with imminent execution. The 1671 statute defining blood brotherhoods as rebellious also contained language treating simple brotherhoods that reflected an increasingly complex understanding of such associations; it discussed the internal organization of the brotherhood and set different penalties for leaders and followers.

Although there were restatements and minor revisions to the laws in 1673 (reducing punishments for those involved in simple brotherhoods) and a new substatute in 1725 (introducing distinctions according to the size of the group),[9] important modifications of the basic laws did not occur until the 1760's and 1770's, after the widespread emergence of secret societies brought renewed attention to the problem. A complex substatute came into force in QL 29 (1764) in response to Dingchang's memorial discussing his experiences with secret societies during his tenure as

Fujian governor.[10] This substatute contained four distinct if overlapping characterizations of brotherhood practices. The first described groups in Fujian who took blood oaths and formed brotherhoods but did not engage in any other criminal or rebellious activities. All members of such brotherhoods were to be strangled after the assizes. The second characterization added the dimension of violence, discussing bands in Fujian who took blood oaths and formed brotherhoods, resisted official arrest, and seized weapons with violent intent. Leaders of such brotherhoods were to be decapitated and followers strangled after the assizes.

The third characterization described bands that secretly manufactured symbols and slogans to cheat the rural people, "abusing the weak and exploiting the few." For some reason, although the manufacture of secret signs and slogans surely falls within the purview of our understanding of "secret society" activities, Qing lawmakers did not identify these practices with oaths of blood brotherhood, and did not use the language of heterodoxy in their discussion of this type of brotherhood. Instead, they considered such activities entrepreneurial rackets, and prescribed sentences according to the "vicious scoundrel" (*xiong'e guntu*) statute, with much lighter punishments than those directed at other types of brotherhoods: leaders of such bands were sentenced to "military exile" in the malarial regions of Yunnan-Guizhou and Guangdong-Guangxi;[11] followers to one less degree; and those innocently seduced into the band were to receive 100 blows of the heavy bamboo and wear the cangue for two months. In the context of these rackets, there was also a good bit of discussion of the involvement of soldiers and yamen underlings, and the tendency of local security personnel to ignore the brotherhoods—again illustrating that Qing officials viewed these activities as racketeering rather than heterodoxy or rebellion.

A final characterization in the 1764 substatute dealt with legal associations, such as the popular idol-carrying processions (*choushen saihui* or *yingshen saihui*), which were not to be confused with others treated in the law, and were not to be punished. The inclusion of language treating legal associations in a law directed against illegal ones again suggests concern on the part of Qing authorities to avoid misapplication of the law.

Another complex substatute was introduced in QL 39 (1774). It contained three separate characterizations of brotherhoods. The first reasserted the depiction of brotherhood associations as rebellious, which had not been explicitly affirmed since YZ 3 (1725). This reaffirmation is not surprising since the substatute was prompted by the arrest of Chen Agao in Chaozhou, Guangdong, and the attempt by some of his blood brothers to break him out of jail.[12] These associations were defined as those made up of people with different surnames, who took blood oaths, burned petitions, and swore brotherhood. Punishment varied with the size of the brotherhood and with the person's position within the group: in groups of less than twenty, leaders were to be strangled after the assizes and followers punished one degree less; in groups larger than twenty, the leaders were to be sentenced to imminent decapitation and followers sent into military exile in a malarial frontier region.

The second characterization of this long substatute distinguished the rebellious blood brotherhood from the simple brotherhood. Simple brotherhoods were to be classified by size, and punishments were fixed accordingly: in simple brotherhoods of more than 40, the leaders were to be strangled after the assizes and followers punished one degree less severely; in brotherhoods numbering between 20 and 40, the leaders were to receive 100 blows of the heavy bamboo, and life exile at a distance of 3,000 *li*, and followers again were to be punished one degree less severely; in brotherhoods containing less than 20 members, the leaders were to receive 100 blows of the heavy bamboo, and wear the cangue for two months, followers one degree less.

A third characterization employed in this substatute introduced language and concepts not previously seen. This section of the substatute dealt with brotherhoods that subverted the age hierarchy in the organization of the group and invested leadership in a youth—clearly a matter of concern to a Confucian state. As I noted in Chapter 2, certain messianic traditions predicted the arrival of young saviors to usher in a new world, but nothing in the language of the clause conclusively indicates which, if either, of these concerns animated Qing lawmakers. This category of brotherhood association is called *qukui*, an ancient term referring to leaders of armed uprisings, yet the punishment prescribed seems somewhat light, if the Qing was indeed worried about violent messianism: leaders were to be sentenced to imminent strangulation, and followers sent into military exile in the malarial regions of Yunnan-Guizhou or Guangdong-Guangxi.

A QL 57 (1792) substatute reflected Qing hypersensitivity concerning secret societies, particularly the Heaven and Earth Society, in the wake of the Lin Shuangwen uprising of 1787–88. Frightened by efforts to revive the Heaven and Earth Society on Taiwan, the law stipulated imminent decapitation for leaders of the society, for those who carried out recruitment, and for those who willingly entered. The sole hint of leniency may not have been particularly soothing to those caught in the dragnet: "As for those who did not recruit others, or who were seduced or coerced into joining and who have always been good subjects, let them be sentenced to imminent strangulation." This law was meant to be an ad hoc response to a temporary situation, and to remain in force only as long as the Heaven and Earth Society bedeviled Taiwan. By making it a temporary measure, the Qing obliquely acknowledged the extreme nature of the punishments.

A JQ 8 (1803) substatute returned to the form and language of the 1774 law, making distinctions and applying differential punishments. The first characterization in the 1803 substatute dealt with brotherhoods marked by the drinking of blood, the burning of petitions, and the taking of blood oaths to form sworn brotherhoods. Punishments for these brotherhoods again varied with the size of the group and the role of the individual in the organization of the group: in groups of less than 20, leaders were to be strangled after the assizes and followers to receive one degree less punishment; in groups of 20 or more, leaders were to suffer imminent decapitation and followers were to be exiled to malarial frontier regions.

A second characterization discussed simple brotherhoods, which again were to be distinguished chiefly by size: in groups larger than 40, leaders were to be strangled after the assizes, followers one degree less; in groups of 20 to 40, leaders were to receive 100 blows of the heavy bamboo, life exile at distance of 3,000 *li*, followers one degree less; in groups smaller than 20, leaders were to receive 100 blows of the heavy bamboo, and wear the cangue for two months.

The third characterization repeated the *qukui* characterization, first seen in 1764, and again marked by subversion of the age hierarchy and investment of leadership in a young person. Once again, the size of the group was to determine the appropriate punishment: in cases involving 40 or more members, leaders were to suffer imminent strangulation and followers were to be sentenced to military exile on distant malarial frontiers; in groups of less than 40, leaders were to be strangled after the assizes; and followers were to receive 100 blows of the heavy bamboo, together with life exile at a distance of 3,000 li.

The substatute of JQ 16 (1811), originally intended to apply only to Guangdong province, was placed under the "robbery" statute in the Code, although other substatutes treating brotherhood associations and secret societies remained under the "rebellion" statute. This substatute contained five characterizations of brotherhoods: as rebellious brotherhoods, simple brotherhoods, *qukui*, criminal rackets, and legal associations. The treatment of rebellious brotherhoods and simple brotherhoods borrowed directly from the language of the 1803 substatute. The discussion of the *qukui* also borrowed the characterization and punishments from the 1803 substatute, but included further discussion of the appropriate punishment should this variety of brotherhood resist arrest. The characterization of brotherhoods that manufactured secret signs and slogans to cheat the rural ignorant repeated the language of the 1764 substatute. The final clause dealt again with seasonal or ephemeral organizations such as *yingshen saihui*, which should not be punished according to this substatute.

The same substatute was repeated the following year (1812) with only minor modifications. One modification provided for less stringent punishment for those who joined an organization led by a youth, so long as they were coerced into joining, and did not resist official arrest, or if they simply contributed money without joining in the violent or rebellious activities of the brotherhood. A second modification omitted discussion of brotherhoods as rackets.

Further research will be required to fill in the gaps between the various substatutes and construct a genuine history of Chinese jurisprudence directed at brotherhood associations and secret societies, but even this brief summary illuminates several important dimensions of the Qing approach. First, punishments prescribed for many varieties of brotherhood were very harsh. To repeat only a few striking examples, the 1774 substatute sentenced to imminent execution all leaders of associations combining 20 or more men of different surnames, who drank blood, pledged oaths, burned petitions, and swore brotherhoods, whether they had engaged in violence or not. The 1803 substatute again sentenced the leader of a mere "simple brotherhood"—one where there was no evidence of blood oaths—of more than 40 men to strangulation after the assizes. The 1792 law, although meant to be temporary, sentenced all those connected with the Heaven and Earth Society to imminent execution in one form or another. Granted, the Qing punished many offenses with death, but most death sentences were designed to repay the loss of life committed during the course of the crime. Many statutes dealing with brotherhood associations and secret societies prescribed death even in the absence of homicide, rebellion, or violence of any kind.

However, the persistent effort to categorize and recategorize the three basic varieties of brotherhood association, the introduction of the dimensions of group size and degree of violence, the different punishments for leaders and followers, and the constant adjustment of the appropriate degree of punishment for association with brotherhoods, all suggest that Qing lawmakers were rarely so frightened by the prospect of nonelite associations or heterodox combinations as to condemn out of hand all varieties of brotherhood formation. The insistence that the *yingshen sai-*

hui be protected from laws against other types of *hui* confirms this same point. The Qing disliked brotherhoods, but grudgingly accepted that some were part and parcel of local society.

A further dimension revealed by this discussion concerns the question of heterodoxy. We assume that the Qing objected to blood brotherhoods because of their "heterodoxy," but neither the Code nor the commentaries of Qing officials on the practice provides much in the way of analysis of this heterodoxy beyond general condemnations of such practices as "absurd" or "uncivilized."[13] The Qing code contained statutes dealing specifically with heterodoxy, but these were not invoked in writing the laws on brotherhoods, nor were the concerns frequently expressed in the writings of Qing officials.[14] Indeed, it is striking that in the 1764 substatute, the description of "secret societies," which largely accords with their depiction in Chapter 4 as religious organizations, does not allude in any way to these dimensions but instead treats secret signs and language as clever ruses to fool the masses. And in the discussion of brotherhoods headed by youths, the relatively light punishment suggests that the Qing was more concerned with violations of the Confucian age hierarchy than with the possibility of messianism. Because violations of Confucian orthodoxy are ipso facto heterodox—note the horrible punishments prescribed for patricide—it may well be that the heterodoxy of blood brotherhoods was so self-evident that it demanded no detailed analysis. In any case, the fact that simple brotherhoods that did not employ a blood oath received lighter punishments proves the Qing antipathy toward the practice, even if written justification for this choice is lacking. By the same token, the different penalties accorded to different kinds of brotherhoods and secret societies and to leaders and followers of these organizations indicate that in the eyes of Qing lawmakers, the heterodoxy of certain kinds of brotherhood associations was, by and large, simply the heterodoxy of the uneducated. Little in the documentary record suggests that Qing officials saw all brotherhood associations and secret societies as devilish threats to the Qing order.

Qing "leniency" toward certain varieties of brotherhoods and secret societies did not stem from a recognition of an abstract "right to association." Qing discussions of brotherhood associations and secret societies are permeated with the same moral condemnation that marks discussions of feuds, gambling, excessive litigation, and a host of social ills that beset the rural society of the Southeast Coast. Qing emperors and officials consistently adopted a tone of elitist distaste, and criticized those who founded or joined brotherhood associations in familiar Confucian terms for their profit seeking (the Mencian condemnation of profit is frequently repeated), willful, unrestrained, uncivilized, and violent behavior (*TDH* 6: 501). In the relatively few instances where Qing officials linked brotherhood associations and secret societies with heterodoxy, secret society "masters" were condemned for chicanery and members for ignorance and naïveté (*TDH* 6: 218–21). Even when discussing those examples of associational behavior that are meant to be legal, such as the *yingshen saihui*, Qing officials frequently condemned the beliefs that underwrote the practices, as well as the conspicuous consumption and gratuitous violence that often accompanied them.*

Qing officials clearly would have preferred a world without brotherhood associations and secret societies, and their efforts to distinguish among various types of societies and to assign punishments appropriate to the various types surely reflected a recognition of the realities of Qing power in rural areas rather than positive sanction for some versions of associational behavior. Differential punishments were part of the Qing calculus of control. The most likely result of any Qing effort to wipe out completely all traces of brotherhood association or secret society activity would have been frequent rebellion. It was far more politic, the Qing reasoned, to persecute the leaders and warn the followers. If Qing officials pushed too hard in their efforts to cleanse the countryside, the result could well be unrest and even rebellion—a fact of life captured in the timeworn expression *guanbi minfan* ("When the officials push hard, the people rise up").

Implementation: When Push Comes to Shove . . .

A full understanding of Qing laws on brotherhood associations and secret societies cannot rely completely on analysis of the text of the Code. In all societies, the abstract expression of the law takes on concrete meaning through implementation, and Qing officials had particularly wide latitude in their interpretation of the statutes and substatutes, since their duties were to adapt the law to local circumstances and to make the punishment fit the crime. An overview of the implementation of Qing laws concerning brotherhood associations and secret societies reveals that the "protections" built into the Qing code for those only marginally involved in brotherhood activities were frequently ignored. Even if Qing lawmakers sought to differentiate—in the formal state-

---

* See, for example, the discussion of *yingshen saihui* in Cheng, Daoguang period, j. 2: 22b–23a: "Once every few years [the people of northern Guangdong] hold a *hui*, where they build ornamental temples and hire young women to dress up and parade through the streets to greet the spirits [*yingshen*]. . . . Men and women mingle together and robbers and thieves are everywhere. Every time they hold this *hui* they spend thousands or tens of thousands of ounces of silver, and it is extremely wasteful."

ments of the law—between practices that merited harsh and lenient punishment, Qing officials, faced with the vexing problems of governing the unruly Southeast Coast, often chose to err on the side of harshness.

Of course, there were examples of leniency. Magistrate Ji Qiguang's discussion of brotherhoods in 1680's Taiwan, presented at some length in Chapter 1, suggests that he saw brotherhoods as little more than regrettable misdemeanors. The treatment received by the Small Knives Society in Taiwan in the 1770's again illustrates that some officials viewed these societies as part of the local social scene. In some cases, the punishment assigned was less than that prescribed by the Code. Jiang Zefang, arrested in 1825 in Qujiang county, Guangdong, as the leader of a simple brotherhood of less than 40 members, had his sentence reduced from the prescribed strangulation after the assizes to life exile at a distance of 3,000 *li* because he voluntarily surrendered to local authorities. Among his followers were two who claimed responsibility for aging mothers; their sentences were reduced from exile to wearing the cangue, which allowed them to remain in their home areas.[15] A recent study of the implementation of Qing homicide laws has identified a kind of "routinized leniency," wherein those convicted were given harsh sentences only to have those sentences reduced on appeal, thus allowing the government to appear simultaneously vigilant and benevolent.[16] Similar principles were probably at work in many unspectacular cases involving named brotherhoods and secret societies.

In addition, there is abundant evidence of the "calculus of control," in which Qing officials sought to balance harsh penalties for brotherhood leaders with lenient treatment of followers. In one instance, the followers of Chen Zuo, one of the leaders of a Small Knives Society that was responsible for the murder of a county magistrate in southern Fujian in 1743, were granted reduction of their sentences. The Fujian-Zhejiang governor-general argued that these followers had been seduced into Chen's band and had volunteered only to rob local villagers. When they found out that Chen planned to lead an attack on the county seat, they abandoned him, proving, in the words of the governor-general, that "they still feared the law."[17] In another instance, a Guangdong governor-general pleaded for leniency for those who turned themselves in following the conclusion of a Three Harmonies Society (*Sanhehui*) case in Shunde county, Guangdong, in JQ 17 (1812). "According to the gentry and elders," the governor-general argued, "these are good people who were led astray [they had merely contributed money to the society, and had not engaged in other activities]. If we do not handle them differently [from the society leaders], then the rest of the fence-sitters will not dare turn themselves in" (*TDH* 6: 502–3).

Even in the tense post–Lin Shuangwen period, when both law and official skittishness dictated extremely harsh punishments for those involved in brotherhood association and secret society activities, we find evidence of "leniency" amid harshness. Yang Zhao set up a Small Knives Society in the twelfth month of JQ 2 (1798) in Danshui, northern Taiwan, intending to organize a rebellion. The 1792 law regarding those who sought to reestablish the Heaven and Earth Society on Taiwan, and prescribing execution for all involved, was still in effect, and Yang in his deposition admitted that there was no difference between his Small Knives Society and the Heaven and Earth Society (*TDH* 6: 80–81). Nonetheless, officials in charge of initial sentencing still requested special consideration for those who played a lesser role in the affair:

> Yang Zhao conceived the idea to establish a secret society and rise up. Once arrests were imminent, he turned himself in hoping to avoid punishment, and to protect his associates. He is particularly treacherous and illegal . . . and should be sentenced to death by slicing [a harsher penalty than that prescribed by the 1792 statute]. [Sixty-six others], some of whom participated in the burning and looting, and some of whom willingly entered the society, should be sentenced according to the "rebellion" statute to imminent decapitation. . . . [There are eleven more] who were coerced into entering the society. The [1792] substatute includes no language about lesser punishments for those who turn themselves in, but it appears that these criminals entered the society only once [i.e., participated in only one initiation ritual], did not engage in burning and looting, and . . . turned themselves in [in a timely manner], so that they are different from those who willingly entered the society.
>
> Moreover, the popular mood of Taiwan is restless, and the people are easily incited to cause disturbances. . . . If we do not spare the lives [of the eleven] we fear that people will not [turn themselves in] in the future. Can we possibly make an analogy to the case of ordinary society bandits who turn themselves in on hearing that arrest is imminent, and sentence them to one hundred strokes of the heavy bamboo and exile at a distance of 3,000 *li*, with the provision that the exile be the harsher punishment of serving as slaves to the military establishment in Heilongjiang? (*TDH* 6 81–82)

Life exile as a slave to the military colonies of Heilongjiang is "lenient" only in a relative sense, of course, and one suspects that the harshness of Qing laws toward brotherhood associations and secret societies made a greater impact on those affected by their implementation. For example, in the late 1720's, Taiwanese officials in Zhuluo county investigating reports of possible queue-clipping and gang violence happened upon two Father and Mother societies unrelated to the original concerns, arrested the members, and executed the leaders—a harsher punishment than the laws prescribed. The evidence does not permit a definitive interpretation of the nature of these Father and Mother societies, but Qing officials, who had faced a string of actual and near-rebellions in Taiwan in the 1720's, had little time for the niceties of the law.[18] Even though local officials argued that the Father and Mother societies "were merely cases of blood oaths and brotherhoods, with no plan for rebellion or weapons involved," which should have been punished with 100 strokes of the heavy bamboo for the leaders, and 80 for the followers, Fujian Governor-General Gao Qizhuo argued for much sterner punishment: "Taiwan is different from the mainland. . . . The [Father and Mother Society] bands were growing. . . . I propose that in these . . . [two cases] we broadcast the proclamations and immediately execute [the leaders] to illustrate the punishments. As for the followers, let them . . . be sentenced to exile."[19] The emperor agreed.

This harshness was particularly obvious in the post–Lin Shuangwen period, as noted in Chapter 4. When Zhang Maqiu rose up on the mainland during Lin Shuangwen's rebellion, claiming association with Lin, punishment for the leaders was increased to death by slicing (*TDH* 5: 371–72). When Zhang Biao and Xie Zhi put together a Heaven and Earth Society and launched a rebellion in the spring of 1791 (QL 56), the official in charge of sentencing argued: "Zhang Biao dared to plot secretly to recruit people to enter his society, and then had his recruits carry out further recruitment, and with Xie Zhi discussed reestablishing rebel Lin Shuangwen's Heaven and Earth Society. This is despicable. All those recruited entered willingly, and are also unlawful. Punishment as stipulated by the [current] law is insufficient" (*TDH* 5: 379).

All this culminated in the extremely harsh 1792 law, which prescribed execution for all those on Taiwan found to have participated in any attempt to revive the Heaven and Earth Society. During this same period, many officials resorted to immediate, on-the-spot execution of large numbers of those involved in secret society activities.[20] These examples of harshness could be multiplied many times over, and one suspects that the provisions in the Code designed to preserve fairness made far less impact on the population (or on the officials) than examples of death by slicing and immediate execution. A thorough study of sentencing of brotherhood association and secret society cases in the seventeenth, eighteenth, and nineteenth centuries would no doubt reveal patterns of alternating harshness and leniency, depending on the disposition of the emperor, the frequency of rebellions or other mass actions, the numbers and quality of troops available, and so on. But if we had evidence of the collective memory of rural communities concerning Qing attitudes toward brotherhood associations and secret societies, these memories would, I have no doubt, revolve around the chilling exercise of absolute power rather than the "fairness" of the Code.[21]

Qing Perspectives on Brotherhoods and Feuds

Since we know relatively little about the theory and practice of Qing law in general, even a thorough examination of Qing laws and their implementation in any one area cries out for a comparative perspective. The following section compares Qing attitudes toward brotherhood associations with Qing attitudes toward feuds (*xiedou*), drawing on legal texts, elite commentary, and implementation of the law. This comparison is useful because officials serving in the Southeast Coast often mentioned these problems together, and the language employed by Qing officials suggests that they noted significant elements of profit seeking in both secret society violence and armed feuding.

At a more formal level, Qing officials did not acknowledge the similarity of the two types of violence. In the eyes of Qing officials, feuds, however violent and disruptive they might be, remained part of "normal," everyday conflict, presumably because of their connections with lineages and villages, the basic structures of late imperial rural society. Brotherhood associations, even if they seemed to be innocent, were suspect because their ties to these basic structures, and to the hierarchies that connected these structures to the imperial state, were uncertain.

THE ENTREPRENEURIAL BROTHERHOOD

The argument that follows hinges on the willingness—or lack thereof—of Qing officials to interpret the activities of brotherhood associations or groups at feud as profit-seeking behavior. Entrepreneurship was by no means the only element in the Qing understanding of brotherhood associations and secret societies, but Qing officials were frequently quite willing to reduce many aspects of brotherhood association and secret society practices to the callous search for profit.

The best example of the Qing willingness to reduce secret society activities to forms of entrepreneurship is their attitude toward the "religious" Heaven and Earth societies discussed in Chapter 4. Although Qing officials acknowledged these magico-religious dimensions in some instances, more frequently they dismissed the rituals, handbooks, and other paraphernalia as "vulgar," and were more comfortable with the notion that secret society leaders were charlatans and secret society members either gullible dupes or bandits. The "teachings" of secret society "masters" were dismissed as a cynical pose masking entrepreneurial intent. A passage from a memorial by Fujian-Zhejiang Governor-General Nasutu, who served in the region in the early 1740's, captures the tone of much Qing writing on this subject: "[The Fujianese] are always forming quasi-religious leagues and putting together associations of various names and denominations, which compete for local power. If there is a squabble anywhere, then these groups immediately send around notices under false names, hoping to delude the commoners into forming gangs and fighting."[22]

The Qing had little difficulty finding evidence to support their belief. In virtually all the secret societies discussed in Chapter 4, the "teachers" charged new members a fee for the initiation ceremony, at which they transmitted secret hand signals and passwords (*TDH* 6: 143, 159, 171, 301–2, 341–42). The fees were justified either as necessary to defray the cost of the items used in the initiation ceremony or as an investment in the written materials that would help in further recruitment (*TDH* 6: 287, 332). Many Qing officials were convinced that the collection of fees was the primary motivation behind secret society formation, and they frequently asked captured society leaders how much money they had made by recruitment and initiation. Sometimes these sums were rather large—such as Li Lingkui's earnings from the sale of White Lotus and Tiandihui scriptures, noted in the last chapter, of 50 Mexican dollars and 200 ounces of silver. Two hundred ounces of silver would have bought over 300,000 cash in North China, roughly equivalent to six months' income from a sinecure clerkship in a district yamen's office.[23]

In addition to the total sums collected, Qing officials found other evidence to confirm that financial considerations figured prominently in the formation of secret societies, even when the society had a clearly religious orientation. Li Lingkui charged different prices for the Buddhist scriptures and the Tiandihui written materials. Other secret society leaders performed more complete rituals and dispensed more materials to those who paid them more money (*TDH* 6: 301–2).

For that reason, Qing officials commonly dismissed the ostensible meaning of society formation with four-character phrases such as *jiehui lianqian* ("setting up societies to collect money") or *chuantu pianqian* ("seeking disciples in order to cheat people out of their money") (*TDH* 6: 142, 245). It is quite certain that entrepreneurship did play an important role in these religiously oriented societies (as it does in many religions), but few Qing officials, as willfully blind as many another secular elite, entertained the possibility that profit-driven behavior could coexist with sincere religious belief.

Qing officials easily found other evidence of entrepreneurship, not only in magico-religious secret societies but also in societies that looked to be more secular. In one instance, a member of an Increase Younger Brothers Society in Longquan, Jiangxi, whose initiation rituals had been marked with great pomp and ceremony, used the charismatic name of the society to bully his way into good burial land for a fellow society member's mother (*TDH* 6: 332–37). In another, a man carrying firewood inadvertently bumped into a Heaven and Earth Society member, who claimed that the firewood had torn his clothes, and used the threat of "mutual aid" to confiscate the firewood as compensation, after which he sold the wood and drank the proceeds (*TDH* 6: 143). Qing officials identified a wide range of activities engaged in by brotherhood associations and secret societies that used the strength of numbers and the threat of violence to engage in more organized varieties of extortion, protection, confidence scams, and, of course, banditry.

In most of these cases, we have little reason to doubt the accuracy of the Qing evidence of entrepreneurship. Most members of these organizations were poor, marginalized people. Had they had greater access to material goods, most would not have been candidates for secret society membership, and it is hardly surprising that the brotherhood association made possible many forms of criminal and violent entrepreneurship. But the Qing by and large worked on the assumption that the motivations of all secret societies were crime, violence, and entrepreneurship, and nothing else.

QING VIEWS OF *XIEDOU*

Some instances of *xiedou* had similarly entrepreneurial aspects, although it overstates the case to identify all feuds in Southeast China as manifestations of criminal entrepreneurship. There is a substantial, and convincing, literature that identifies the Chinese *xiedou* with the feud as practiced in other parts of the world. This literature depicts feuds as a means of settling conflict in an acephalous society, carried out by groups generally organized through kinship, occurring in cycles of violence frequently expressed in the language of "blood" or honor, and functioning ecologically to maintain a rough balance of contending forces.[24] Chinese society of course differed greatly from the examples of acephalous societies highlighted in the anthropological literature on feuding; no one would confuse the bureaucratized Chinese polity with the nomadic societies of Northern Africa, the hill tribes of Montenegro, or feuding Corsican villages.[25] But some of the rural areas of the Southeast Coast appear to have been relatively independent of the Chinese state, and Qing officials often depicted *xiedou* as a means of conflict resolution.[26] Other passages make the complementary point connecting frequent *xiedou* violence to the inadequate and overburdened Qing legal system.[27] As one official serving in Minnan in the early 1760's noted: "The people of Zhaoan are always fighting over trivial matters concerning marriages and fields. They do not come to the yamen . . . but rather engage in *xiedou*."[28]

These same commentators identify the groups involved in *xiedou*, chiefly lineages and villages. One Qing official discussed "a great *xiedou* case involving thousands of people. This results from large lineages living together. The larger lineages have several thousand households, and the smaller several hundred. None of them speak to other lineages, except to set a time to *xiedou*."[29] One Qing governor once proposed dealing with the problem of *xiedou* by destroying lineage temples and confiscating genealogies.[30] Many of the battles in this form of *xiedou* were preceded by mobilization of forces at the ancestral hall, at which time the venue and date of the upcoming battle were announced, and leaders selected those who were to undertake the brunt of the fighting.[31]

The conflicts themselves frequently involved issues of honor:

> In . . . Tongan [county], Quanzhou [prefecture], and Zhangpu [county], Zhangzhou [prefecture], the lines of enmity have been drawn for many years. Grudges over murdered fathers and elder brothers are everywhere. In the worst cases [lineages engaged in *xiedou*] will dig up the graves of several generations of ancestors [of their enemy lineage] and take the bones to the market, displaying them with a sign saying: "For Sale: The Bones of Several Generations of the Ancestors of X [lineage]." They display this in the marketplace where everyone can see.[32]

There are also records of lineages that kept the bloodied clothing of the lineage members killed at feud in lineage halls to nourish the collective memory of the conflict.[33] These enmities often continued for generations, becoming "inherited grudges" (*shichou*).

Chinese lineages involved in *xiedou* also "kept score" in the way that feuding groups in other cultures did: "If the numbers of killed and wounded in the *xiedou* are equal [on both sides], then middlemen can mediate. But if my side has killed two of your men, and your side has killed three of my men, then we have to set a time to fight again, because you are still holding what I need to balance the scale."[34] The numbers of deaths recorded in this type of *xiedou* seem to have been limited, and also to have been regulated by the idea of achieving balance, even if "balancing the scale" might conflict with dispute resolution under certain conditions. In some cases, balancing the scale was achieved by sacrificing the appropriate number of "substitutes"—men paid to admit their guilt in deaths resulting from feud violence—to the state. Since the state ignored most *xiedou*, official records do not contain much information about the resolution of *xiedou* conflict that did not involve the state.

In sum, there is considerable evidence that the Chinese *xiedou* can be viewed as the equivalent of the feud. Even though late imperial Chinese society had a more complex political structure than the acephalous societies in which the classical feud is generally found, it is clear nonetheless that *xiedou* and feud overlap. The Chinese *xiedou* was to some degree a form of conflict resolution, spawned by an inadequate legal system, carried out largely by kinship groups, often in cycles of recurring "blood" violence, with balanced numbers of casualties. This has in fact been the central interpretation of the Chinese *xiedou* in Western literature on the subject, although scholars have been careful to note differences between *xiedou* and feud.[35]

At the same time, one finds support in the observations of Qing officials for other interpretations of *xiedou* that link it to the entrepreneurial activities of brotherhoods and secret societies. For example, many commentaries linking *xiedou* with large lineages and surname groups also indicate that the leadership of *xiedou* was not in the hands of lineage elders. One passage makes this point explicitly:

> The Shen and Cai lineages linked up [their members across] townships and fought. They killed each other and dug up each other's graves for eight or nine years without cease. If one asked them why they enjoyed *xiedou*, they would reply that it was a sorrow rather than a joy. If you asked them why they did not stop, they would answer that there were no *jiazhang* [lineage heads]. If you asked them why they did not select a *jiazhang* to manage these affairs, they would answer that the yamen underlings had to have their bribes, that people's lives had to be paid for [i.e., bribes given to deflect prosecution of member fighters], that court cases were never resolved, and that lineage property [*jiachan*] had all been exhausted through *xiedou*.[36]

Elsewhere in the same essay the official notes that "the good *jiazhang* are inadequate to restrain their evil younger members [*zidi*], and the bad ones enjoy stirring up trouble so that they can make money." Too many powerful lineages remain in today's Southeast Coast for this to stand as a general statement, but the theme is repeated often enough that we should not dismiss it out of hand.

Another passage makes a similar point in discussing the leadership exercised by local elites:

> Some say that those with education [*xiucai*] should be held responsible for *xiedou*, but today in the more remote rural areas the level of culture [*wenfeng*] diminishes daily, and there will be no *xiucai* for thousands of men. Moreover, common-surname groups are divided into strong and weak branches, and if a licentiate belongs to a weak branch he will not dare interfere in the affairs of a stronger branch.[37]

Other evidence identifies junior members of lineages or other groups at feud as the leaders. A well-documented instance of *xiedou* from late nineteenth-century Guangdong highlights the role of these younger members.[38] Similarly, officials investigating a Fujian-Hakka conflict in Fengshan county, southern Taiwan, in the winter of QL 33–34 (1769–70), found that lineage elders lacked sufficient power to control their communities: these elders directed officials to "junior members" of the community who presumably were in charge of the violence.[39]

In some instances, it appears that these young toughs had little formal relationship to the group for which they fought:

> *Xiedou* are the greatest source of disorder in Guangdong and Fujian. The ancestral halls of all the great lineages accumulate a great deal of resources. Troublemakers, viewing this accumulation of money to which they do not have access, cause incidents with other lineages in order to bring about *xiedou*. Once a *xiedou* begins, the officials are showered with bribes, so the officials are happy for the troublemakers' *xiedou*, while the troublemakers are pleased with the bribes, for they start the lineage resources flowing. Thus once there is a *xiedou*-related case, the lineage resources begin to disperse throughout the lineage. The only thing that remains is the fund set aside for sacrifices.[40]

If this evidence is accurate, then at least in some instances, *xiedou* were not the result of deliberate actions by traditional lineage or village leaders but rather were the work of strongmen who had simply asserted control. Another commentary supports this view:

> The people of Guangdong are willful and perverse. In every trivial incident, every affair involving fields and mountains, they do not await official adjudication, but rather hire outside bandits, choose a time and engage in *xiedou*. Those who lead the fighting are, in the main, people despised by the lineage heads, lineage gentry, and ritual leaders [*sizhang*]. They say it is a matter of two lineages or two cantons fighting, but in fact it is a bunch of temporarily hired bandits and salt smugglers, plus a kind of professional mercenary dare-to-die. Those called together number in the hundreds if not thousands, involving several if not several tens of villages.[41]

The absence of traditional lineage leadership went hand in hand with the frequent hiring of outside mercenaries to fight the actual *xiedou* engagements.

> If [lineages engaged in *xiedou*] are lacking in numbers, then they pay large sums of money to hire people to help. If a helper dies in the *xiedou*, his family is given a sum of money, and if he is injured, he is given money with which to convalesce. These fees come out of the ancestral coffers, or are assessed per amount of land owned. The idle [*youshou*] and the un-

employed are happy to receive such employment. Even if they die they do not regret it.[42]

Another source is more revealing about the practice of hiring mercenaries. This source suggests that the leaders of *xiedou* were referred to by a special term, "Great Fighter" (*doukui*); those who followed him into battle were known as his "fighting soldiers" (*doutu*), made up of his own (?) "younger agnates" (*zidi*) and tenants of the lineage as well as outside mercenaries who were hired through a *qinfen*, a sort of boss. The hired forces were called "birds" and were placed at the front lines. If they died they were said to have "flown."[43] The mercenaries even developed their own terminology: "Death" was called, for taboo reasons, "auspicious prosperity" (*daji lishi*); the loss of a head was termed "flying [away with the?] wind" (*feifeng*); the loss of a corpse was called "going to water" (*zoushui*).[44]

Later in the nineteenth century, with the accelerated import of more Western arms, the mercenaries, by then called *chongshou* or *qiangshou*, actually trained in the use of the new guns; but mercenary groups themselves are an old phenomenon in the region, dating back to at least mid-Ming times. The 1612 *Quanzhou fuzhi* notes: "There are also strongmen, like panthers and tigers, who gang up in tens or one hundred . . . and who assemble at one call. Some of those with grudges against the great families use [hire?] these [gangs] as shields and spears [i.e., a vanguard] in order to vent their anger. The result is that these gangs scour the countryside looking for grievances."[45] From this perspective, the *xiedou* looks more like a racket than a feud, and some commentators note that the entire process came to be commercialized:

> Lineage strongmen [*zuhao*] delight in *xiedou* activity because it gives them the opportunity to line their pockets. . . . Lineage toughs [*zugun*] take delight in *xiedou* activity because it gives them a chance to divide profits among themselves. . . . Pettifoggers delight in *xiedou* because they make money through their machinations. . . . Evil gentry delight in *xiedou* activity because they can manipulate the situation to their advantage. Yamen underlings delight in *xiedou* activity because it offers them an opportunity to trade on their influence.[46]

Brotherhood associations and secret societies also participated in *xiedou*, confirming the participation of outsiders in *xiedou* and suggesting the similarity between associational violence and *xiedou*. As already noted, Qing officials frequently linked *xiedou* and brotherhood associations. On taking up his post as Fujian Governor in 1797, Wang Zhiyi memorialized that people in Zhangzhou and Quanzhou formed associations in order to engage in *xiedou* (*TDH* 1: 136–40). In the Daoguang period, Xie Jinluan noted, in a discussion of Zhangzhou and Quanzhou: "In feuds of previous days, there were very few *huishe*. Now there are *huishe* everywhere, and whenever a *she* is involved in a feud, then those of the same *hui* will bring out their weapons to help them. Consequently, more and more people become involved [in each incident]."[47] There are a few documented cases of the involvement of societies in *xiedou*: the Small Knives Society was involved in the 1782 *xiedou* described in detail below; the Red and Black Flags, surely the rough equivalent of associations or secret societies, incited *xiedou* in the Lufeng-Huilai border areas in Guangdong in the 1870's.[48]

In sum, Qing officials discuss *xiedou* as racket as frequently as they do *xiedou* as feud, and they often depict leadership of *xiedou* violence as having fallen into the hands of young toughs who used the process to enrich or empower themselves. Lineages or villages at feud reportedly hired secret societies and other mercenaries to fight "their" battles for them. This interpretation does not deny the importance of lineages, honor, and balanced violence, but simply suggests that marginalized young men manipulated these forces to their own ends.

THE ARCHIVAL DEPICTION OF *XIEDOU*

Lacking full evidence, it may not be possible to arrive at a definitive interpretation of the Chinese *xiedou*. To piece together the interpretations of *xiedou* as feud *and xiedou* as racket, we have a collection of general statements about *xiedou* in literati writings (both letters and government documents), local gazetteers, and other sources familiar to Qing historians. Few of these statements give a specific context for their observations. Statecraft essays comment on "the nasty habits of the people of southern Fujian." The "customs and habits" sections of local gazetteers provide equally unanchored statements, as do collections of literati commentary such as the *Qingbai leichao* or Chen Shengshao's *Wensulu*. Since these statements rarely describe particular *xiedou* incidents in detail, we cannot be certain of the accuracy of their conclusions.

The sole exception to this vague testimony is a small number of *xiedou* cases recorded in the archives. In these cases, Qing officials investigated and recorded information about specific incidents, providing some sense of the chronological and sociological development of the violence. Although archival records hardly constitute ethnographic observations, because Qing officials, for the usual reasons, worked within prescribed frameworks, these records are valuable supplements to the more numerous but more general statements contained in the sources just discussed.

Most archival material on Chinese feuds discusses the "subethnic feud" (*fenlei xiedou*) on Taiwan.* As noted in the discussion of the Lin Shuangwen rebellion, ethnicity—or "subethnicity"—describes the organization of *xiedou* violence by membership in one of three ethnic groups: people from Zhangzhou prefecture, people from Quanzhou prefecture (both in southern Fujian), and Hakkas. The majority of Chinese immigrants to Taiwan during the early Qing period belonged to one of these three groups, and ethnicity provided an important axis of social identity during the frontier period of Taiwan's history. I have argued elsewhere that the role of ethnicity has been overemphasized as an explanation for *xiedou* on Taiwan, but there is no question that ethnic ties had a great deal to do with the expansion of small, local conflicts into large-scale *xiedou* that sometimes involved large numbers of villages across wide geographical expanses.[49] Indeed, the size of many Taiwanese *fenlei xiedou*—considerably larger than their mainland counterparts—demanded the official attention that resulted in archival records. As a whole, these archival records support the "entrepreneurial" rather than the conventional interpretation of *xiedou*, although again, the two interpretations are not necessarily mutually exclusive. The best illustration of this is a discussion of the most thoroughly documented instance of *xiedou* violence uncovered to date, the Zhang-Quan *xiedou* of 1782.

The 1782 *xiedou* broke out following seemingly random violence in Zhanghua county in the eighth month of QL 47 (1782). Organized hostilities on a small scale began within five days. Officials intervened in the following month, achieving a temporary lull in the fighting, but later in the ninth and early part of the tenth months, the *xiedou* exploded in many areas of Zhanghua county, as some 200 villages were attacked, burned, and looted.[50] Late in the ninth month, the violence spread south to Zhuluo county and Qing authorities transferred troops from Zhanghua to Zhuluo.[51] The violence in Zhuluo was as destructive as that in Zhanghua, and required the transfer of mainland officials to assist in its suppression. Discussion of reconstruction efforts began only in the twelfth month.[52] Thus the *xiedou* lasted more than two months, spread rapidly throughout both Zhanghua and Zhuluo counties, and involved several thousand people. Four hundred villages were damaged, thousands of refugees fled their homes seeking protection from more power-

* Archival information on mainland *xiedou* is sorely lacking. There are scattered references, but little that adds to the rich body of material on Fujianese and Cantonese *xiedou* activity available in more traditional sources. I found virtually no evidence of *xiedou* in the *shishu* (summary memorials) of the routine memorials of the Board of Punishment that I perused in the Number One Archives in Beijing in search of information on *xiedou* in eighteenth- and nineteenth-century Southeast China. This surely indicates that *xiedou* were seldom reported as routine conflict.

ful neighbors, hundreds of deaths resulted, and the state eventually executed almost three hundred.

The events that led to the *xiedou* began on QL 47.8.23, with an incident at a local opera, customarily the scene of drinking, gambling, and frequent violence. On this occasion, people from Zhangzhou and people from Quanzhou were gambling together at a celebration in a Zhangzhou village in an area of mixed Zhang-Quan settlement between the Zhanghua county seat and the coast.[53] A gambling dispute between Zhangzhou and Quanzhou people led to a quarrel and an unintentional death.[54]

The subsequent violence escalated in several stages. County authorities were informed, but the Zhanghua county magistrate merely went through the motions of an investigation and failed to arrest the accused assailants.[55] Meanwhile, efforts were begun to organize private vengeance, both by the families on their own and by hired mercenaries (the leader of the Zhangzhou mercenaries, Lin Shiqian, came from Lin Shuangwen's village of Daliyi), and finally by the mobilization of entire ethnic communities. Within a week to ten days of the original incident, narrowly focused acts of vengeance carried out by surname groups expanded to organized offensive and defensive violence, expressed along ethnic lines.[56]

An examination of this escalation reveals elements of the *xiedou* as feud and the *xiedou* as racket. The confession of Quanzhou leader Xie Xiao contains many elements that suggest *xiedou* as feud.[57] Xie was the leader of the early Zhanghua Quanzhou efforts to defend against Zhangzhou attacks. Xie, 65 years old, was a longtime resident of Taiwan, having migrated from Jinjiang county, Quanzhou, with his father in QL 12 (1747). Like most migrants, Xie's family had started out as farmers, but at some point had made enough money for Xie to open a dyeing shop in Fanzigou (the first village attacked by Zhangzhou mercenaries). In fact, Xie appears to have been at least moderately wealthy: his eldest son had purchased a *jiansheng* degree. Moreover, despite his leadership of the Quanzhou forces in this *xiedou* engagement, Xie was apparently not ethnically rigid, for his daughter was married to a man from Guangdong.[58]

Xie agreed that the original death at the festival had been "accidental," and placed some of the blame for the ensuing violence on the failure of the Zhanghua authorities to honor the Quanzhou community's request for an investigation, noting that the "mutual grudge" that led to the *xiedou* developed as a result of the magistrate's failure to act on the Quanzhou complaints. According to Xie's deposition: "On . . . [QL 47.8.28] the Zhangzhou villagers . . . readied themselves to organize the Zhangzhou [gang from] Daliyi to plunder and kill throughout the [Quanzhou] villages [around] Fanzigou. They let it be known that they would kill every

Quanzhou person they saw. . . . [A worried Quanzhou man] told . . . [me] about all this, and asked me what to do."[59] This suggests that Xie had not been party to any of the surname-group violence, and that he had remained passive up to a certain point.

Xie also argued that violence should have ceased following Quanzhou "victories" early in the *xiedou*. He seems to have been motivated by an obvious need to defend his village against outside aggressors, rather than by entrepreneurial considerations, and he had planned only to exact revenge for the Quanzhou deaths and injuries suffered during the Zhangzhou attacks and, with the achievement of balanced losses, to call a halt to the *xiedou*. Given the regional tradition of *xiedou* and the rough-and-ready conditions on the Taiwan frontier, private violence was legitimate.

It is possible to see in Xie's actions an attempt to follow the rules of the feud by engaging in pre-set battles and by achieving balanced losses. Xie, and perhaps the Zhangzhou leaders too, also expected that if the tacit rules were kept, the authorities would leave them alone. But indiscriminate looting and attack were not part of what Xie accepted as legitimate violence, and when he realized that the violence was continuing to expand and that the government would become involved in its suppression, he abandoned his Taiwan community and returned to the mainland. There is no way of knowing what would have happened to the course of Quanzhou violence if he had stayed behind. But his flight left a vacuum of leadership, to be filled either by mercenaries or by the local underclass. From this perspective, the archival records of Taiwanese *xiedou* reveal continuities with the tradition of legitimate private violence that ought to have limited the sort of violence that began to occur around the time of Xie's exodus. The legitimate private violence waged by Xie Xiao should have worked to contain the open-ended *xiedou* practiced by the Zhangzhou mercenary Lin Shiqian.

Although Lin Shiqian left no confession, it is difficult to see him as anything other than a mercenary strongman. Within one day after being approached by the Zhangzhou parties to the initial violence, he organized a force of over 100 men who went on the attack the next day in an area at some distance from Lin's home base. Government documents single Lin out as a major force in the escalation of *xiedou* violence in Zhanghua, and his desire for revenge helped to change the focus of violence from specific targets within the Quanzhou community to the Quanzhou community at large. If Xie Xiao exemplifies a community leader concerned with the protection of community security and honor, Lin Shiqian exemplifies a mercenary whose business was violence. It seems clear, moreover, that Lin's stance was more common than Xie's in this conflict.[60]

Several of those connected with the leadership of the Zhangzhou side of the violence were Small Knives Society members: two had been arrested for their society connections some years before the 1782 *xiedou*, and Lin Shiqian recruited at least one—and probably more—Small Knives Society members to his mercenary band. In the wake of the feud, Qing authorities executed nine Small Knives Society members for having looted and killed, and arrested 24 others (who apparently had not been involved in the feud).[61] The participation of these secret society elements strengthens the contention that *xiedou* in this case mixed ethnic and entrepreneurial motives.

Documents describing the violence in Zhuluo also highlight the role of another set of actors: the underclass. Taiwan brigade general Jin Dangui noted this in a memorial:

> When I arrived at Zhuluo city, I learned that the villages to the south of Bengang along the seacoast on the Zhuluo-Zhanghua border had all been burned. When I inquired about the reason I learned that Taiwan had long been troubled by a great many no-goods [*feilei*], which are called locally "*luohanjiao*" ["arhat's feet"]. These are the people's greatest enemies. They take advantage of any disturbance. Recently, they took advantage of the feuding between the Zhangzhou and Quanzhou villages, and egged them on. In Zhangzhou villages they would cry that the Quanzhou people were coming to kill them. In Quanzhou villages they would cry that the Zhangzhou people were coming to surround and kill them. The result was that everyone became more and more troubled, and small villages fled to seek the protection of large villages. This left the houses in the small villages empty, and the *luohanjiao* burned and looted.[62]

A check through the lists of participants in various phases of the *xiedou* violence in both Zhanghua and Zhuluo reveals references at virtually every point to "hangers-on" (*fuhe*) who apparently had no clear relationship to the defensive organization or the community to which it was attached. Lin Shiqian's recruitment efforts, for example, are described in the following terms: "Lin Shiqian . . . sent . . . [deputies] to recruit [*zhaoji*] Huang Quan from Fangqiaotou village, as well as Lin Asai and Lin Ma, Lin Shiqian's lineage members from near Daliyi, assembling some 45 people in all. In addition, there were also 36 people from a neighboring village and also some Zhangzhou men from outer villages who had heard about it and wanted to join in."[63] Whatever else these volunteers were, they were not part of a defense corps attached to a solidary ethnic community.

In sum, the well-documented Zhang-Quan *xiedou* of 1782 permits us to identify the major participants in the violence and to chart the trajectory of the feud. In this particular instance, it seems quite clear that entrepreneurial considerations directed the course of the violence. The leadership was in the hands of mercenaries and hangers-on, and considerations of honor and balanced violence were only pretexts for their looting and robbery.

One of the earliest Qing examples of *xiedou* activity in the region, the 1769–70 Fujian-Hakka violence in Fengshan county, Taiwan, displays several elements of the same sort of profit seeking. The violence broke out during the Huang Jiao uprising, which diverted Qing troops and provided the Fengshan Hakka community with a pretext to reactivate their *yimin* status, earned through loyal service to the state in helping to suppress the Zhu Yigui rebellion in 1721, and to organize for violence against the local Fujian community.[64] Such opportunism was probably not unusual in the context of feud violence, ethnically organized or otherwise. In addition, when officials sought out village elders to try to get them to agree to stop the violence, many elders indicated that they lacked sufficient power to control their communities. They directed officials to "junior members" of the community, who presumably were in charge of the violence.[65] Drifters (*wulai*) also made their appearance, taking advantage of the lapse of social order to loot and pillage.[66]

The exploitation of the feud process for gain is particularly evident in a Zhang-Quan *xiedou* that broke out in Danshui, northern Taiwan, in the spring of 1809 (JQ 14). This instance of violence built on tensions created three years before when an incipient *xiedou* was suppressed by the authorities before local feelings of vengeance had been satisfied. In part, the 1809 violence was encouraged by a Zhangzhou man who had been implicated in secret society activities in late winter and had fled to the mountains to evade arrest, and then led a gang that killed Quanzhou people in a number of different locations. Naturally enough, the Quanzhou community responded with attacks on Zhangzhou communities. At this point, villages throughout the area began to hire local hangers-on (*feitu*) to protect themselves. Those hangers-on who were not engaged for "protective purposes" broadcast false rumors to stir things up even more. The cycle of militarization intensified. Stronger communities reacted to this by organizing to fight. Weaker communities fled. Thereupon, the *feitu* took advantage of the situation to loot, apparently at random, for, as the documents note, "There were those who took advantage of the situation to plunder the villages of their own ethnic identity."[67]

These archival sources permit us to ground official commentary concerning the nature of *xiedou* in specific events rather than disconnected observations. They include observations to support the entrepreneurial interpretation of *xiedou*, although we certainly find elements of the feud as more traditionally understood. Of course, I am not suggesting that these instances are representative of all Qing *xiedou*. Balanced violence on a smaller scale, which surely characterized many cases of *xiedou*, did not invite official intervention and is thus underrepresented in the archives. Nonetheless, Qing officials grouped these large incidents together with other *xiedou*, and in the absence of richer sources on "classical" aspects of the Chinese feud, attention to these larger incidents seems justified. In any case, it is not my intention to dismiss the complexity of the factors that contributed to feud violence, or to reduce *xiedou* to entrepreneurship pure and simple. My goal has been to show that Qing officials themselves made observations concerning *xiedou* that support the sort of entrepreneurial interpretation they often put forward concerning brotherhood associations, but at the same time failed to draw the obvious conclusions from those observations.

Qing Representations of Xiedou

Turning from historical interpretation of Qing feuds to an examination of how Qing authorities understood and dealt with *xiedou*, one is struck first by the relative scarcity of laws treating the problem. Of the numerous laws on the books directed at collective violence resembling *xiedou*, few mentioned *xiedou* by name. The term "*xiedou*" appears to have come into common usage only in the 1720's (as a contraction of such four-character phrases as *chixie xiangdou*—"to fight each other with weapons"), suggesting that *xiedou* were a Qing phenomenon even if feudlike violence had a longer history (in the same way that *hui* were a Qing phenomenon, even though brotherhoods dated back to antiquity). The frequent mention of *xiedou* in memorials to the throne and in the statecraft writings of officials who served in Southeast China also suggests that they were a frequent occurrence and a moderately serious social problem in the region. It is therefore curious that in the mushrooming number of substatutes in Qing law, designed to deal with every conceivable problem, including brotherhood associations, the same sort of legal remedies were not employed for *xiedou*.

There were, as noted, laws directed at collective violence: the "quarrels and blows" (*dou'ou*) section of the code prescribes penalties for fights between individuals and between groups, premeditated or spontaneous, using hands and feet or weapons, resulting in the loss of teeth, fingers, hair, eyes, genitals or life itself.[68] The laws on premeditated murder apply even more directly to the kinds of feuds that were the product of community leadership.[69] In 1741, a substatute that appears to be aimed directly at *xiedou* was added to the Qing code:

When those who inhabit riverine and coastal areas* attack each other with spears and clubs, let the ringleaders of each side and those who sounded the gong to call the people together be sentenced to 100 strokes of the heavy bamboo and exile at a distance of 3,000 *li*. Those criminals who committed injury to others should be sentenced to 100 strokes of the heavy bamboo and three years imprisonment; as for hangers-on who injured no one, let them wear the cangue for one month and receive 40 blows of the bamboo.[70]

This substatute was originally proposed in 1659, and was designed, according to Xue Yunsheng, compiler of the authoritative *Duli cunyi*, to "punish feuds heavily."[71]

Nonetheless, the 1741 substatute does not use the term *xiedou* and might apply to any number of forms of violence. It was not until the early 1820's that laws directed specifically at *xiedou* were added to the Code. These laws are quite detailed, attempt to distinguish *xiedou* from routine collective violence (defining *xiedou* as requiring prior collection of fees and determination of the time to fight), and, like the laws directed at brotherhood associations and secret societies, seek to determine appropriate penalties for various levels of violence. The important provisions of the first laws include:

In Guangdong, Fujian, Guangxi, Jiangxi, Hunan, and Zhejiang when groups assemble to attack each other, unless it is a routine case of collective assault . . . [and] if it is determined that there was prior collection of fees and the establishment of a time to feud and kill each other; and if the number of people amassed amounts to 10 or 20 or more, resulting in the death of four or more members of the opposing group, then the ringleader in the organization of the group[s] should be punished with death by strangulation. When the number of group members exceeds 30, and the number of dead exceeds four, or if the number of group members is less than 30, but the number of dead exceeds 10, then let the ringleader in the organization of the group[s] be sentenced to beheading. . . . If two or three members of one family are killed, then the ringleader . . . should die either by strangulation or beheading. . . . As for those who were called in the excitement of the moment to aid in the battle, and who had not intended to join in the feud, then assign their guilt according to the original joint assault [*gong'ou*] statute. If local officials do not try the ringleaders, but rather protect them, and handle feud cases as if they were [other kinds of] cases, then the viceroy or governor should impeach such officials.[72]

The second substatute promises even more state intervention into local institutions:

* Xue 1970: 893 speculates that this refers to the south in general.

When *xiedou* occur in Guangdong and Fujian, if those involved employ lineage land or moneys to purchase [lit. bribe—*huimai*] a substitute, thus creating the conditions for a feud,* then in addition to the strict sentencing of the chief purchaser, investigate the property of the lineage hall in question, and after leaving several tens of *mou* of sacrificial land to provide the wherewithal to continue the ancestral sacrifices, distribute the remainder of the land and monies to the [other] branches of the lineage. If the lineage heads [*zuzhang*] or community compact leaders [*xiangyue*] are unable to point out those who collected property for the purchase of criminals, then sentence the lineage heads to beating and exile [*zhangliu*] according to the statute dealing with premeditated collective assault. . . . Give the community compact leaders 60 strokes of the heavy bamboo and imprison them for one year.[73]

These provisions were aimed directly at the *xiedou* of the Southeast Coast and might have been effective in coping with certain forms of *xiedou* violence. I have not done enough research in nineteenth-century sources to know whether the laws were effective, or were even used; but if the memorials and statecraft writings of officials who served in the region are to be believed, decades of feuding had passed before the state formulated laws that mentioned *xiedou* by name and designed provisions specifically for this type of violence—an obvious contrast to the legal hyperactivity in the case of brotherhoods and secret societies.

One suspects that legal remedies were slow in coming because legal methods were rarely employed in dealing with *xiedou*, common though they were. Officials who served in Southeast China in the late eighteenth and early nineteenth centuries were well aware of their frequency. Xie Jinluan wrote:

There is not one feud-free county in Quanzhou or Zhangzhou, and . . . there is no feud-free year in either of the counties. In each county, if the number of feud-related deaths does not exceed one hundred, then there are at least several tens; many cases are not reported, so the officials have no way of knowing [the actual number]. . . . If one could stop one county from feuding and kidnapping, then each year several tens of deaths could be avoided. . . . A prefect could save several thousand people.[74]

Yao Ying observed that in Pinghe county in southern Fujian "there are no less than a thousand accumulated cases [of *xiedou*], most of which involve homicide committed during robbery, feuds, and abductions."[75] Wang Zhiyi reported that since taking up his post as governor of Fujian in 1796 (QL 60), he had processed several tens of cases of local feuding.[76]

* Substitutes promised to admit guilt and turn themselves in to the authorities in the event that the *xiedou* resulted in deaths and prompted official intervention.

Virtually everyone who wrote about the Minnan-Yuedong region listed *xiedou* as one of the major problems of governance faced by officials who served there.

And yet, in contrast to the frequent mention of the headaches caused by *xiedou*, records of official prosecution of actual *xiedou* incidents are rare. Some of the officials who bemoaned the problems *xiedou* caused did mention, in anecdotal fashion, particular cases in which they were involved. Gazetteers occasionally list *xiedou* in their "military affairs" section. Genealogies make infrequent mention of difficulties with surrounding lineages. Archival records of *xiedou* incidents are surprisingly sparse. If it were not for the writings of the officials who served in the region and the general reputation of the inhabitants as "perverse" and "quarrelsome," the historian would never suspect that *xiedou* constituted an important social problem. But *xiedou* must have been pervasive and troublesome; there is no reason for officials to fabricate vexing problems and confess their inability to deal with them. And if *xiedou* constituted frequent, vexing problems and yet left little record of official intervention, the most plausible explanation is that officials rarely intervened in *xiedou* violence.

Why not? First, feuds were messy affairs, embedded in the local social landscape, frequently connected with local elites—in sum, unlikely to be resolved quickly and permanently by the decisive action of "alien" officials whose tenure in the region was likely to be short. Intervention in *xiedou* violence was risky for an official's career, and no doubt in many cases moralistic criticism of the perverse locals substituted for direct action. Second, local militarization for purposes of self-defense received limited sanction in the Chinese statecraft tradition,[77] and the Southeast Coast had a long history of piracy and banditry and of local organization to combat pirates and bandits.[78] Under these conditions, officials expected to find groups of armed men in the backwaters of Southeast China where state presence was at a minimum, and they recognized that a certain amount of violence was inevitable. Chen Shengshao's comment about the southern Fujianese county of Zhaoan captures some of this attitude:

> The second township is a long way from the county seat. The inhabitants of this area are stubborn and wild, and will not answer a government summons. The runners are unable to get a single cent, a single meal, or a single interview out of them, and if they manage to arrest someone, he is often forcibly taken back, so they simply refuse to go. If the army goes in, then the inhabitants flee and return according to the troop movements, which only bankrupts the army. They live in mountain villages, and dare not

enter the county town, so people grow old and die without knowing what the yamen is. The officials are unable to settle disputes, and the people do not report disputes to the officials. So they take revenge on one another, which leads to kidnappings and *xiedou*.[79]

Third, some officials were probably not altogether unhappy to see powerful local groups deplete their resources in ways that were generally self-regulating. Maurice Freedman has pointed out the fundamental ambivalence of the Chinese state toward powerful lineages, which could be at once conservative agents of socialization and control as well as competitors with the state for local influence.[80] In the wake of a nasty bout of *xiedou* violence in Taiwan in 1809, Fujian-Zhejiang Governor-General Fang Weidian noted that although everyone hoped that Taiwan's ethnic problems would be overcome with time, subethnic *xiedou* nonetheless remained more tolerable than uprisings. "It would not be appropriate," Fang continued, "if the three groups [i.e., Zhangzhou people, Quanzhou people, and Hakkas] banded together in an important overseas area. In addition, we are fortunate that the different groups are divided and will not yield to each other. Whenever evil people rise up, their ethnic enemies become *yimin* and fight them." Fang suggested that officials continue to make use of this antagonism—while attempting to solve the problem of recurrent violence.[81] It is rare that officials admit to such a cynical, Machiavellian view of violent acts that, in the case Fang is discussing, resulted in dozens of deaths and possibly hundreds of injuries, and it is unlikely that all officials shared these views. Nonetheless, conditions in the Southeast Coast destroyed the idealism of at least one other official. Yao Ying, who served as a magistrate of several Fujian counties in the early nineteenth century, noted:

> The people live in walled forts. They are completely equipped with all the implements they need. . . . If the troops arrive with great numbers to attempt an arrest, then the accused flees, leaving an empty house. If the troops are few, then the locals loiter around their doors [openly] resisting arrest. . . . If the arrest of criminals requires the use of troops, and . . . even leads to armed affrays [between the people and the] officials, then how are these people different from rebels [*luanmin*]? Thus it reaches the point that we destroy their lairs and burn their houses; there is no room for permissiveness.[82]

It is not difficult to imagine that an official like Yao, no matter how much he might deplore such practices as *xiedou*, could also grasp their utility in maintaining a certain balance of power.

These considerations may explain the reticence of local officials to intervene in ongoing *xiedou* violence, and the reticence itself may account for the relative lack of laws dealing with *xiedou*, since imperial comments, which would have been prompted by official documents, are the major sources for new substatutes. In addition, I suspect that no special effort was made to enact laws to contain *xiedou* simply because *xiedou* conformed to the social language of the Southeast Coast—territory and lineage (and indeed to much Chinese thought about social organization in general). In spite of a good deal of evidence to the contrary, when Chinese officials looked at *xiedou*, they saw lineage and village leaders, not marginal young toughs. Lineage and village leaders were part of the Confucian hierarchy, which was governed by "the rule of men" rather than by "the rule of law." Indeed, if Qing officials and lawmakers *had* adopted the "entrepreneurial" view of *xiedou* put forward in this chapter, it would have been a chilling admission of the lack of state control over the rural areas. Without the Confucian hierarchy, real or imagined, parts of late imperial China were essentially ungovernable.

Qing representations of brotherhood associations and secret societies were complex. On the one hand, laws against such "combinations" were extremely harsh, prescribing the death penalty in many instances. Such harshness suggests Qing concern over heterodoxy and rebellion, although detailed discussions of the nature of the heterodoxy of brotherhood associations are largely absent. On the other hand, Qing lawmakers constantly fiddled with the laws against brotherhood associations, attempting to bring crime and punishment into accord and pointing out legal practices not covered by the laws. At some level, Qing officials recognized that brotherhood associations were a part of the local social order and were not going away, even while they remained prudently concerned about the criminal and rebellious aspects of many brotherhood associations.

The comparison of Qing attitudes toward brotherhood associations and feuds suggests the source of the Qing inconsistency toward associations. In many instances, brotherhood associations and groups at feud could be equally violent, and the violence could be directed by the same marginal elements. Nonetheless, Qing officials generally treated brotherhood associations much more harshly than groups at feud, despite their similarities. The failure of Qing authorities to acknowledge the similarities between the activities of brotherhood associations and groups at feud alerts us to an important reason for the Qing fixation on brotherhood associations. Brotherhood associations, part of the fragmented, mobile, sometimes desperate social order of late imperial China, fell outside the hierarchies through which the Qing sought to understand and rule their far-flung, overpopulated empire. From the ideological perspective of the Qing state, the marginal status of most brotherhood and secret society members suggested a dangerous absence of control, and therefore carried connotations of heterodoxy and rebellion—even when their daily activities appeared relatively innocuous.

CHAPTER 6

Chinese Brotherhood Associations
and Late Imperial China

Had this book been written a generation ago, its emphasis would have been on Chinese brotherhood associations as examples of simmering popular discontent, fueled either by class or by bureaucratic oppression, or by both. In the background would have sounded the beat of the approaching revolution, the major event of modern Chinese history. Indeed, the activities of brotherhood associations and secret societies lend themselves readily to interpretations based on collective violence. There are indications, for example, that brotherhood associations and secret societies were largely the creations of *young* men. The observation of Ji Qiguang, magistrate of Zhuluo county, Taiwan in the late seventeenth century, that brotherhood associations were "evil customs" practiced by "young no-goods" is only one of many such comments.[1] To the extent that this is true, it provides a partial explanation of the relationships between population growth, social structural change, and violence: high birth rates produced more young men than could be absorbed into the institutions of family, lineage, or village, and these young marginals turned to violence.[2] From another perspective, the persistent linkage of brotherhood associations to the lineages and villages of Southeast China—one of the major themes of this volume—suggests that the violence of brotherhood associations might be best understood as a sort of low-grade virus, in which the displacement produced by population growth on a static resource base was channeled back into the heart of community life by way of "survival strategies" of "alienated" brotherhood associations.

I have not attempted to test these hypotheses in the present work, in part for lack of evidence but more fundamentally because of conceptual concerns. The huge literature analyzing and comparing collective vio-lence and rebellion is intimately linked to the discourse of modernity, and seeks to unravel the complex causes and effects of the industrial and political revolutions that have marked our modern experience. It is not obvious that the categories employed in this literature are appropriate to the analysis of late imperial China. This is doubly true because the rise of Industrial East Asia and the spectacular collapse of Soviet commu-nism in the late twentieth century have complicated our understanding of both "modernity" and "revolution."

If this study shies away from global comparisons, it nonetheless per-mits consideration of the power and influence of the Chinese state vis-à-vis local society in late imperial China. In this context, the history of brotherhood associations chronicled here yields two opposing perspec-tives. The first emphasizes the power of the Chinese state, as seen par-ticularly in the Qing reaction to the Lin Shuangwen rebellion of 1787–88. As already noted, Lin's uprising can be seen as a defining moment in the history of Chinese brotherhood associations. Simple brotherhoods, named brotherhoods, and secret societies had all proliferated before Lin's uprising and had excited the intermittent hostility of the state, but Lin's year-long rebellion firmly established the secret society as a powerful force in the minds of Qing officials and the common people. Qing offi-cials during the 1790's understood all brotherhoods in the Southeast Coast to be dangerous expressions of heterodoxy and sedition, and the popular influence of the Tiandihui grew enormously—in part because of the relative success of Lin Shuangwen, in part because Qing suppression forced Tiandihui members out of their original home base and into new areas, where they found new recruits. Indeed, it is a plausible argument that Lin's rebellion, and the decade of suppression that followed, helped to transform eighteenth-century brotherhoods, devoted to mutual aid and criminal entrepreneurship, into nineteenth-century secret societies, pledged to anti-Manchu rebellion. In a sense, the paranoid Qing state created a force of opposition out of an informal institution, an ironic tes-timony to the power of the state.

At the same time, we should be careful not to overemphasize the power of the Qing state to shape local society, and herein lies the other perspective one can draw from this study. Historians writing in the late twentieth century take the power of the Chinese state very seriously, as might be expected given the history of the People's Republic of China and the tragic events of June 1989. However, important differences sepa-rate the eighteenth-century Chinese state from the present Communist regime. Although committed to autocracy and capable of spurts of fear-some power, the Qing state of the late eighteenth century was also be-coming increasingly *superficial* in its relationship to local society. In spite of increasing numbers of supernumeraries, overworked Qing officials were often simply overwhelmed by the undisciplined mobile order brought about by population growth and commercialization.

Many of the findings of this volume highlight the local interpretations given to brotherhood associations that paid little heed to the history of Qing persecution. The clearest examples of these local interpretations are of course the Tiandihui groups of the early nineteenth-century western Fujian–eastern Jiangxi region, who understood the Tiandihui as a set of magico-religious practices that invested members with supernatural power and protection, even though the Tiandihui was brought to the region by society members fleeing Qing persecution. Some of the magico-religious practices of the western Fujian–eastern Jiangxi region were not unrelated to anti-Manchu rebellion, but they clearly did not originate in rebellious concerns, nor was rebellion the primary motivation for joining the regional Tiandihui. Even the founding of the Heaven and Earth Society, which has frequently been linked to anti-Manchu consciousness or Qing persecution, might just as easily be understood as a repackaging of familiar elements of Chinese popular culture, directed as much at religious, or "cosmic," concerns as at particular Manchu policies.

Both these perspectives are valid. Narratives seeking to trace the evolution of the twentieth-century Chinese state, as well as interpretations emphasizing the mutability and flexibility of Chinese society—or even the emergence of forces that might constitute a "civil society" in China—can draw on the material presented here. Surely one of the defining features of the late imperial order was that the state lacked the resources to realize its authoritarian vision, which permitted the development of a freewheeling social order—within limits.

A closer consideration of these "limits" may be in order, to sharpen our appreciation of the distinctive character of late imperial China. One valuable way to gain perspective on these "limits" is to compare the experiences of Chinese brotherhood associations in Southeast Asia with brotherhood experiences in China proper. As is well known, virtually the entire population of the Chinese communities of Southeast Asia traced their roots to the Southeast Coast, the majority having migrated during the eighteenth and nineteenth centuries. The social habits of these migrant Chinese were similar if not identical to those examined in this volume who remained in China proper, and the brotherhood association clearly traveled with the migrants as part of their cultural and organizational heritage. However, in the relatively underpopulated, undergoverned societies of precolonial and even colonial Southeast Asia, the Chinese brotherhood associations assumed economic and political roles unavailable to them in China proper.

In some parts of Southeast Asia, small-scale mutual aid organizations imported from China became *corporations* based on shareholding. The Chinese mining kongsis (the Southeast Asian equivalent of brotherhood associations) of the Dutch West Indies possessions of West Borneo and Bangka, for example, built directly on the ritual traditions of brotherhood associations and secret societies; the oaths of brotherhood that accompanied initiation into the kongsi promised the reconstruction of kinship relations in an environment of unrelated young men in a way that is completely familiar to the Chinese situation. The difference was that membership in these kongsis was based on shares. The shares could be procured through labor as well as by purchase, and they offered the promise of participation in the economic fortunes of the mine or plantation. Moreover, to facilitate large-scale economic activity, and to provide protection from native or colonial military challengers, the Chinese kongsis readily came together to form large federations (also called kongsis), which organized substantial networks to keep the mines supplied with new labor, or fielded thousands of fighters to meet military opponents.[3]

Another example of the larger roles available to Chinese brotherhood associations outside China is the history of the Ngee Heng kongsi (mandarin, *yixing*) in precolonial and colonial Malaya. The rituals of this kongsi clearly identify it as part of the Tiandihui tradition; members joined the kongsi in elaborate initiation rituals that involved blood oaths and anti-Manchu symbols. Nonetheless, the Ngee Heng was instrumental in the development of the pepper and gambier plantation agriculture in the Johore and Riau regions of the Malay peninsula, which eventually became Singapore. Here, as in the Dutch East Indies, the brotherhood association provided an element of social cohesion in a frontier community of new migrants, and at the same time lent a structure on which to build larger economic organizations.[4] One could easily cite similar examples for Chinese communities in Thailand, Cambodia, the Philippines, and elsewhere in Southeast Asia (indeed, elsewhere in the worldwide Chinese diaspora).[5]

The social and political roles assumed by the Chinese brotherhood associations in Southeast Asia are equally revealing. The flexible kongsi, often translated as "district and clan association"[6] or "dialect association,"[7] satisfied the religious needs of émigrés by establishing temples to the gods of the locality from which a particular migrant group hailed and providing a community within which to celebrate the festivals of the Chinese ritual calendar.[8] The kongsi also provided lodging for new arrivals, aid in securing employment, medical care, and sometimes free burial—all classic offerings of mutual aid societies.

From a political perspective, one should note that leadership of the mining kongsis in Borneo was temporary and by popular election, an egalitarian aspect of brotherhood practices rarely noted in the Chinese context. It is also significant that although the secret societies of the region maintained their ostensibly anti-Manchu initiation rituals (in spite of their new political context), rebellion was not a constant focus of their activities. Instead, both kongsis and "secret societies" helped to arbitrate conflict within the Chinese community, and they produced community leaders who could act as intermediaries between the colonial state and the Chinese population.[9] Early colonial Singapore legally recognized kongsis and secret societies as a form of voluntary association—to which the vast majority of Chinese belonged—with a legitimate role in the governance of the Chinese community.

To balance this rosy picture, one should note as well the involvement of secret societies in opium distribution and smuggling, gambling, prostitution, and protection rackets. Not all these activities were illegal (particularly in Southeast Asia) until fairly late in the nineteenth century, and it was only after colonial governments undertook a consistent policy of suppression of the societies that, as had happened earlier in Qing China, the societies became criminal.

Even this brief sketch of the experiences of Chinese brotherhood associations in Southeast Asia vindicates an interpretation of such organizations as emerging, nonelite social institutions. In a less crowded, less competitive environment, oceans away from the Confucian state and the Confucian elite, Chinese brotherhood associations provided the organizational, social, political, and cultural means by which the poor, marginalized migrants of the Southeast Coast forged new lives. It is obvious that the brotherhood association represented far more than parasitic banditry or political dissent. By the same token, many of the "limitations" of Chinese brotherhoods in China proper—their ephemeral character, their small size, their penchant for crime and racketeering—stand out less as characteristics of Chinese brotherhoods in general than as products of the specific context of the late imperial Chinese state. Even if the state was not powerful enough to stamp out brotherhood associations completely or even to impose its own meanings on associational practices, it retained sufficient power to influence the environment in which brotherhood associations functioned, and to shape the historical trajectory of a popular practice firmly embedded in local society.

Appendixes

APPENDIX A

Participation in the
Lin Shuangwen Uprising

The following data are drawn from the confessions of those arrested for their involvement in the Lin Shuangwen uprising. The data base includes 161 confessions, 138 from members of Lin Shuangwen's forces, and 23 from members of Zhuang Datian's forces. Eighty-nine of these 161 had joined the Tiandihui, while the others participated in the violence associated with the rebellion without having taken the oaths of membership. The tables that follow illustrate the value of such sources in constructing a social profile of brotherhoods, secret societies, and rebel groups. In particular, these data are helpful in assessing the degree to which such groups diverged from the norms of mainstream society in terms of marital and family relations. Throughout, I divide the data into "all rebels," which includes all 161 confessions, and "society members," which includes only those 89 who confessed to having joined the society.

A.1 *Were rebels married?*

	Number	Pct. of total	Pct. of total known
	ALL REBELS		
No	19	11.8	33.3
Yes	38	23.6	66.6
No data	104	64.6	
	SOCIETY MEMBERS		
No	10	11.2	40
Yes	15	16.9	60
No data	64	71.9	

A.2　Did rebels have children?

	Number	Pct. of total	Pct. of total known
ALL REBELS			
No	31	19.3	57.4
Yes	23	14.3	42.6
No data	107	66.5	
SOCIETY MEMBERS			
No	16	18	64
Yes	9	10.1	36
No data	64	71.9	

A.3　Did rebels have living parents?

	Number	Pct. of total	Pct. of total known
ALL REBELS			
No	31	19.3	55.4
Yes	25	15.5	44.6
No data	105	65.2	
SOCIETY MEMBERS			
No	11	12.4	44
Yes	14	15.7	56
No data	64	71.9	

A.4　Rebel Occupations

Occupation	No.	Occupation	No.
ALL REBELS			
Barber	1	Shaman	1
Butcher	1	Teacher	2
Clerk	3	Tenant	5
Diviner	1	Lineage head	1
Farmer	3	No data	123
Jiansheng/			
Estate mgr.	1	**SOCIETY MEMBERS**	
Landlord	2	Butcher	1
Laborer	2	Farmer	1
Merchant	5	Landlord	1
Mil official	1	Merchant	3
Painter	1	Painter	1
Peddler	2	Yamen runner	2
Peddler-monk	1	Bully	1
Porter	2	Tradesman	1
Runner	3	No data	77

A.5 *Average age*

All rebels = 37.3 *sui*, based on response of 106 of 161, or 65.8%.
Society members = 36.92 *sui*, based on response of 38 of 89 TDH members, or 42.7%.

A.6 *Average length of residence on Taiwan*

All rebels = 24 yrs, based on response of 34 of 161, or 21.1%.
Society members = 21.19 years, based on response of 16 of 89 TDH members, or 18%.

A.7 *Ethnic identification (by native prefecture)*

Prefecture	No.	Pct. of total	Pct. of total known
ALL REBELS			
Chaozhou	4	2.5	3.7
Taiwan	1		
Fuzhou	1		
Quanzhou	23	14.3	21
Tingzhou	3	1.9	2.8
Xinghua	1		
Zhangzhou	76	47.2	69.7
No data	52	33.3	
SOCIETY MEMBERS			
Chaozhou	2	2.2	5.1
Quanzhou	5	5.6	12.8
Tingzhou	3	3.4	7.7
Xinghua	1		
Zhangzhou	28	31.5	71.2
No data	50	56.1	

Chronology of the Lin Shuangwen Rebellion

QL 51.11.28	Lin Shuangwen's Tiandihui attacks Dadun.
QL 51.11.29	Lin Shuangwen leads successful attacks on Zhanghua and Lugang.
QL 51.12.6	Lin Shuangwen leads Li Qi, Su Po, et al. in successful attack on Zhuluo.
QL 51.12.7	Lin Shuangwen sends Wang Zuo and Lin Xiaowen north to attack Danshui.
QL 51.12.11	Lin Shuangwen leads an unsuccessful attack on the prefectural city.
QL 51.12.12	Second Captain Chen Bangguang retakes Lugang and Zhanghua for the Qing, capturing rebel general Gao Wenlin.
QL 51.12.13	Zhuang Datian leads successful attack on Fengshan.
QL 52.1.4	Naval Commander-in-Chief Huang Shijian leads 2,000 troops to the prefectural city.
QL 52.1.6	Commander-in-Chief of the Land Forces Ren Cheng'en leads 2,000 troops to Lugang.
QL 52.1.22	Brigade General Chai Daji retakes Zhuluo for the Qing, and the rebel armies retreat to the Zhuluo suburbs.
QL 52.1	Lin Shuangwen sets up his government at Zhanghua, later moving it to Daliyi.
QL 52.2.12	Lin Shuangwen, Chen Pan, and Zhou Zhenxing lead 5,000+ rebels to attack Puxinzhuang and Zhuluo.
QL 52.2.21	Brigade General Hao Zhuangyou retakes Fengshan.
QL 52.3.8	Zhuang Datian retakes Fengshan for the rebels, destroying 2,000+ Qing troops.
QL 52.3.9	The Qianlong emperor orders Huang Shijian and Ren Cheng'en removed from their posts and appoints Fujian-

	Zhejiang Governor-General Chang Qing as general to replace Huang Shijian as commander of military affairs in Taiwan.
QL 52.3.26	Lin Shuangwen sends Xu Shang and Lin Yong to lead troops in a coordinated, unsuccessful attack with Zhuang Datian on the prefectural city.
QL 52.4.4	Lin Shuangwen leads an unsuccessful three-pronged attack on Zhuluo.
QL 52.4.15	The Qing court sends Jiangnan Commander-in-Chief Lan Yuanmei to lead 2,000 troops to Taiwan, replacing the commander-in-chief of the land forces.
QL 52.4.28	Lin Shuangwen leads 9,000 men in an unsuccessful attack on Zhuluo.
QL 52.4	Fuzhou general Heng Rui leads 4,000 troops from the mainland to the prefectural city.
QL 52.5	Lin Shuangwen and Zhuang Datian lead unsuccessful coordinated attacks on the prefectural city.
QL 52.6.1	Lin Shuangwen leads a successful attack on Bengang.
QL 52.7.28	Lin Shuangwen leads an unsuccessful attack on Zhuluo.
QL 52.8.7	Lin Shuangwen leads more than 10,000 men in an unsuccessful attack on Zhuluo.
QL 52.8.9	The Qianlong emperor removes Chang Qing as general, replacing him with Fukang'an, accompanied by 9,000 additional men.
QL 52.9.12	Chen Pan leads 5,000 rebels in an unsuccessful attack on Puxinzhuang.
QL 52.9.16	Brigade General Pu Zibao retakes Bengang for the Qing.
QL 52.9.30	Lin Shuangwen leads an unsuccessful attack on Zhuluo.
QL 52.10.6	1,000 additional troops to Taiwan.
QL 52.11.1	Fukang'an arrives in Lugang.
QL 52.11.8	Councillor Hailancha breaks the siege of Zhuluo.
QL 52.11.10	Fukang'an arrives in Zhuluo.
QL 52.22.21	Fukang'an takes Douliumen.
QL 52.11.25	Fukang'an takes Daliyi.
QL 53.1.4	Lin Shuangwen captured at Laoquqi.
QL 53.2.5	Zhuang Datian captured at Langjiao, executed in the prefectural city.
QL 53.3.10	Lin Shuangwen executed in Beijiang.

SOURCE: Taken from Liu Ruzhong, *Taiwan Lin Shuangwen qiyi*, pp. 55–58, with modifications.

Reference Matter

Notes

Introduction

1. Isaacs 1962: 111–24.
2. Sewell 1980; Godsden 1967.
3. Zhuang 1982: 183–268.
4. Ownby 1993: 18–21.
5. Murray 1994.
6. Ma 1990; Schiffrin 1968; Wilbur 1976.
7. Tao 1943; Hirayama 1912.
8. Murray 1994: 116–50 describes this historiography. For representative works, see Xiao 1935; Luo Ergang 1943.
9. Chesneaux 1972: 2.
10. Ward and Stirling 1925; Wynne 1941; Blythe 1969; Morgan 1960; Milne 1826; Williams 1849.
11. Wynne 1941; Comber 1959; Blythe 1969.
12. With some significant exceptions, such as Pickering 1878, 1879, where Pickering, as Protector of the Chinese in the Straits Settlements, reported his commentary as participant-observer in a five-hour secret society initiation ceremony.
13. Schlegel 1866 is an excellent example.
14. Representative works include Zhou and Shao 1993, Qin 1988, Cai 1990, 1987, Zhuang 1981.
15. Wagner 1982; Muramatsu 1960.
16. Perry 1980: 208–47; Wou 1994: 51–97.
17. Ownby forthcoming.
18. Li Guoqi 1982: 2.
19. Wang Yeh-chien 1986: 82.
20. On the late Ming court, see Struve 1984; for an English-language introduction to the vast literature on Zheng Chenggong, see Croizier 1977. A more recent English-language treatment of the Zheng period is Shepherd 1993: 91–104.

21. Hsieh 1932; Ura 1954; Luo Xianglin 1973; R. Watson 1985: 21–23.

22. On commercial prosperity, see Ng 1983; on Han colonization of Taiwan, see Shepherd 1993; on commercial relations between the mainland and Taiwan, see Lin Renchuan 1983.

23. On commercial contracts, see Yang Guozhen 1988; on lineages, see Freedman 1958, 1966; Fu 1961; Mori 1986; and Zheng 1992; on land ownership, see Fujii 1984; on local religious traditions, see Schipper 1985; ter Haar 1990; and Dean 1993.

24. Ng 1983: 12.

25. Rawski 1972.

26. Shepherd 1993: 161–62.

27. Cited in Wang Yeh-chien 1986: 92, n. 35. For more general information on emigration, see Wen 1984.

28. Averill 1983.

29. Entenmann 1982: 78–86.

30. Ng 1983: 179–82.

31. Ibid., 38.

32. Ibid.

33. Gardella 1976.

34. Skinner 1977: 229.

35. See So 1975.

36. Most recently in Shepherd 1993: 91–104.

37. Vermeer 1990b: 10. Vermeer cites the figures 1.74 to 1.4 million, but these clearly refer to taxpayers rather than population. I have multiplied by 5.5 to estimate population.

38. Zhu 1986, 2: 411.

39. See, for example, Yao Qisheng, Kangxi period, *youweixuan, wengao* 2: 47a–b.

40. Yang and Chen 1985, 1987.

41. See Zhuang and Wang 1985: 426–30 for an illustration of the effects of the evacuation of Minnan lineages; Vermeer 1990a: 120–32 discusses the evacuation in the context of Xinghua prefecture, Fujian; R. Watson 1985: 21–24 provides a discussion of similar events in Guangdong.

42. Zhu 1986, 2: 427–31.

43. See Zhuang 1989: 6–15.

44. Ownby 1989: 356–63, based on Chen Ch'i-nan 1987: 95–97; Huang Xiuzheng 1976: 85–86; Zhang 1970: 35–43; Kong 1986: 387–95.

45. Zhang 1970: 35–43.

46. Tong 1991: 74.

47. Buoye 1990: 252–53, tables 6 and 7.

48. Ibid., 246.

49. Cited in Vermeer 1990b: 6.

50. Chen Shengshao 1983: 86.

51. Yao Ying 1963a: 5–8. Yao Ying, from Tongcheng, Anhui, earned his *jinshi* degree in 1808. From 1816 to 1818 he served as Pinghe county magistrate, from 1818 to 1819 as Longqi county magistrate, from 1819 to 1823 as Taiwan county magistrate, and from 1838 to 1843 as Taiwan *daotai*. For more details on Yao's life, see Polachek 1992: 68–71.

52. Shepherd 1993: 4.
53. Ibid. 430.
54. Perkins 1969: 207.
55. Ho 1959: 266.
56. Ng 1983: 15–16.
57. Boxer 1953: 248.
58. Chen Ch'iu-k'un 1978; Wang Yeh-chien 1986; Ho 1959: 268.
59. Cited in Zhao 1928: j. 314/95: 1190.
60. Rawski 1972: 51; Ng 1983: 21, 131.
61. Elvin 1973: 208.
62. Cited in Tang 1987: 10.
63. Cited in ibid., 15.
64. Ibid. See also Harrell 1974.
65. Cited in Tang 1987: 21–22.
66. Cited in ibid., 23.
67. Lamley 1981: 302–3; Chen Ch'i-nan 1987: 52–54.
68. Hsu 1980: 88.
69. Wang Shih-ch'ing 1974.
70. J. Watson 1988.
71. Chen Shengshao 1983: 137–38.
72. Cheng, Daoguang period, j. 2: 21a–36a.
73. Ibid.
74. *JJCLF, NYFQ* 3312.8. QL 48.2.23 (1783).
75. Lamley 1981; Ownby 1990.
76. See Zhuang 1989: 6–15.
77. See *TDH* 1980–88. Of course, not all these documents are of equal value. Most of the first five volumes of this series are devoted to the Lin Shuangwen uprising, and the majority of the documents treating the uprising are more valuable for research in Qing military capacity or elite politics than for brotherhood associations.
78. For an excellent evocation of this legal culture, see Kuhn 1990.
79. See Naquin 1976.

Chapter 1

1. Tong 1991.
2. Zhuang 1990a: 112–41.
3. C. K. Yang 1975: 197.
4. Sangren 1984.
5. Clawson 1989 notes similar developments in the context of brotherhoods in nineteenth-century America.
6. Naba 1938: 41.
7. *Zhongwen dacidian* 1973, 9: 263.
8. Naba 1938: 43.
9. Ibid., 41.
10. Shimizu 1951: 392–93, 397–98.
11. Ibid., 394–97.
12. Cited in ibid., 418–19.

13. Cited in ibid., 419.
14. Cited in ibid., 456.
15. Cited in ibid., 457.
16. Cited in ibid., 460.
17. Cited in ibid., 463–64.
18. Cited in ibid., 466.
19. Perry 1980: 53; Kulp 1925: 196–203.
20. Cited in Shimizu 1951: 469.
21. Shimizu 1951: 499. See also Wang Zongpei 1931: 1–9.
22. Cited in Shimizu 1951: 487.
23. Cited in ibid., 500.
24. On the rotating credit society in contemporary Taiwan, see Winn 1994: 214–19; and *Taiwan* 1985. Other treatments of twentieth-century Chinese rotating credit societies include Wang Zongpei 1931; Kulp 1925, 1: 190–96; Fei 1939: 267–74; and Gamble 1944. For cross-cultural comparison, see Geertz 1962.
25. Shimizu 1951: 489–90, 496–97.
26. Zhou Mi 1872.
27. Naquin and Yü 1992.
28. *Xinghua fuzhi* (Fujian) Ming Hongzhi edition j. 15 p. 6b; *Huian xianzhi* (Fujian) Qing Jiaqing edition, j. 4: 3a; *Funing zhouzhi* (Fujian) Ming Wanli edition, j. 2: 5a.
29. Cohen 1990: 521–28.
30. Wang Shih-ch'ing 1974: 80, 85.
31. Shimizu 1951: 519–60, 610–42.
32. Ibid., 462.
33. Lewis 1990: vii, 7.
34. Ibid., 43.
35. Ibid.
36. Ibid., 45.
37. Ibid., 46.
38. A detailed description of a Triad ceremony, including blood oath, from early nineteenth-century Singapore is in Abdullah 1970: 204–17. Murray 1994: 29, 93–100, 239–46 offers several examples of Chinese blood oaths. Jordan 1985: 254–62 provides a more modern version of ritual brotherhood in contemporary Taiwan.
39. Lewis 1990: 78.
40. Ter Haar n.d.
41. The early history of the *Shuihuzhuan* is treated in Irwin 1966: 23–60. Plaks 1987: 279–303 discusses the evolution of the novel to its present form, and also (361–76) the evolution of the *Sanguo yanyi*.
42. Egerton 1939: 6–31.
43. Ter Haar n.d.
44. Mention of Deng's blood oath is in Zhu 1986, 2: 134. Pages 113–52 of this same volume offer an extensive treatment of the uprising. An English-language introduction to the extensive Japanese studies of Deng Maoqi is Tanaka Masatoshi 1984: 202–4. The uprising is also treated in Twitchett and Grimm 1988: 312–14.

45. Specifically, by the sixteenth-century Fujianese pirate Lin Daoqian. Ter Haar n.d.

46. Fu 1961: 106.

47. *Enping xianzhi* (1825) 3: 15a.

48. Qu 1985: 248.

49. Although there are scattered references to *hui* in the late Ming and during the Ming-Qing transition (Tanaka Masatoshi 1984: 197; Wakeman 1985: 637; and Ter Haar, n.d.), there is no mention of *hui* in such standard sources as Li Wenzhi 1966 or Parsons 1970. Wang Lianmao 1987 treats what appears to be a *hui* in his study of late Ming tax resistance, but a close reading of his evidence reveals that at no point did the peasants in question refer to their organization as a *hui*.

50. Yao Qisheng, Kangxi period, *wengao* sections 2–4; Ownby 1989: 215–20.

51. *GZD YZ* 19: 37–41, 493–94.

52. *Shiliao xunkan* 1963, sec. *di*: 409b–450a.

53. Qin and Li 1986: 30–34.

54. Ibid., 34–37.

55. Zhuang 1974–75.

56. Zhuang 1981: 34–36; Shepherd 1993: 194–95.

57. *Taiwan shihō* 1910, 1, *xia*: 362–63; see Sangren 1984 on leadership terminology.

58. Pasternak 1972: 64–66; Kulp 1925: 196–203. Freedman 1966: 93 discusses the implications of Kulp's findings.

59. Zhuang 1988, 1990b; Murray 1993.

60. *Taiwan xianzhi* 1961: 230–32.

61. Ibid.

62. A Zhang-Quan *xiedou* erupted in Zhanghua in QL 40 (1775), although details are scarce. See Zhang 1970: 12; Huang Xiuzheng 1976: 85.

63. Zhuang 1974–75: 295–96.

64. Yang almost certainly acquired his *jiansheng* degree by purchase. Ho 1962: 33–34 notes that the enrollment of the Imperial Academy (Guozijian)—the institution to which *jiansheng* were supposedly attached—under the Qing "seldom exceeded 300," and that "practically anyone who could afford a little over 100 taels could obtain the *chien-sheng* title and the right to wear the scholar's gown and cap."

65. Ho 1962: 34.

66. Qin and Li 1986: 30–34.

67. For example, one of the Fumuhui discussed above was established on the date of the dragon boat festival, and the other held a meeting on Guanyin's birthday. *GZD YZ* 11: 167–69.

68. Ter Haar 1993: 164.

69. *GZD YZ* 19: 37–41. Another ostensibly criminal Fumuhui is discussed in De Groot 1972–73, 2: 472.

70. *GZZP, NMYD* 677.1, QL 7.6.12 (1742).

71. Yao Qisheng, Kangxi period, *youweixuan, wengao* section 3: 14a–15b. Ownby 1989: 215–22 provides an English-language discussion of these brotherhoods.

72. Qin and Li 1986: 34–37.

Chapter 2

1. For analysis of the military aspects of the suppression of the rebellion, see Zhuang 1982: 183–268; and Lai 1984: 37–43, 126–40, 248–54.

2. Zhuang 1981: 254; Lai 1984: 134, 385–86.

3. The actual number is recorded as 9,486, including some lost in battle and some merely injured. Zhuang 1981: 64–65.

4. Qi 1985, 1: 192, n. 55b.

5. Shepherd 1993: 161, table 6.4.

6. The single largest source of information is found in the series of documentary collections jointly edited by Zhongguo renmin daxue Qingshi yanjiusuo and Zhongguo diyi lishi dang'anguan and published under the title *Tiandihui* (seven volumes). This series includes material from the Number One Archives in Beijing relating to Tiandihui activities from the earliest reported activities through the Daoguang period. The length and size of the Lin Shuangwen uprising were such that most of the first five volumes deal with that particular uprising; nearly 1,100 documents are made available, including memorials, edicts, confessions of participants in the uprising and of civil and military officials convicted of negligence, as well as depositions of *yimin* who contributed to the suppression of Lin Shuangwen. The *Tiandihui* volumes are better indexed, easier to use, and more complete than the more traditional *Qinding pingding Taiwan jilüe*, the imperially commissioned record of the quelling of the Lin Shuangwen rebellion. This volume begins with poetry and literature treating the rebellion and proceeds to a detailed documentary chronology. There is a considerable degree of overlap with the *Tiandihui* collection, since both contain memorials, edicts, confessions, and depositions. A further valuable collection of documents is the *TAHLGJ*. This collection is divided into five chapters, the first three consisting of memorials and edicts excerpted from the *Ming-Qing shiliao* series dealing with various aspects of the reconstruction efforts following the quelling of the rebellion and with military expenditures. The last two chapters are imperial edicts sent to general Fukang'an, who eventually quelled the rebellion, in QL 52–53. Again, there is some overlap with the coverage of the two collections discussed above. Further confessions from the Palace Museum archives in Taiwan are found in Liu Ruzhong and Miao Xuemeng, eds., *Taiwan Lin Shuangwen qiyi ziliao xuanbian*. This same edition also reprints relevant passages from the *Qingshilu* and *Donghualu*, from Taiwan gazetteers, and from funerary and other literati writings. Another important source on the rebellion, Yang Tingli's *Dongying jishi*, is reprinted in Zhongguo shehui kexueyuan lishi yanjiusuo and Mingshi yanjiushi, eds., *Qingdai Taiwan nongmin qiyi shiliao xuanbian*: 113–37. Important secondary treatments include Qin 1988: 238–73; Cai 1987: 66–122; Zhuang 1981: 34–77; Liu 1982, 1989; and Zhou and Shao 1993: 48–65.

7. *Zhanghua xianzhi* 1962: 383–86.

8. Ibid., 384–85.

9. *GZD QL* 22: 804.

10. Murray 1994: 5–37 provides a useful history of the search for Tiandihui origins as well as an assessment of recently uncovered archival evidence on the topic. Recent Chinese treatments of the origins question include Zhou and Shao 1993: 3–12; Qin 1988: 61–107; and Cai 1987: 45–65, among many others.

11. Hong Xiuquan's vision is a case in point. See Kuhn 1977.

12. Ter Haar 1993: 157, notes that the characters *mudou* refer to the wooden rice measure, an essential Triad ritual item, and, as split characters, represent the character *zhu*, the surname of the Ming imperial house. A literal translation of the phrase is thus "when 'wood' (*mu*) stands and it is the age of 'the bushel' (*dou*), [somebody] will rule all under Heaven." The connotation of the split characters *mudou* strongly suggest that this "somebody" will be the Ming.

13. Ter Haar 1993 and forthcoming.

14. Ter Haar 1993: 163, 165 argues that Ma Jiulong refers to Ma Chaozhu, who was alleged to have led a Ming-restorationist rebellion in 1752 in Hubei. Ma Chaozhu is also discussed in Kuhn 1990: 62–65.

15. See Mollier, 1990: 22–25, 56–58; Seidel 1969–70: 216–47; and ter Haar 1992: 115–16.

16. See ter Haar 1993.

17. See Zürcher 1982.

18. Murray 1994: 197–228 provides translations of several versions of the *Xiluxu*.

19. See the discussion in Zhou and Shao 1993: 89.

20. In *TDH* 1: 161, the characters are given as *mengzhu*—"alliance leader." In Qin 1988: 153, however, the characters are given as *mingzhu*, "Ruler of Light," or "Ming ruler-emperor." Qin, personal communication, informed me that a re-check of the archival originals determined that *mingzhu* is accurate. In some contexts, of course, the two characters can be used interchangeably.

21. *Shiliao xunkan* 1963, sec. *di*: 443a

22. Shepherd 1993: 138.

23. Hong 1984, 2, xia: 103.

24. *TDH* 4: 340–41; *TAHLJJ* 1964: 260–61.

25. Meskill 1979: 38–56 offers a general description of Zhanghua county.

26. *JJCLF, NYFG* 3312.8. QL 48.2.23 (1783).

27. Yu 1953: 27; Yang Tingli 1983: 117.

28. Personal interviews in Dali, summer 1990.

29. Esherick 1987: 327.

30. *TDH* 1: 116. On military romances, see Hsia 1974.

31. LM: 218–19, 262–66. The difficulty stems partly from the determination of Yan's interrogators to establish a clear and simple conspiracy illustrating the spread of the Tiandihui, much as they did with Chen Biao and Xing Yi (see Chapter 4). Such an effort might have prompted them to seek an earlier rather than a later date of transmission from Yan Yan to Lin Shuangwen, one that would also reduce the local officials' behavior as one of the causes of the uprising. Because much the same initiation ceremony seems also to have been carried out at each transmission of the Tiandihui, it is very difficult to pin down the date of the founding of the Taiwan branch of the Tiandihui by Lin Shuangwen.

32. Reprinted in Zhongguo shehui kexueyuan lishi yanjiusuo and Mingshi yanjiushi 1983: 113–37. For a brief biography of Yang Tingli, see the *Fujian tongzhi* 1871: 486–87.

33. Yang Tingli 1983: 117.

34. Reprinted in LM: 112.

35. Skinner 1964: 39; Freedman 1966: 95.

36. For a more detailed discussion, see Ownby 1989: 293–97.

37. Studies like Liu 1982 conflate society members with hangers-on who joined after the rebellion was under way.

38. Jung 1979: 368–75.

39. Shepherd 1993: 215–30; Ch'en Ch'i-nan 1987: 37.

40. Some sources say recruitment began in the sixth month. See *TDH* 1: 176.

41. The basic narrative of these events is supplied in *TDH* 1: 170–75. The quote is from 171.

42. Antony 1993: 208, n. 8, argues cogently that "imminent" is a more accurate translation than the conventional "immediate," since the decision passed through several levels of review before being implemented.

43. Zhuang 1981: 39.

44. Yang Tingli 1983: 117.

45. See, for example, *Zhanghua xianzhi* 1962: 112–13.

46. See Faure 1979 on conspiracy theories.

47. For criticisms of Liu and Li, see two imperial edicts in *TDH* 5: 16–18. Li Yongqi's own account of his investigation into the case is in *TDH* 1: 175–77.

48. See Shepherd 1993: 355; Zhuang 1981: 34–36.

49. See the many instances in *TDH* 6 and 7.

Chapter 3

1. *Zhanghua xianzhi* 1962: 114. Eberhard 1986: 41–42 notes: "When Shi Huang-di, the first Emperor of China, had defeated the red Zhou Dynasty he chose black as the colour of his dynasty, since water (associated with black) puts out fire (red). His successors in the Former Han Dynasty . . . let all of a hundred years elapse before they opted for red again. . . . Black was chosen by later historians as the symbolic colour of the first of the three ancient dynasties—Xia; the second—Shang—was symbolised by white. . . . As a symbol, black stands for darkness, death, honour. In the Chinese theatre eight heroes with blackened faces represent men who are honourable, if rough and ready."

2. LM: 32–33. The importance of seals as legitimating objects is well known. See Wagner 1982: 41.

3. In this respect, Lin differed little from most rebel leaders in Chinese history. Muramatsu 1960: 242 observes that in addition to Daoist and Buddhist beliefs, most rebels, or at least rebel leaders, shared in worship of benevolent heaven and were thus "drawn into the historical constellation of Confucian ideas. Most of the rebels openly expressed hatred of . . . the local officials—who were usually alleged to be hopelessly corrupt and hard on the common people. These denunciations did not exclude the possibility of compromise with the emperor as long as he was acknowledged to hold a residue of the 'mandate.'"

4. See Esherick 1987: 63–67; Hsia 1974.

5. *TDH* 5: 12; Hucker 1985: 218.

6. LM: 244; Hucker 1985: 168.

7. LM: 241; Hucker 1985: 176.

8. Lamley 1981: 305. One could further subdivide Lamley's "severe phase" into four subperiods of ethnic feuding. The first lasted from 1782 through 1791, consisted mostly of Fujian-Hakka violence, and took place in mid- and northern Tai-

wan. The second period, 1805–10, was confined to Zhang-Quan *xiedou*, and was again concentrated in mid- and north Taiwan, with some activity also in the northeast (Gemalan). The third period, 1826–34, was almost exclusively Fujian-Hakka violence, and occurred throughout Taiwan. The final period ran from the mid-1840's through the end of the 1850's, was chiefly Zhang-Quan violence, and was with few exceptions limited to northern Taiwan. See Ownby 1989: 150, 370.

9. See Lamley 1981: 302–3.

10. Ibid., 291–96; Shi 1987: 66–90.

11. Ownby 1990: 79.

12. *Ping Tai jishi benmo* 1958: 29.

13. Yang Tingli 1983: 120–21.

14. See Nan 1980: 51–87.

15. Sasaki 1970: 221. The earthquake occurred on KX 59.10.1 (1720) with aftershocks following on KX 59.12.8 (1721) and for several days thereafter.

16. *Ming-Qing shiliao*, wubian, 1: 21a–21b. The majority of the houses in the area were destroyed, and many people were crushed to death.

17. Ibid.

18. Ibid.

19. Lan 1983: 8. Rebel strength may well be exaggerated: Li Guoqi 1982: 47 gives a population estimate for Taiwan in 1700 of between 200,000 and 250,000, and Shepherd 1993: 161 gives an estimate for 1684 of 130,000.

20. Xiao 1986, 1: 497. These particular Hakka *yimin* are quite famous: their militia organization lasted all the way to the nineteenth century. See Chen Ch'i-nan 1987: 98–101; Nan 1980: 38–45.

21. Zhang 1970: 35–36.

22. Kong 1986: 338–39.

23. Cited in ibid., 347.

24. *Fengshan xianzhi* 1962, j. 10: *yimin*.

25. Kong 1986: 339.

26. *Ming-Qing shiliao*, wubian, 1: 21a–21b.

27. Muramatsu 1960: 258.

28. Ter Haar 1993: 165.

29. Ibid., 163.

30. Ibid.

31. Qin and Li 1986: 30–34.

32. *Fujian tongzhi* 1768, j. 267: 32a.

33. Hucker 1985: 298.

34. Ibid., 544.

35. Van der Loon 1977: 154 notes that military titles were used in religious processions in the Song, although he provides no information on the particular titles.

36. Huang Xiuzheng 1975: 149–51.

37. Wakeman 1985: 1043.

38. Ruhlmann 1960.

39. Muramatsu 1960 remains among the most useful.

40. Tong 1991.

41. Crowell 1983.

42. Shih 1956.

Chapter 4

1. Jones and Kuhn 1978: 137; Naquin 1976.
2. C. K. Yang 1975: 197.
3. See Antony 1988.
4. Van der Loon 1977: 168.
5. *TDH* 5: 99. See also Shepherd 1993: 333; Meskill, 1979: 73; and Huang Fu-san 1987: 82.
6. *TDH* 5: 98. There was, of course, much more to the reconstruction of Taiwan than the confiscation of weapons. See, for example, Peng 1976; Shepherd 1993: 330–32.
7. Qin and Li 1986: 38.
8. Another source suggests that Lu used a Ming descendant rather than a Song descendant. See *Fujian shengli* 1964: 893–95.
9. Qin and Li 1986: 30–39.
10. Ibid., 37–39.
11. Efforts were made to track the Tiandihui to Sichuan. See, for example, *TDH* 1: 113, 126–29. Barend ter Haar connects Ma Jiulong to Ma Chengzhu, and suggests that the formation of the Tiandihui was in some way connected with Ma's earlier rebellion. See ter Haar 1993: 163.
12. Qin and Li 1986: 37.
13. Zhang Maqiu, who led an uprising in Zhangpu, Zhangzhou in late QL 52 (1788)—while the Lin Shuangwen rebellion was still under way—cited both Lu Mao and Lin Shuangwen as "inspirations," and noted that both used the *shuntian* slogan. See *TDH* 5: 368.
14. See ter Haar 1993.
15. Qin and Li 1986: 38.
16. Many of these are brought together in *TDH* 5: 424–50.
17. Richard J. Smith, personal communication.
18. Yang Tingli 1983: 183.
19. Qin 1988: 283.
20. See, for example, the cases of Zheng Guangcai, *TDH* 6: 73–78; and Xu Zhang, *TDH* 6: 86–90.
21. Many scholars have commented on this development. See, for example, Cai 1987: 132–38.
22. Antony 1993: 201–2.
23. See chart in Zhuang 1990a. Zhuang 1990b and Zhuang 1988 provide further elaboration of the relationship between migration and secret societies.
24. See chart in Zhuang 1990a.
25. See chart in ibid.
26. Calculations based on Cai 1987: 142–47.
27. See Antony 1988.
28. Cai 1987: 124–32 echoes these basic findings.
29. Feuchtwang 1992: 46. A photograph of an altar and its ritual objects is on p. 192.
30. Lagerwey 1987: 48, and Weller 1987: 92, as well as many other ethnographic treatments.
31. Dean 1993: 46.

32. *TDH* 6: 212, 301. Smith 1991: 224 also discusses "inviting the gods."

33. Lagerwey 1987: 23.

34. *TDH* 6: 359. These particular *"tian," "di,"* and *"hong"* characters were all fabricated within the Tiandihui tradition.

35. Lagerwey 1987: 28–29.

36. Ibid., 59.

37. *TDH* 6: 336, 361; Lagerwey 1987: 61.

38. Lagerwey 1987: 61–67, gives an excellent example of only a few of the documents that must accompany performance of a classical *jiao* ritual. See also Schipper 1974; and ter Haar 1992: 148.

39. Schipper 1985: 47.

40. *TDH* 6: 360. Ter Haar 1992: 167, mentions the "karma mirror technique," which is a method of seeing past and future incarnations in a bowl of water or a mirror; 181 discusses "fireballs" in the context of the great panic of 1557, based on widespread fears of flying objects, "which were rampant in the entire coastal region from the Yangzi river down to Canton." Feuchtwang 1992: 175–76 notes: "In southern Taiwan . . . the purification of the altar reaches a dramatic climax with an irruption of a demonic tiger figure. . . . To furious gonging and drumming, the Daoist master rushes into the altar space. With a bowl of ritually purified spirit water in his left hand and a sword in his right he takes giant steps across the space, then swivels and, facing north, from his mouth sprays water taken from the bowl."

41. Examples of these manuals and the charms can be seen in the photolithographic reproductions of Tiandihui documents in the front matter of *TDH* 6.

42. Lian 1988: 29–111.

43. Ibid., 67–68.

44. Ibid., 81.

45. Zhou and Shao 1993: 103–4.

46. *TDH* 6: 208. For commentary on the role of dreams and visions in Chinese popular religion, see Wagner 1982: 21–23; and Brown 1988.

47. *TDH* 6: 301, 332; Lagerwey 1987: 57; Schipper 1985: 29; ter Haar 1993: 167.

48. Classic statements of this perspective may be found in Wolf 1974; and C. K. Yang 1961, but variations on the general theme are legion.

49. See Naquin 1976; and Kelley 1982. Ter Haar 1992 has challenged this identification of a "sectarian" tradition, arguing that the millenarian "White Lotus" was the creation of an overzealous Chinese state, and that the tradition of millenarian rebellion is more properly understood as the history of state persecution.

50. See *TDH* 6: 233. In another instance, a Tiandihui member was ousted from his home by his father and mother after entering the society. See *TDH* 6: 267. Whatever else this suggests, the member surely was not an outsider until after his initiation.

51. Ter Haar 1992: 183 discusses "descriptions of the strange objects in local gazetteers from the Shanghai area and Wujiang. The pasting of feathers, or hairs, on the backs of the paper objects served to bring them alive."

52. Lagerwey 1987: 48.

53. Ter Haar n.d. Ter Haar is currently completing a book-length manuscript on this general topic.

54. DeBernardi 1987.

55. Joseph Esherick's work on the Boxers illustrates that Qing officials were familiar with and knew how to describe these practices. Esherick 1987: 56.

56. Seidel 1969–70: 216.

57. Feuchtwang 1992: 46.

58. Ibid.

59. Later on, the Xiaodaohui came to be another name for the Tiandihui. It is not clear whether this is true for this early version of the Xiaodaohui. For information on the case, see *GZD QL* 55: 859.

Chapter 5

1. Bodde and Morris 1973: 102–4.

2. Ter Haar n.d. argues that the Manchus themselves, as well as other border peoples, practiced the blood oath in much the same way as described in Chapter 1.

3. Lamley 1977: 1.

4. See, for example, Wagner 1982: 7.

5. The following section draws on Zhuang 1990a: 111–41, where he brings together all Qing statutes and substatutes dealing with brotherhoods and secret societies.

6. Antony 1993: 192.

7. Bodde and Morris 1973: 97 note: "Whipping, used side by side with, or as a substitute for, beating with the stick, appears in the Code of 503 of the Liang dynasty, as well as in many subsequent codes. In Ch'ing times, the whip replaced the bamboo as a punishment for Manchus, the designated number of blows of the light or heavy bamboo being convertible to the same number of blows of the whip. Otherwise, it did not constitute a legal punishment."

8. Bodde and Morris 1973: 77 provide a table indicating the customary reduction of the number of blows. A sentence of 100 blows, for example, was reduced to 40.

9. Antony 1993: 193.

10. See discussion in Chapter 1 above, and in Anthony 1993: 196–98.

11. Bodde and Morris 1973: 88–91 note that most of the "military" aspects of "military exile" had disappeared by Qing times.

12. Antony 1993: 198–99.

13. For one example, see *TDH* 6: 216.

14. See discussion in Kuhn 1990: 84–91. An exception is in *TDH* 6: 145, where Fujian-Zhejiang Governor-General Yude sentences a Tiandihui leader for having used "heterodox doctrines [*zuodao yiduan*] to seduce the people." In another example, a proclamation by Fujian Provincial Director of Education Wang Runzhi identified secret societies as "heterodox teachings" (*xiejiao*) and those who joined the societies as "heterodox bandits" (*xiefei*). See *TDH* 6: 219.

15. Antony 1993: 200–201.

16. Buoye n.d.

17. *GZZP, NMYD qita* 947.1, 947.2, and 947.10. The citation is from the last document.

18. Sasaki 1970: 232.

19. *GZD YZ*, 11: 69–70.

20. See examples in Chapter 4.

21. See J. Watson 1991 for an example of peasant impressions of the imperial state.

22. *GZZP, NMYD, mimi jieshe* 677.3.

23. Naquin 1976: 281.

24. On feuds as conflict resolution, see Wilson 1988; on kinship, see Black-Michaud 1975; on honor, see Hallpike 1977; on ecology, see Boehm 1984.

25. Muir 1993 discusses feuds in Renaissance Italy, hardly an "acephalous" society.

26. See, for example, Chen Shengshao 1983: 95–96.

27. See Cheng 1963, j. 9: 13a–16b.

28. *Fujian shengli* 1964: 862–63.

29. Cited in Niida 1954: 375–76, n. 13.

30. Cited in ibid., 373, n. 2.

31. See, for example, *MZLY* 1757: 49a–49b; j. 18.

32. Xie 1959: 102–4.

33. *Quanzhou jiufengsu ziliao huibian* 1985: 144.

34. Xie 1959: 98.

35. The Western scholar most closely identified with the study of Chinese *xiedou* is Harry J. Lamley, who essentially equates *xiedou* with feud and highlights the communal aspects of the violence. See Lamley 1977, 1981, 1990a, and 1990b. Ownby 1989: 92–98 gives a fuller presentation of the evidence equating *xiedou* and feud. Discussion of mainland *xiedou* can also be found in Freedman 1958: 105–13; Hsiao 1960: 419–33; Kuhn 1970: 77–79; Perry 1980: 75–78; and Ng 1983: 26–37, among others. Important Chinese studies include Lang 1935 and Xu Xiaowang 1986. In Japanese see Niida 1954 and Kitamura 1950. There is a larger literature on the "subethnic" *xiedou* on Taiwan. In English see Lamley 1981; Hsu 1980; Meskill 1979: 62–67; Ownby 1990; and Shepherd 1993: 308–61. In Chinese and Japanese see Inō 1928; Huang Qimu 1954; Dai 1963; Zhang 1969, 1970, 1974, 1976; Huang Xiuzheng 1976; Chen Ch'i-nan 1980, 1987; Kong 1985, 1986; Li Yiyuan 1980; and Lin Weisheng 1988.

36. Xie 1959: 103.

37. Ibid.

38. See Ownby 1989: 112–32; Marks 1984: 66–75.

39. *GZZP, NMYD, qita* 959.2, QL 33.12.8.

40. Cited in Niida 1954: 377–78, n. 29.

41. Cited in Lang 1935: 144.

42. Cited in Niida 1954: 375–76, n. 13.

43. Niida 1942: 24.

44. Cited in Niida 1954: 393, n. 10.

45. *Quanzhou fuzhi* 1612, j. 3: 57b–58a.

46. Cheng 1963, j. 9: 14b.

47. Xie 1959: 104.

48. Xu Gengjie 1908, j. 4: 5b–6a.

49. See Ownby 1990.

50. *JJCLF, NYFQ* 3310.6, QL 47.10.15; *JJCLF, NYFQ* 3311.3, QL 48.01.09.

51. *JJCLF, NYFQ* 3309.12, QL 47.11.29.

52. See, for example, *Da Qing lichao shilu*, 39: 17151.

53. *TAHLJ* 1964: 277–80. For a map of the area where the *xiedou* began, see Lin Weisheng 1988: 32.

54. The most complete report of the origin of the hostilities is found in *TAHLJ* 1964: 277–80. Other sources indicate that the argument began because the Quanzhou gambler attempted to pay his losses with "foreign money" (Mexican Spanish dollars) in which the silver content looked suspiciously low. See *JJCLF, NYFQ* 3309.1, QL 47.10.21.

55. *TAHLJ* 1964: 277–80. See also *JJCLF, NYFQ* 3310.10, QL 47.12.22. In this document, Yade is impeaching Zhanghua county magistrate Jiao Changgui, and claims to have learned from merchants at Xiamen that the Quanzhouers' anger was brought about by Jiao's failure to act on their complaint. Yade himself had been the target of criticism from the Qianlong emperor, and his remarks concerning Jiao's alleged incompetence must be viewed in this context. Nonetheless, the information that the Quanzhou people brought suit with the authorities is repeated in the paraphrased confession of Xie Xiao, one of the Quanzhou leaders. See *JJCLF, NYFQ* 3311.10 QL 48.1.21; and Sasaki 1970: 94–103. In the last four months of QL 46 (1781–82), eight high officials on Taiwan were impeached, mainly for negligence in pursuit of criminal cases, or in the case of censors who were impeached, negligence in overseeing the local officials who should have been guarding the public trust. None of these local officials was serving in Zhanghua. In QL 47.9 (1782), Governor-General Chen Huizu, who had been instrumental in five of the earlier impeachments, was himself impeached for financial irregularities. Shepherd 1993: 319 observes that the impeachments, plus the *xiedou*, "mark a low point in administrative effectiveness."

56. *TAHLJ* 1964: 277–80.

57. The chief document on which the following account is based is *JJCLF, NYFQ* 3311.10, QL 48.01.21. The text of the same document is also in *TAHLJ* 1964: 250–53. Other documents concerning Xie Xiao, and confirming the information found in the above memorial, are *JJCLF, NYFQ* 3311.4, QL 48.01.12; and *JJCLF, NYFQ* 3311.9, QL 48.01.17.

58. Either a Minnan-speaker from coastal Guangdong or a Hakka.

59. *JJCLF, NYFQ* 3311.10, QL 48.1.21. The text of the same document is also in *TAHLJ* 1964: 250–53. Xie's confession is cited indirectly.

60. See details in Ownby 1990.

61. *GZD QL* 55: 858–60.

62. *JJCLF, NYFQ* 3310.6, QL 47.10.15.

63. See *TAHLJ* 1964: 269.

64. Referred to in the documents as *jiagong baosi*. See *GZZP, NMYD qita* 959.1, QL 33.11.28. The documents discussing this case do not use the terms "*fenlei*" or "*xiedou*" but only describe the conflict as "mutual vengeance burning and killing" (*xiechou huxiang fensha*); but there is little doubt that the violence belongs to the same category under discussion here.

65. *GZZP, NMYD qita* 959.2, QL 33.12.8.

66. Ibid., 959.3, QL 34.2.2.

67. Ibid., 961.11, JQ 15.3.8.

68. See Boulais 1966: 586–89.

69. "If several individuals plan a collective assault on a person, and kill him in the process, then he who struck the mortal blow shall be punished with strangu-

lation after the assizes. The chief planner, whether or not he participated in the assault, will receive one hundred blows of the heavy bamboo and life exile at a distance of 3,000 *li*. The other aggressors will receive 100 blows of the heavy bamboo." Cited in Boulais 1966: 559.

70. Xue 1970: 893.

71. Ibid. The compiler does not explain the long delay between the proposal of the substatute and its adoption.

72. Ibid., 841–42.

73. Ibid.

74. Xie 1959: 110.

75. Yao Ying 1963b.

76. Wang Zhiyi 1963, 1, j. 23, *lizheng, shouling xia*: 42–46.

77. See Kuhn 1970: 30–31.

78. See Yang and Chen 1985.

79. Chen Shengshao 1983: 95–96.

80. Freedman 1958: 114–25.

81. *GZZP, NMYD qita* 961.11. JQ 15.3.8.

82. Yao Ying 1963a: 6.

Chapter 6

1. *Taiwan xianzhi* 1961: 230.

2. One should also note that similar evidence exists for periods not marked by rapid population growth. Tong 1991: 153 writes: "Suzhou in the early seventeenth century was infested with juvenile gangs. Young and untender, they operated in small squads in different territories, for hire to kill or terrorize, and preyed on either the local populace or country folk who came to the city to trade. Similar juvenile gangs existed in nearby Changshu and Jiading counties, as well as in Fuzhou in Fujian." Billingsley 1988: xvi also notes that many Republican-period bandits were quite young.

3. Heidhues 1993.

4. Trocki 1993.

5. See, for example, Skinner 1957, Wilmott 1967, 1970, and Wickberg 1968, among others.

6. Purcell 1951: 303.

7. Yen 1986: 44.

8. Ibid., 44–56.

9. Carstens 1993.

Bibliography

Abdullah bin Abdul Kadir, Munshi. 1970. *The Hikayat Abdullah*. Kuala Lumpur: Oxford University Press.

Antony, Robert James. 1988. "Pirates, Bandits, and Brotherhoods: A Study of Crime and Law in Kwangtung Province, 1796–1839." Ph.D. diss., University of Hawaii.

———. 1993. "Brotherhoods, Secret Societies, and the Law in Qing Dynasty China." In David Ownby and Mary S. Heidhues, eds., *"Secret Societies" Reconsidered: Perspectives on the Social History of Early Modern South China and Southeast Asia*, pp. 190–221. Armonk, N.Y.: M. E. Sharpe.

Averill, Stephen C. 1983. "The Shed People and the Opening of the Yangzi Highlands." *Modern China* 9.1: 84–126.

Billingsley, Phil. 1988. *Bandits in Republican China*. Stanford, Calif.: Stanford University Press.

Black-Michaud, Jacob. 1975. *Cohesive Force: Feud in the Mediterranean and the Middle East*. Oxford: Basil Blackwell.

Blythe, Wilfred. 1969. *The Impact of Chinese Secret Societies in Malaya*. London: Oxford University Press.

Bodde, Derk, and Clarence Morris. 1973 (reprint). *Law in Imperial China*. Philadelphia: University of Pennsylvania Press. Original edition 1967.

Boehm, Christopher. 1984. *Blood Revenge: The Anthropology of Feuding in Montenegro and Other Tribal Societies*. Lawrence: University Press of Kansas.

Boulais, Le P. Guy, S.J. 1966 (reprint). *Manuel du Code Chinois* (Text of the Chinese Code). Taipei: Chengwen. Original edition 1924.

Boxer, C. R., trans. 1953. *South China in the Sixteenth Century*. London: University of Glasgow Press.

Brown, Carolyn T., ed. 1988. *Psycho-Sinology: The Universe of Dreams in Chinese Culture*. Washington, D.C.: Woodrow Wilson International Center.

Buoye, Thomas. 1990. "Economic Change and Rural Violence: Homicides Related to Disputes over Property Rights in Guangdong During the Eighteenth Century." *Peasant Studies* 17.4: 233–60.

———. n.d. "'Suddenly Murderous Intent Arose': Bureaucratization and Benevolence in Eighteenth-Century Qing Homicide Reports." Unpublished manuscript.

Cai Shaoqing. 1987. *Zhongguo jindai huidangshi yanjiu* (Research on the modern history of Chinese secret societies). Beijing: Zhonghua shuju.

———. 1990. *Zhongguo mimi shehui* (Chinese secret societies). Hangzhou: Zhejiang renmin chubanshe.

Carstens, Sharon A. 1993. "Culture and Polity in Nineteenth-Century Malaya: The Case of Yap Ah Loy." In David Ownby and Mary Somers Heidhues, eds., *"Secret Societies" Reconsidered: Perspectives on the Social History of Early Modern South China and Southeast Asia,* pp. 120–52. Armonk, N.Y.: M. E. Sharpe.

Ch'en Ch'i-nan (Chen Qi'nan). 1980. "Qingdai Taiwan shehui de jiegou bianqian" (Social structural change in Qing dynasty Taiwan). *Bulletin of the Institute of Ethnology, Academia Sinica* 49: 115–47.

———. 1987. *Taiwan de chuantong Zhongguo shehui* (Traditional Chinese society in Taiwan). Taipei: Yunchen congkan.

Ch'en Ch'iu-k'un (Chen Qiukun). 1978. "Qingchu Taiwan diqu de kaifai, 1700–1756" (The opening of Taiwan in the early Qing period, 1700–1756). *Shihuo yuekan* 8: 221–33.

Chen Shengshao. 1983 (reprint). *Wensulu* (Inquiry into customs). Beijing: Shumu wenxian chubanshe. Author's preface to original edition dated 1827.

Cheng Hanzhang. Daoguang period. *Yuechuan weishigao* (The uncertain drafts of [Cheng] Yuechuan [Hanzhang's courtesy name]). Yunnan, Jingdong: Cheng family woodcut edition.

———. 1963 (reprint). "Lun xidou shu" (A letter on quelling feuds). In He Changling, ed., *Huangchao jingshi wenbian,* j. 9, pp. 13a–16b. Taipei: Guofeng chubanshe. Original edition 1886.

Chesneaux, Jean, ed. 1972. *Popular Movements and Secret Societies in China, 1840–1950.* Stanford, Calif.: Stanford University Press.

Clawson, Mary Ann. 1989. *Constructing Brotherhood: Class, Gender, and Fraternalism.* Princeton, N.J.: Princeton University Press.

Cohen, Myron L. 1990. "Lineage Organization in North China." *Journal of Asian Studies* 49.3: 509–34.

Comber, L. F. 1959. *Chinese Secret Societies in Malaya: A Survey of the Triad Society from 1800 to 1900.* Locust Valley, N.Y.: J. J. Augustin.

Croizier, Ralph C. 1977. *Koxinga and Chinese Nationalism: History, Myth, and the Hero.* Cambridge, Mass.: Harvard University, East Asian Research Center.

Crowell, William G. 1983. "Social Unrest and Rebellion in Jiangnan During the Six Dynasties." *Modern China* 9.3: 319–54.

Da Qing lichao shilu (Veritable records of successive reigns of the Qing dynasty). 1937. Mukden.

Dai Yanhui. 1963. "Qingdai Taiwan xiangzhuang zhi shehui de kaocha" (Investigation into the village society of Qing dynasty Taiwan). *Taiwan yinhang jikan* 14.4: 198–228.

De Groot, J. J. M. 1972–73 (reprint). *Sectarianism and Religious Persecution in China.* 2 vols. Shannon, Ireland: Irish University Press. Original edition 1903, 1904.

Dean, Kenneth. 1993. *Taoist Ritual and Popular Cults of Southeast China.* Princeton, N.J.: Princeton University Press.

DeBernardi, Jean. 1987. "The God of War and the Vagabond Buddha." *Modern China* 13.3: 310–32.

Eberhard, Wolfram. 1986. *A Dictionary of Chinese Symbols: Hidden Symbols in Chinese Life and Thought.* London: Routledge.

Egerton, Clement, trans. 1939. *The Golden Lotus.* London: Routledge and Kegan Paul.

Elvin, Mark. 1973. *The Pattern of the Chinese Past.* Stanford, Calif.: Stanford University Press.

Enping xianzhi (1825).

Entenmann, Robert Eric. 1982. "Migration and Settlement in Sichuan, 1644–1796." Ph.D. diss., Harvard University.

Esherick, Joseph W. 1987. *The Origins of the Boxer Uprising.* Berkeley: University of California Press.

Faure, David. 1979. "Secret Societies, Heretic Sects, and Peasant Rebellions in Nineteenth Century China." *Journal of the Chinese University of Hong Kong* 1: 189–206.

Fei Hsiao-t'ung. 1939. *Peasant Life in China: A Field Study of Country Life in the Yangtse Valley.* New York: E. P. Dutton.

Fengshan xianzhi. 1962 (reprint). Taipei: Taiwan wenxian congkan #124. Original edition 1764.

Feuchtwang, Stephan. 1992. *The Imperial Metaphor: Popular Religion in China.* London: Routledge.

Freedman, Maurice. 1958. *Lineage Organization in Southeastern China.* London: Athlone Press.

———. 1966. *Chinese Lineage and Society: Fukien and Kwangtung.* London: Athlone Press.

Fu Yiling. 1961. *Ming-Qing nongcun shehui jingji* (The social economy of the Ming-Qing rural village). Beijing: Sanlian Press.

Fujian shengli (Statutes of the province of Fujian). 1964 (reprint). Taipei: Taiwan wenxian congkan #199. Original edition 1768.

Fujian tongzhi. 1768 edition.

Fujian tongzhi. 1964 (reprint). Taipei: Taiwan wenxian congkan #84. Original edition 1829, reissued 1871.

Fujii Hiroshi. 1984. "Ichiden-ryōshushi no kihon kōzō" (The basic structure of the one-field two-owners system) in *Kindai Chūgoku* (Modern China) 15: 46–107.

Funing zhouzhi. Ming Wanli edition.

Gamble, Sidney D. 1944. "A Chinese Mutual Savings Society." *Far Eastern Quarterly* 4: 41–52.

Gardella, Robert P. 1976. "Fukien's Tea Industry and Trade in Ch'ing and Republican China: The Developmental Consequences of a Traditional Commodity Export." Ph.D. diss., University of Washington.

Geertz, Clifford. 1962. "The Rotating Credit Association: A 'Middle Rung' in Economic Development." *Economic Development and Cultural Change* 10: 241–74.

Godsden, P. H. J. H. 1967. *The Friendly Societies in England, 1815–1875.* New York: Augustus M. Kelley.

GZD QL . *Gongzhongdang Qianlongchao zouzhe* (Imperially rescripted memorials from the Qianlong reign period). 1977–80. Taipei: Guoli gugong bowuyuan.

GZD YZ. *Gongzhongdang Yongzhengchao zouzhe* (Imperially rescripted memorials from the Yongzheng reign period). 1977–80. Taipei: Guoli gugong bowuyuan.

GZZP, NMYD. *Gongzhong zhupi, nongmin yundong* (Imperially rescripted palace memorials, peasant movements, anti-Qing struggles). Archival documents held in the First Historical Archives of China, Beijing.

Hallpike, Christopher R. 1977. *Bloodshed and Vengeance in the Papuan Mountains: The Generation of Conflict in Tauade Society.* Oxford: Clarendon Press.

Harrell, Steven C. 1974. "When a Ghost Becomes a God." In Arthur P. Wolf, ed., *Religion and Ritual in Chinese Society,* pp. 193–206. Stanford, Calif.: Stanford University Press.

Heidhues, Mary Somers. 1993. "Chinese Organizations in West Borneo and Bangka: *Kongsi* and *Hui.*" In David Ownby and Mary S. Heidhues, eds., *"Secret Societies" Reconsidered: Perspectives on the Social History of Early Modern South China and Southeast Asia,* pp. 68–88. Armonk, N.Y.: M. E. Sharpe.

Hirayama Shū. 1912. *Zhongguo bimi shehuishi* (History of China's secret societies). Shanghai: Shangwu yinshuguan.

Ho Ping-ti. 1959. *Studies on the Population of China, 1368–1953.* Cambridge, Mass.: Harvard University Press.

———. 1962. *The Ladder of Success in Imperial China.* New York: Columbia University Press.

Hong Minlin. 1984. *Taiwan jiu diming zhi yan'ge* (The evolution of former place-names in Taiwan). Taizhong: Taiwansheng wenxian weiyuanhui.

Hsia, C. T. 1974. "The Military Romance." In Cyril Birch, ed., *Studies in Chinese Literary Genres,* pp. 339–90. Berkeley: University of California Press.

Hsiao Kung-ch'üan. 1960. *Rural China: Imperial Control in the Nineteenth Century.* Seattle: University of Washington Press.

Hsieh Kuo-ching [Xie Guozhen]. 1932. "Removal of the Coastal Population in Early Tsing Period." *Chinese Social and Political Science Review* 15: 559–96.

Hsu Wen-hsiung. 1980. "Frontier Social Organization and Social Disorder in Ch'ing Taiwan." In Ronald G. Knapp, ed., *China's Island Frontier: Studies in the Historical Geography of Taiwan,* pp. 87–105. Honolulu: University of Hawaii Press.

Huang Fusan. 1987. *Wufeng Linjia de xingqi* (The rise of the Lins of Wufeng). Taipei: Zili wanbao.

Huang Qimu. 1954. "Fenlei xiedou yu Mengjia" (Ethnic xiedou and Mengjia). *Taibei wenwu* 2.1: 55–58.

Huang Xiuzheng. 1975. "Zhu Yigui de chuanshuo yu geyao" (Legends and songs about Zhu Yigui). *Taiwan wenxian* 26.3: 149–51.

———. 1976. "Qingdai Taiwan fenlei xiedou shijian zhi jiantao" (An examination of ethnic xiedou incidents in Qing Taiwan). *Taiwan wenxian* 27.4: 78–86.

Hucker, Charles O. 1985. *A Dictionary of Official Titles in Imperial China.* Stanford, Calif.: Stanford University Press.

Huian xianzhi. Qing Jiaqing edition.

Inō Yoshinori (Kanori). 1928. *Taiwan bunkashi* (A record of Taiwan's culture). Tokyo: Tōkōshoin.

Irwin, Richard G. 1966. *The Evolution of a Chinese Novel*. Cambridge, Mass.: Harvard University Press.

Isaacs, Harold R. 1962. *Images of Asia: American Views of China and India*. New York: Capricorn Books.

JJCLF, NYFQ. Junjichu lufu, nongyun fanQing (Grand council file copies of memorials, peasant movements, anti-Qing struggles). Documents held in the First Historical Archives of China, Beijing.

Jones, Susan Mann, and Phillip A. Kuhn. 1978. "Dynastic Decline and the Roots of Rebellion." In John K. Fairbank, ed., *The Cambridge History of China*, vol. 10, *Late Ch'ing, 1800–1911*, Part I, pp. 107–62. Cambridge: Cambridge University Press.

Jordan, David. 1985. "Sworn Brothers: A Study in Chinese Ritual Kinship." In Chuang Yin-chang and Chester Hsieh-Jih Ch'eng, eds., *The Chinese Family and Its Ritual Behavior*, pp. 232–62. Taipei: Academia Sinica Institute of Ethnology.

Jung, Richard Lee Kuen. 1979. "The Ch'ien-Lung Emperor's Suppression of Rebellion: The White Lotus and the Triads, 1774–1788." Ph.D. diss., Harvard University.

Kelley, David E. 1982. "Temples and Tribute Fleets: The Luo Sect and Boatmen's Associations in the Eighteenth Century." *Modern China* 8.3: 361–91.

Kitamura Hironao. 1950. "Shindai kaitō no ichi kōsatsu" (An examination of Qing dynasty *xiedou*). *Shirin* 33.1: 64–77.

Kong Li (Chen Kongli). 1985. "Qingdai Taiwan xiedou shishi bianwu" (Distinguishing errors among the facts concerning *xiedou* in Qing Taiwan). *Taiwan yanjiu jikan*, 1985.4: 68–72.

———. 1986. "Zhu Yigui qiyi yu Wu Fusheng qiyi gongce de bijiao yanjiu" (Comparative study of confessions from the Zhu Yigui and Wu Fusheng uprisings). In Chen Zaizheng, Kong Li, and Deng Kongzhao, eds., *Qingdai Taiwanshi yanjiu* (Studies in the history of Qing Taiwan), pp. 338–49. Xiamen: Xiamen University Press.

Kuhn, Philip A. 1970. *Rebellion and Its Enemies in Late Imperial China*. Cambridge, Mass.: Harvard University Press.

———. 1977. "Origins of the Taiping Vision: Cross Cultural Dimensions of a Chinese Rebellion." *Comparative Studies in Society and History* 19.3: 350–66.

———. 1990. *Soulstealers: The Chinese Sorcery Scare of 1768*. Cambridge, Mass.: Harvard University Press.

Kulp, Daniel H. 1925. *Country Life in South China: The Sociology of Familism*. Vol. 1, *Phenix Village, Kwantung, China*. New York: Columbia University Press.

Lagerwey, John. 1987. *Taoist Ritual in Chinese Society and History*. New York: Macmillan.

Lai Fushun. 1984. *Qianlong zhongyao zhanzheng zhi junxu yanjiu* (A study of the military requirements of Qianlong's important military battles). Taipei: National Palace Museum.

Lamley, Harry J. 1977. "Hsieh-tou: The Pathology of Violence in Southeastern China." *Ch'ing-shih wen-t'i* 3.7: 1–39.

———. 1981. "Subethnic Rivalry in the Ch'ing Period." In Emily M. Ahern and

Hill Gates, eds., *The Anthropology of Taiwanese Society*, pp. 282–318. Stanford, Calif.: Stanford University Press.

———. 1987. "*Hsieh-tou* Violence and Lineage Feuding in Southern Fukien and Eastern Kwangtung." *Newsletter for Modern Chinese History*, 1987.3: 43–60.

———. 1990a. "Lineage and Surname Feuds in Southern Fukien and Eastern Kwangtung Under the Ch'ing." In Kwang-Ching Liu, ed., *Orthodoxy in Late Imperial China*, pp. 255–78. Berkeley: University of California Press.

———. 1990b. "Lineage Feuding in Southern Fujian and Eastern Guangdong Under Qing Rule." In Jonathan N. Lipman and Stevan Harrell, eds., *Violence in China*, pp. 27–64. Albany: State University of New York Press.

Lan Dingyuan. 1983 (reprint). *Dongzhengji* (Record of the eastern campaign). In Zhongguo shehui kexueyuan, lishi yanjiusuo, and Mingshi yanjiushi, eds., *Qingdai Taiwan nongmin qiyi shiliao xuanbian*. Fuzhou: Fujian renmin chubanshe. Original edition 1722.

Lang Jingxiao. 1935. "Qingdai Yuedong xiedou shishi" (Historical facts concerning *xiedou* in eastern Guangdong during the Qing). *Lingnan xuebao* 4.2: 103–51.

Lewis, Mark Edward. 1990. *Sanctioned Violence in Early China*. Albany: State University of New York Press.

Li Guoqi. 1982. *Zhongguo xiandaihua de quyu yanjiu: Min-Zhe-Tai diqu, 1860–1916* (Studies of the modernized regions of China: The Fujian-Zhejiang-Taiwan area, 1860–1916). Taipei: Zhongyang yanjiuyuan jindaishi yanjiusuo.

Li Wenzhi. 1966. *Wan Ming minbian* (Popular uprisings in the late Ming). Hong Kong: Yuandong tushu gongsi.

Li Yiyuan. 1980. "Taiwan chuantong shehui zhidu de yuanliu" (The origin and evolution of Taiwan's traditional social system). In Chen Qilu (Chen Chi-lu), ed., *Zhongguo de Taiwan*, pp. 307–36. Taipei: Zhongyang wenwu gongyingshe.

Lian Lichang. 1988. *Fujian mimi shehui* (Secret societies in Fujian). Fuzhou: Fujian renmin chubanshe.

Lin Renchuan. 1983. "Qingdai Taiwan yu zuguo dalu de maoyi jiegou" (The structure of trade between Taiwan and the mainland in the Qing). *Zhongguo shehui jingjishi yanjiu*, 1983.2: 31–42.

Lin Weisheng. 1988. "Fenlei xiedou manyan quanTai de fenxi" (Analysis of the spread of ethnic feuding throughout Taiwan). *Taiwan fengwu* 38.3: 27–52.

Liu Niling. 1982. "Youmin yu Qingdai Taiwan minbian" (Drifters and uprisings in Qing Taiwan). *Taiwan fengwu* 32.1: 1–22; 32.2: 15–44.

———. 1989. *Taiwan de shehui dongluan—Lin Shuangwen shijian* (Social instability in Taiwan: The Lin Shuangwen incident). Taipei: Jiuda wenhua.

Liu Ruzhong and Miao Xuemeng, eds. 1984. *Taiwan Lin Shuangwen qiyi ziliao xuanbian* (Selected materials on the Lin Shuangwen uprising on Taiwan). Fuzhou: Fujian renmin chubanshe.

LM. See Liu Ruzhong.

Luo Ergang. 1943. *Tiandihui wenxianlu* (Documents on the Heaven and Earth Society). Shanghai: Zhengzhong shuju.

Luo Xianglin. 1973. *Kejia yuanliukao* (Research into the origins of the Hakka). Hong Kong: Shijie Keshu dierci kenqin dahui choubei weiyuanhui.

Ma, L. Eve Armentrout. 1990. *Revolutionaries, Monarchists, and Chinatowns:*

Chinese Politics in the Americas and the 1911 Revolution. Honolulu: University of Hawaii Press.

Marks, Robert. 1984. *Rural Revolution in South China: Peasants and the Making of History in Haifang County, 1570–1930.* Madison: University of Wisconsin Press.

Meskill, Johanna Menzel. 1979. *A Chinese Pioneer Family: The Lins of Wu-feng, Taiwan, 1729–1895.* Princeton, N.J.: Princeton University Press.

Milne, Dr. William. 1826. "Some Account of a Secret Association in China, entitled the Triad Society." *Transactions of the Royal Asiatic Society of Great Britain and Ireland,* vol. 1, part 2.

Ming-Qing shiliao (Historical materials of the Ming and Qing dynasties). 1930–36. Edited by the Research Institute of History and Philology of the Academia Sinica. Shanghai: Commercial Press.

Mollier, Christine. 1990. *Une Apocalypse taoïste du Ve siècle: le livre des incantations divines des grottes abyssales* (A Daoist apocalypse of the fifth century: the book of divine spells from the grottos). Paris: Collège de France, Institut des Hautes Etudes Chinoises.

Morgan, W. P. 1960. *Triad Societies in Hong Kong.* Hong Kong.

Mori Masao. 1986. "Weirao 'xiangzu' wenti" (Some problems about the patriarchal clan). *Zhongguo shehui jingjishi yanjiu,* 1986.2: 1–8.

Muir, Edward. 1993. *Mad Blood Stirring: Vendetta and Factions in Friuli during the Renaissance.* Baltimore: Johns Hopkins University Press.

Muramatsu, Yuji. 1960. "Some Themes in Chinese Rebel Ideologies." In Arthur F. Wright, ed., *The Confucian Persuasion,* pp. 240–67. Stanford, Calif.: Stanford University Press.

Murray, Dian H. 1993. "Migration, Protection, and Racketeering: The Spread of the Tiandihui Within China." In David Ownby and Mary S. Heidhues, eds., *"Secret Societies" Reconsidered: Perspectives on the Social History of Early Modern South China and Southeast Asia,* pp. 177–89. Armonk, N.Y.: M. E. Sharpe.

———. 1994. *The Origins of the Tiandihui: The Chinese Triads in Legend and History.* Stanford, Calif.: Stanford University Press.

MZLY. *Minzheng lingyao* (Essentials for the governance of Fujian). 1757 original. *Chaoben* from the library of the Fujian Provincial Teacher's College in Fuzhou.

Naba Toshisada. 1938. "Tōdai no shayo ni tsuite" (On Tang dynasty *sheyi*). *Shirin* 23.2: 223–65; 23.3: 495–534; 23.4: 729–93.

Nan Binghe. 1980. *Taiwan yimin* (Taiwan's yimin). Taipei: Zhongyang wenwu gongyingshe.

Naquin, Susan. 1976. *Millenarian Rebellion in China: The Eight Trigrams Uprising of 1813.* New Haven, Conn.: Yale University Press.

Naquin, Susan, and Chün-fang Yü, eds. 1992. *Pilgrimages and Sacred Sites in China.* Berkeley: University of California Press.

Ng Chin-keong. 1983. *Trade and Society: The Amoy Network on the China Coast, 1683–1735.* Singapore: Singapore University Press.

Niida Noboru. 1942. "Shina kinsei dōzoku buraku no kaitō" (*Xiedou* between single-lineage villages in recent Chinese history). *Shina kanko chosa ihō,* pp. 23–35. Tokyo.

———. 1954. *Chūgoku no nōson kazoku* (Peasant families in China). Tokyo: Tokyo University Press.

Ownby, David. 1989. "Communal Violence in Eighteenth Century Southeast China: The Background to the Lin Shuangwen Uprising of 1787." Ph.D. diss., Harvard University.

———. 1990. "The 'Ethnic Feud' in Qing Taiwan: What Is This Violence Business Anyway? An Interpretation of the 1782 Zhang-Quan Xiedou." *Late Imperial China* 11.1: 75–98.

———. 1993. "Secret Societies Reconsidered." In Ownby and Mary S. Heidhues, eds., *"Secret Societies" Reconsidered: Perspectives on the Social History of Early Modern South China and Southeast Asia*, pp. 3–33. Armonk, N.Y.: M. E. Sharpe.

———. Forthcoming. "Mutual Benefit Societies in Chinese History." In International Society of Labour History, ed., *Proceedings of the Colloque international sur l'histoire de la mutualité*. Amsterdam.

Parsons, James B. 1970. *Peasant Rebellions of the Late Ming Dynasty*. Tucson: University of Arizona Press.

Pasternak, Burton. 1972. *Kinship and Community in Two Chinese Villages*. Stanford, Calif.: Stanford University Press.

Peng Xianlin. 1976. "Lin Shuangwen shijian hou de Qingting zhiTai cuoshi" (The Qing court's policies toward Taiwan after the Lin Shuangwen incident). *Taiwan wenxian* 27.3: 183–99.

Perkins, Dwight. 1969. *Agricultural Development in China, 1369–1968*. Chicago: Aldine.

Perry, Elizabeth J. 1980. *Rebels and Revolutionaries in North China, 1845–1945*. Stanford, Calif.: Stanford University Press.

Pickering, W. A. 1878, 1879. "Chinese Secret Societies and Their Origin." *Journal of the Straits Branch of the Royal Asiatic Society* 1: 63–84; 3: 1–18.

Ping Tai jishi benmo (The complete story of the suppression [of the Lin Shuangwen uprising] on Taiwan). 1958 (reprint). Taipei: Taiwan wenxian congkan #16.

Plaks, Andrew H. 1987. *The Four Masterworks of the Ming Novel*. Princeton, N.J.: Princeton University Press.

Polachek, James M. 1992. *The Inner Opium War*. Cambridge, Mass.: Harvard University Council on East Asian Studies.

Purcell, Victor. 1951. *The Chinese in Southeast Asia*. London: Oxford University Press.

Qi Jialin. 1985. *Taiwan shi* (Taiwanese history). Taipei: Zili wanbao.

Qin Baoqi. 1988. *Qing qianqi Tiandihui yanjiu* (A study of the early Qing Heaven and Earth Society). Beijing: People's University Press.

Qin Baoqi and Li Shoujun, eds. 1986. "Youguan Tiandihui qiyuan shiliao" (Historical materials on the origins of the Heaven and Earth Society). *Lishi dang'an* 1: 30–39.

Qinding pingding Taiwan jilüe (The imperially commissioned record of the suppression [of the rebellion on] Taiwan). 1961 (reprint). Taipei: Taiwan wenxian congkan #102.

Qu Dajun. 1985 (reprint). *Guangdong xinyu* (New commentary on Guangdong). Beijing: Zhonghua shuju. Original edition 1700.

Quanzhou fuzhi. 1612 edition.

Quanzhou jiufengsu ziliao huibian (Collected materials on old customs in Quanzhou). 1985. Quanzhou: Quanzhou City Government.

Rawski, Evelyn S. 1972. *Agricultural Change and the Peasant Economy of South China*. Cambridge, Mass: Harvard University Press.

Ruhlmann, Robert. 1960. "Traditional Heroes in Chinese Popular Fiction." In Arthur F. Wright, ed., *The Confucian Persuasion*, pp. 141–76. Stanford, Calif.: Stanford University Press.

Sangren, P. Steven. 1984. "Traditional Chinese Corporations: Beyond Kinship." *Journal of Asian Studies* 18.3: 391–415.

Sasaki Masaya. 1970. *Shinmatsu no himitsu kessha; zempen, Tenchikai no seiritsu* (Secret societies in the late Qing period: The founding of the Tiandihui). Tokyo: Gannanto shoten.

Schiffrin, Harold Z. 1968. *Sun Yat-sen and the Origins of the Chinese Revolution*. Berkeley: University of California Press.

Schipper, Kristofer M. 1974. "The Written Memorial in Taoist Ceremonies." In Arthur P. Wolf, ed., *Religion and Ritual in Chinese Society*, pp. 309–24. Stanford, Calif.: Stanford University Press.

———. 1985. "Vernacular and Classical Ritual in Taoism." *Journal of Asian Studies* 45.1: 21–57.

Schlegel, Gustave. 1866. *Thian Ti Hwui: The Hung League or Heaven-Earth League*. Batavia: Langue and Co.

Seidel, Anna K. 1969–70. "The Image of the Perfect Ruler in Early Taoist Messianism: Lao-Tzu and Li Hung." *History of Religions* 9.2,3: 216–47.

Sewell, William H. 1980. *Work and Revolution in France: The Language of Labor from the Old Regime to 1848*. Cambridge: Cambridge University Press.

Shepherd, John Robert. 1993. *Statecraft and Political Economy on the Taiwan Frontier*. Stanford, Calif.: Stanford University Press.

Shi Tianfu. 1987. *Qingdai zai Tai Hanren de zuji fenbu he yuanxiang shenghuo fangshi* (Distribution of Han population on Qing Taiwan by mainland origin and lifestyles in the home regions). Taipei: National Taiwan Normal University Department of Geography.

Shih, Vincent Y. C. 1956. "Some Chinese Rebel Ideologies." *T'oung-pao* 44: 150–226.

Shiliao xunkan (Historical Documents). 1963 (reprint). Taipei: Guofeng Press. Original edition 1930.

Shimizu Morimitsu. 1951. *Chūgoku kyōson shakairon* (On Chinese village society). Tokyo: Ganba shoten.

Skinner, G. William. 1957. *Chinese Society in Thailand: An Analytical History*. Ithaca, N.Y.: Cornell University Press.

———. 1964. "Marketing and Social Structure in Rural China." *Journal of Asian Studies* 24.1: 3–43.

———. 1977. "Regional Urbanization in Nineteenth Century China." In G. William Skinner, ed., *The City in Late Imperial China*, pp. 211–49. Stanford, Calif.: Stanford University Press.

Smith, Richard J. 1991. *Fortune-Tellers and Philosophers: Divination in Traditional Chinese Society*. Boulder, Colo.: Westview Press.

So Kwan-wai. 1975. *Japanese Piracy in Ming China During the Sixteenth Century*. Lansing: Michigan State University Press.

Struve, Lynn A. 1984. *The Southern Ming, 1644–1662*. New Haven, Conn.: Yale University Press.

TAHLGJ. Taian huilu gengji (Taiwanese cases, collection number seven). 1964. Taipei: Taiwan wenxian congkan #200.

TAHLJJ. Taian huilu jiji (Taiwanese cases, collection number six). 1964. Taipei: Taiwan wenxian congkan #191.

Taiwan. 1985. *Taiwan diqu minjian hehui xianzhuang zhi yanjiu* (Studies on the current situation regarding popular rotating credit societies in the Taiwan region). Taipei: Legal Affairs Bulletin Press.

Taiwan shihō, dai ikkan, fudōsan (Taiwan private law, part one, real estate). 1910. Kobe: Rinji Taiwan kyūkan chōsakai.

Taiwan xianzhi. 1961 (reprint). Taipei: Taiwan wenxian congkan #103. Original edition 1720.

Tanaka Issei. 1985. "The Social and Historical Context of Ming-Ch'ing Local Drama." In David Johnson, Evelyn S. Rawski, and Andrew J. Nathan, eds., *Popular Culture in Late Imperial China*, pp. 143–60. Berkeley: University of California Press.

Tanaka Masatoshi. 1984. "Popular Uprisings, Rent Resistance, and Bondservant Rebellions in the Late Ming." In Linda Grove and Christian Daniels, eds., *State and Society in China: Japanese Perspectives on Ming-Qing Social and Economic History*, pp. 165–214. Tokyo: Tokyo University Press.

Tang Yu. 1987. "Qingdai Taiwan yimin shenghuoshi zhi yanjiu, shang" (Research into the history of the lives of Qing period immigrants to Taiwan, part one). *Taiwan wenxian* 38.1: 1–87.

Tao Chengzhang. 1943. "Jiaohui yuanliu kao" (Examination of the origin and development of sects and secret societies). In Luo Ergang, comp., *Tiandihui wenxianlu*, pp. 61–76. Shanghai: Zhengzhong shuju.

TDH. Tiandihui (The Heaven and Earth Society). 7 vols. 1980–88. Zhongguo renmin daxue Qingshi yanjiusuo and Zhongguo diyi lishi dang'anguan, joint eds. Beijing: Zhongguo renmin daxue chubanshe.

Ter Haar, Barend J. 1990. "The Genesis and Spread of Temple Cults in Fujian." In E. B. Vermeer, ed., *Development and Decline of Fukien Province in the 17th and 18th Centuries*, pp. 349–96. Leiden: E. J. Brill.

———. 1992. *The White Lotus Teachings in Chinese Religious History*. Leiden: E. J. Brill.

———. 1993. "Messianism and the Heaven and Earth Society." In David Ownby and Mary S. Heidhues, eds., *"Secret Societies" Reconsidered: Perspectives on the Social History of Early Modern South China and Southeast Asia*, pp. 153–76. Armonk, N.Y.: M. E. Sharpe.

———. n.d. "Sources of the Heaven and Earth Gathering Tradition." Unpublished paper presented at the Conference of the Association for Asian Studies, New Orleans, La., April 1991.

———. Forthcoming. *The Role of Myth and Ritual: The Case of the Chinese Triads.*

Tong, James W. 1991. *Disorder Under Heaven: Collective Violence in the Ming Dynasty*. Stanford, Calif.: Stanford University Press.

Trocki, Carl A. 1993. "The Rise and Fall of the Ngee Heng Kongsi in Singapore." In David Ownby and Mary S. Heidhues, eds., *"Secret Societies" Reconsidered: Perspectives on the Social History of Early Modern South China and Southeast Asia*, pp. 89–119. Armonk: N.Y.: M. E. Sharpe.

Twitchett, Denis, and Tilemann Grimm. 1988. "The Cheng-t'ung, Ching't'ai, and T'ien-shun Reigns, 1436–1464." In *The Cambridge History of China*, vol. 7, *The Ming Dynasty, 1368–1644, Part 1*, pp. 305–42. Cambridge: Cambridge University Press.

Ura Ren'ichi. 1954. "Shinsho no senkairei no kenkyū" (Study of the coastal evacuation in the early Qing). *Hiroshima daigaku bungakubu jiyō* 5: 124–58.

Van der Loon, Piet. 1977. "Les origines rituelles du théâtre chinois" (The ritual origins of Chinese theater). *Journal Asiatique* 265.1,2: 143–68.

Vermeer, E. B. 1990a. "The Decline of Hsing-hua Prefecture in the Early Ch'ing." In Vermeer, ed., *Development and Decline of Fukien Province in the 17th and 18th Centuries*, pp. 101–62. Leiden: E. J. Brill.

———. 1990b. "Introduction: Historical Background and Major Issues" In Vermeer, ed., *Development and Decline of Fukien Province in the 17th and 18th Centuries*, pp. 5–34. Leiden: E. J. Brill.

Wagner, Rudolf G. 1982. *Reenacting the Heavenly Vision: The Role of Religion in the Taiping Rebellion*. Berkeley: University of California Institute of East Asian Studies.

Wakeman, Frederic, Jr. 1985. *The Great Enterprise: The Manchu Reconstruction of Imperial Order in Seventeenth-Century China*. Berkeley: University of California Press.

Wang Lianmao. 1987. "Minmatsu Senshu no tensō shudatsu to 'torokai' tōsō" (Rent exploitation and the Doulaohui revolt in Quanzhou in the Late Ming period). *Shiho* 17: 39–52.

Wang Shi-ch'ing. 1974. "Religious Organization in the History of a Taiwanese Town." In Arthur P. Wolf, ed., *Religion and Ritual in Chinese Society*, pp. 71–92. Stanford, Calif.: Stanford University Press.

Wang Shiqing. 1958. "Qingdai Taiwan de mijia" (Rice prices on Qing Taiwan). *Taiwan wenxian* 9.4: 11–20.

Wang Yeh-chien. 1986. "Food Supply in Eighteenth Century Fukien." *Late Imperial China* 7.2: 80–117.

Wang Zhiyi. 1963 (reprint). "Jingchen zhihua Zhang-Quan fengsu shu" (Memorial respectfully outlining how to manage and alter the customs of Zhangzhou and Quanzhou). In He Changling, ed., *Huangchao jingshi wenbian*, j. 23, lizheng, shouling xia, pp. 42–46. Taipei: Guofeng chubanshe. Original edition 1886.

Wang Zongpei. 1931. *Zhongguo zhi hehui* (Chinese associations). Nanjing: Zhongguo hezuo xueshe.

Ward, J. S. M., and W. G. Stirling. 1925. *The Hung Society or the Society of Heaven and Earth*. London.

Watson, James L. 1988. "Self Defense Corps, Violence, and the Bachelor Subculture in South China: Two Case Studies." *Proceedings of the Second International Conference on Sinology*. Academia Sinica, Taiwan.

———. 1991. "Waking the Dragon: Visions of the Chinese Imperial State in Local Myth." In Hugh D. R. Baker and Stephan Feuchtwang, eds., *An Old State in New Settings: Studies in the Social Anthropology of China in Memory of Maurice Freedman*, pp. 162–77. Oxford: Journal of the Anthropological Society of Oxford.

Watson, Ruby S. 1985. *Inequality Among Brothers: Class and Kinship in South China*. Cambridge: Cambridge University Press.

Weller, Robert. 1987. *Unities and Diversities in Chinese Religion*. Seattle: University of Washington Press.

Wen Guangyi, 1984. "Fujian huaqiao chuguo di lishi he yuanyin fenxi" (History and causes of Fujianese emigration). *Zhongguo shehui jingjishi yanjiu* 2: 75–89.

Wickberg, Edgar. 1968. *The Chinese in Philippine Life, 1850–1898*. New Haven, Conn.: Yale University Press.

Wilbur, C. Martin. 1976. *Sun Yat-sen: Frustrated Patriot*. New York: Columbia University Press.

Williams, S. Wells. 1849. "Oath Taken by Members of the Triad Society, and Notice of Its Origins." *Chinese Repository* 18: 281–95.

Willmott, William E. 1967. *The Chinese in Cambodia*. Vancouver: University of British Columbia Press.

———. 1970. *The Political Structure of the Chinese Community in Cambodia*. London: Athlone Press.

Wilson, Stephan. 1988. *Feuding, Conflict, and Banditry in Nineteenth-Century Corsica*. Cambridge: Cambridge University Press.

Winn, Jane Kaufman. 1994. "Relational Practices and the Marginalization of Law: Informal Financial Practices of Small Businesses in Taiwan." *Law and Society Review* 28.2: 193–232.

Wolf, Arthur P. 1974. "Gods, Ghosts, and Ancestors." In A. Wolf, ed., *Religion and Ritual in Chinese Society*, pp. 131–82. Stanford, Calif.: Stanford University Press.

Wou, Odoric Y. K. 1994. *Mobilizing the Masses: Building Revolution in Henan*. Stanford, Calif.: Stanford University Press.

Wynne, M. L. 1941. *Triad and Tabut: A Survey of the Origin and Diffusion of Chinese and Mohamedan Secret Societies in the Malay Peninsula A.D. 1800–1935*. Singapore: Government Printing Office.

Xiao Yishan. 1935. *Jindai mimi shehui shiliao* (Historical materials on modern secret societies). Beijing: Beiping yanjiuyuan.

———. 1986 (reprint). *Qingdai tongshi* (General history of the Qing). Beijing: Zhonghua shuju.

Xie Jinluan. 1959 (reprint). "Quan-Zhang zhifalun" (On governing Quanzhou and Zhangzhou). In Ding Yuejian, comp., *Zhi Tai bigaolu*, pp. 97–113. Taipei: Taiwan wenxian congkan.

Xinghua fuzhi (Fujian). Ming Hongzhi edition.

Xu Gengjie. 1908. *Buqiezhai mancun* (Occasional notes from the dissatisfied studio). Shanghai: Nanyang shuju.

Xu Xiaowang. 1986. "Qingdai Minnan de xiangzu xiedou jiqi yuanyin tanzheng" (Lineage *xiedou* in southern Fujian in the Qing and their reasons). *Fujian gong-an zhuanke xuexiao xuebao* 1.1: 47–53.

Xue Yunsheng. 1970 (reprint). *Duli cunyi* (Doubts and suspicions on reading the statutes). Taipei: Chinese Materials and Research Aids Service Center, Research Aids Series. Original edition 1905.

Yang, C. K. 1961. *Religion in Chinese Society*. New York: Columbia University Press.

———. 1975. "Some Preliminary Patterns of Mass Actions in Nineteenth-Century China." In Frederic Wakeman, Jr., and Carolyn Grant, eds., *Conflict and Control in Late Imperial China*, pp. 174–210. Berkeley: University of California Press.

Yang Guozhen. 1988. *Ming Qing tudi qiyue wenshu yanjiu* (Research on land contract documents of the Ming and Qing). Beijing: People's Press.

Yang Guozhen and Chen Zhiping. 1985. "Ming-Qing shidai Fujian de tubao" (Local fortresses in Ming-Qing Fujian). *Zhongguo shehui jingjishi yanjiu* 2: 45–57.

———. 1987. "Ming Qing Fujian tubao bulun" (Supplemental discussion of local fortresses in Ming and Qing Fujian). In Fu Yiling and Yang Guozhen, eds., *Ming-Qing Fujian shehui yu xiangcun jingji* (Fujian society and village economy in Ming and Qing times). Xiamen: Xiamen University Press.

Yang Tingli. 1983 (reprint). *Dongying jishi* (Record of a voyage to the east). In Zhongguo shehui kexueyuan lishi yanjiusuo, Mingshi yanjiushi, eds., *Qingdai Taiwan nongmin qiyi shiliao xuanbian*, pp. 113–37. Fuzhou: Fujian renmin chubanshe. Original edition 1790.

Yao Qisheng. Kangxi period. *Minsong huibian* (Collected praise of Fujian). Fujian: Woodcut edition.

Yao Ying. 1963a (reprint). "Fu Fang Benfu qiuyan zhazi" (Letter in reply to Fang Benfu's inquiry). In He Changling, ed., *Huangchao jingshi wenbian*, j. 23, lizheng sec. 9, shouling xia, pp. 4–9. Taipei: Guofeng chubanshe. Original edition 1886.

———. 1963b (reprint). "Shang Wang Zhijun shu" (A letter to Wang Zhijun). In He Changling, ed., *Huangchao jingshi wenbian*, j. 23, lizheng, shouling xia, pp. 27–29. Taipei: Guofeng chubanshe. Original edition 1886.

Yen, Ching-hwang. 1986. *A Social History of the Chinese in Singapore and Malaya, 1800–1911*. Singapore: Oxford University Press.

Yu Lihua. 1953. "Lin Shuangwen geming yanjiu" (A study of Lin Shuangwen's revolution). *Taiwan wenxian* 4.3: 27–36.

Zhang Tan. 1969. "Tongji xiedou de Wu Alai shijian" (The intra-ethnic Wu Alai incident). *Taiwan wenxian* 20.4: 118–36.

———. 1970. "Qingdai chuqi zhi Tai zhengce de jiantao" (An examination of early Qing policies toward Taiwan). *Taiwan wenxian* 21.1: 19–44.

———. 1974. "Qingdai Taiwan fenlei xiedou pinfan zhi zhuyin" (The chief reasons for the frequency of ethnic *xiedou* in Qing Taiwan). *Taiwan fengwu* 24.4: 75–85.

———. 1976. "Yilan liangci xiedou shijian zhi pouxi" (Analysis of two *xiedou* incidents in Yilan). *Taiwan wenxian* 27.2: 54–71.

Zhanghua xianzhi. 1962 (reprint). Taipei: Taiwan wenxian congkan #156. Original edition 1834.

Zhao Yi. 1928. *Qingshigao* (Draft history of the Qing). Beijing: Qingshiguan.

Zheng Zhenman. 1992. *Ming Qing Fujian jiazu zuzhi yu shehui bianqian* (Ming Qing Fujian lineage organization and social change). Hunan: Hunan Educational Press.

Zhongwen dacidian (Comprehensive Chinese dictionary). 1973. Taipei: Zhonghua xueshuyuan.

Zhou Mi. 1872 (reprint). *Wulin jiushi* (Old Hangzhou), in Bao Tingbo, comp., *Zhi buzu zhai congshu* (Collectanea from the "aware of inadequacy" studio), j. 3, shehui section. Original edition Song dynasty.

Zhou Yumin and Shao Yong. 1993. *Zhongguo banghuishi* (The history of Chinese secret societies). Shanghai: Shanghai renmin chubanshe.

Zhu Weigan. 1986. *Fujian shigao* (Draft history of Fujian). Fu'an, Fujian: Fujian Educational Publishing Press.

Zhuang Jifa. 1974–75. "Taiwan Xiaodaohui yuanliukao" (A study of the origins of the Taiwan Small Knives Society). *Shihuo yuekan fukan* 4.7: 293–303.

———. 1981. *Qingdai Tiandihui yuanliukao* (Studies in the origin of the Qing Heaven and Earth Society). Taipei: Gugong congkan bianji weiyuanhui.

———. 1982. *Qing Gaozong shiquan wugong yanjiu* (A study of the ten great military campaigns of the Qing Gaozong emperor). Taipei: National Palace Museum.

———. 1988. "Qingdai Min-Yue diqu de renkou liudong yu mimi huidang de fazhan" (Population movement in Qing dynasty Fujian and Guangdong and the development of secret societies). In *Jindai Zhongguo chuqi lishi yantaohui lunwenji*, pp. 737–73. Nangang: Academia Sinica.

———. 1989. "Development of Secret Societies in the Ch'ing Dynasty and Changes in Ch'ing Statutes Governing Them." Paper delivered at the 104th Annual Meeting of the American Historical Association, December 27–30, San Francisco.

———. 1990a. "Cong Qingdai lüli de xiuding kan mimi huidang de qiyuan jiqi fazhan" (The origin and development of secret societies from the perspective of changes in Qing laws). *Guoli Taiwan Shifan Daxue lishi xuebao* 18: 107–68.

———. 1990b "Qingdai Hu-Guang diqu de renkou liudong yu mimi huidang de fazhan" (Population movement in Qing dynasty Hu-Guang and the development of secret societies). *Danjiang shixue* 2: 149–76.

Zhuang Weiji and Wang Lianmao, eds. 1985. *Min-Tai guanxi zupu ziliao xuanbian* (Selected genealogical materials on Fujian-Taiwan relations). Fuzhou: Fujian renmin chubanshe.

Zürcher, Erik. 1982. "'Prince Moonlight,' Messianism and Eschatology in Early Medieval Buddhism." *T'oung Pao* 68: 1–59.

Glossary

annan dajiangjun 安南大將軍
ba 霸
baiba 拜把
bao 保
baochai 包差
baojia dajiangjun 保家大將軍
baojiahui 保家會
bashiyuan hui 八十元會
baxianhui 八仙會
beidihui 北帝會
ben 本
bianqianhui 邊錢會
biaohui 標會
bu'an benfen 不安本分
chanping wang 鏟平王
chengge hudi 稱哥呼弟
chifuhui 吃福會
chixie xiangdou 持械相鬥
chongshou 銃手
choushen 酬神
choushen saihui 酬神賽會
chuantu pianqian 傳徒騙錢
chushe 鋤社
da 大
daitian xingdao 代天行道
daitian xinghua 代天行化
daji lishi 大吉利市
Dajiejing 大戒經
dang 黨

dasao 大嫂
Dashengjing 大乘經
dayuanshuai 大元帥
dili 地理
ding 訂
dingxiong 訂兄
dixi 弟媳
doukui 鬥魁
dou'ou 鬥毆
doutu 鬥徒
duanwujie 端午節
dudu 都督
duijihui 堆積會
Enbenjing 恩本經
erbaiyuan hui 二百元會
eryu 餌魚
fang 房
fangsheng 放生
fanQing-fuMing 反清復明
fashe 法社
feifeng 飛風
feilei 匪類
feitu 匪徒
fenlei xiedou 分類械鬥
fu 符
fubu 符簿
fuguo jiangjun 副國將軍
fuhe 附合
fumuhui 父母會

gong'ou 公甌
gongsheng 公生
guanbi minfan 官逼民反
guandihui 關帝會
guanshenghui 關聖會
guluzi 咽嚕子
guogong 國公
guoyuanshuai 國元帥
gutou 骨頭
haoming haoshi zhi xin
好名好勢之心
haoqiang 好強
haoshi zhengqi 好事爭奇
hei 黑
hong 洪
hongbaihui 紅白會
Honger heshang 洪二和尚
honghao 洪號
honghao dajiangjun 洪號大將軍
honghao fuguo dayuanshuai
洪號副國大元帥
honglishe 紅禮社
hongmaohui 紅帽會
huanwo jiangshan 還我江山
huguo jiangjun 護國將軍
hui 會
huiguan 會館
huigui 會規
huijue 會訣
huimai 賄買
huishe 會社
huitou 會頭
hunjiahui 婚嫁會
jia 甲
jiachan 家產
jiagong baosi 假公報私
jiangjun 將軍
jiansheng 監生
jiao ("rite of cosmic renewal") 醮
jiao (teaching) 教
jiazhang 家長
jiazi 甲子
jie 結
jiebai 結拜
jiehui lianqian 結會斂錢
jiehui shudang 結會樹黨

jieyi 結義
jijinhui 集金會
jing 敬
jinshi 進士
jinwu jiangjun 金吾將軍
jiumen tidu 九門提督
junzihui 君子會
juren 舉人
kaikou buli ben, chushou buli san
開口不離本，出手不離三
kainan dajiangjun 開南大將軍
kangkai 慷慨
kanqinghui 看青會
ketou 磕頭
leigonghui 雷公會
li 里
Lin Shuangwen 林爽文
luanmin 亂民
luohanjiao 羅漢腳
luzhu 爐主
meng 盟
mengzhu 盟主
midou 米斗
ming 明
mingzhu 明主
mitong 米桶
mou 畝
moupan 謀叛
muli doushi zhitianxia
木立斗世知天下
neidi 內地
nu 奴
pingxi dajiangjun 平西大將軍
polian'gou 破臉狗
qi 氣
qiangshou 強手
qianhui 錢會
qigong 氣功
qinfen 親份
qing 青
qinghui 請會
qingminghui 清明會
qingshen 請神
Qingtian duoguo 清天奪國
qixianhui 七賢會
qixinghui 七星會

qukui 渠魁
ri 日
saobei dajiangjun 掃北大將軍
she 社
shehui 賒會
shenghui 聖會
shengling 生靈
shenminghui 神明會
shenqu 神曲
shi (master) 師
shi (unit of measure) 石
shichou 世仇
shishu 史書
shuikou fu 水口符
shunguo yuanfen 順國源分
shuntian xingdao 順天行道
Shuntiangong 順天宮
sizhang 祀長
sui 歲
sujiang 俗講
Taishang Laojun 太上老君
tanggui 堂規
taoyuanhui 桃園會
tian–di–hong 天地洪
tiandihui (Heaven and Earth Society) 天地會
tiandihui (Add Younger Brother Society) 添弟會
tianqiao 天橋
tianyun 天運
tianyun kainian 天運開年
tiechihui 鐵尺會
Tixi 提喜
tuhao 土豪
tuji 圖記
Tuxi 涂喜
wan 萬
Wan Tixi 萬提喜
wangyehui 王爺會
weidi 未弟
wenfeng 文風
wudian ershiyi 五點二十一
wugu baiba 無故拜把
wuhuhui 五虎會
wuji zhi min 無籍之民
wulai 無賴

wuzonghui 五總會
xiang 鄉
xianghui 香會
xiangyue 鄉約
xiaodaohui 小刀會
xiaoyihui 孝義會
xiechou huxiang fensha 挾仇互相焚殺
xiedou 械鬥
xiefei 邪匪
xiejiao 邪教
Xiluxu 西魯序
xingke tiben 刑科題本
xiong'e guntu 兇惡棍徒
xishe 喜社
xiucai 秀才
xueshi dafu 學士大夫
Yan Ruohai 嚴若海
Yan Yan 嚴烟
yang 陽
yaohui 搖會
yaqianhui 牙籤會
yi 代
yi an minxin, yi bao nongye shi 以安民心, 以保農業事
yimin 義民
yin 陰
yingshen saihui 迎神賽會
yingzang dili 營葬地理
yinhui 銀會
yinji wuse 陰記物色
yin mao 寅卯
yiqi 義氣
yiqianhui 一錢會
yishe 邑社
Yiwang 義王
yixing 義興
yonghe 永和
youhui 遊會
youshou 游手
youshou youshi 游手游市
youyinggong 有應公
yue (bond) 約
yue (moon) 月
yufohui 浴佛會
zafan 雜犯

zangqinshe 葬親社
zhafu 札付
zhaihui 齋會
zhangliu 杖流
zhaoji 招集
zhenbei dajiangjun 振北大將軍
zhenguo dajiangjun 振國大將軍
zhiji 知己
zhongyu 種芋
zhongwu jiangjun 重武將軍
zhou 周
zhu 朱
Zhu Yigui 朱一貴

zidi 子弟
zilonghui 子龍會
zong 總
zongli 總理
zongshou 總手
zongzhi shuaifu qianyin
　　總制帥府鈐印
zongzuo 總左
zugun 族棍
zuhao 族豪
zuodao yiduan 左道異端
zuzhang 族長

Index

In this index an "f" after a number indicates a separate reference on the next page, and an "ff" indicates separate references on the next two pages. A continuous discussion over two or more pages is indicated by a span of page numbers, e.g., "57–59." *Passim* is used for a cluster of references in close but not consecutive sequence.

Aboriginal peoples, Taiwan, 20, 50, 65, 89
Aligang (Taiwan), 69
Anhui, 35

Baiba (informal brotherhood), 25, 83, 95
Bailiancai (lay Buddhist religion), 135
Bailianhui (lay Buddhist religion), 135
Bailianjiao (lay Buddhist religion), 135
Bailianzong (lay Buddhist religion), 135
Baixianghui (Worship Incense Society), 138
Bangka, 182
Beijing, 56, 117
Beishiwei (Taiwan), 90
Bengang (Taiwan), 90, 170
Brotherhood associations: definition, 2f; socioeconomic reasons for proliferation, 11–22; pre-Qing history, 30, 33–42
Buddhism, 26, 37, 135, 202n3
Burial societies (*Fumuhui*), 2, 32–38 *passim*, 42–47 *passim*, 53, 112, 157

Cai Fu, 75
Cambodia, 182
Chai Daji, Taiwan Brigade General, 73–80 *passim*
Changqing, Fujian-Zhejiang Governor-General, 77
Changtai county (Fujian), 97
Chaoyang county (Guangdong), 98, 113
Chaozhou prefecture (Guangdong), 53, 96, 98, 111ff, 122, 127, 130
Chen Agao, 150
Chen Biao, 62, 113–16
Chen Dong, 113
Chen Guang'ai, 118, 121
Chen He, Taiwan sub-lieutenant, 73f
Chen Huizu, Fujian-Zhejiang Governor-General, 208n55
Chen Pang, 67
Chen Pi, 113f
Chen Shaoyun, 133
Chen Shengshao, author of *Wensulu*, 16, 166, 175
Chen Sulao, 120–26 *passim*
Chen Tan, 123, 127

Library of Congress Cataloging-in-Publication Data

Ownby, David
Brotherhoods and secret societies in early and mid-Qing China :
the formation of a tradition / David Ownby
    p. cm.
    Includes bibliographical references and index.
    ISBN 0-8047-2651-5 (alk. paper)
    1. Secret societies—China—History. 2. China—History—Ch'ing
dynasty, 1644–1912. I. Title.
HS310.086 1996
398'.0951—dc20
95-31759 CIP

⊗This book is printed on acid-free, recycled paper.

Original printing 1996
Last figure below indicates year of this printing:
05 04 03 02 01 00 99 98 97 96